GODS OF
ANCIENT
EGYPT

For Juan, Juana and Paul

GODS OF ANCIENT EGYPT

BARBARA WATTERSON

SUTTON PUBLISHING

First published in 1984 by
Batsford Academic and Educational
a division of B.T. Batsford Ltd
4 Fitzharding Street · London · WIH 0AH

First published in this edition in 1996 by
Sutton Publishing Limited · Phoenix Mill
Thrupp · Stroud · Gloucestershire · GL5 2BU

Paperback edition first published in 1999

British Library Cataloguing in Publication Data

A catalogue record for this book is available from the British Library

ISBN 0 7509 2225 7

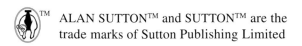

Typeset in 10/14 Sabon.
Typesetting and origination by
Sutton Publishing Limited.
Printed in Hong Kong by
Midas Printing Limited.

CONTENTS

PART I

CHAPTER ONE

CHAPTER TWO

PART II
THE MAJOR GODS OF EGYPT

PART III

LIST OF
ILLUSTRATIONS

ACKNOWLEDGEMENTS

I should like to thank the following for their help in the production of this book:

my husband, Juan, for his constant support and encouragement; my daughter, Juana, for the line drawings; my son-in-law, Paul, for the photograph of the scarab-beetle on page 52; and my friend, Hugh Evans, for the photograph of Min on page 194.

All other photographs were taken by the author.

PREFACE

The artefacts of the ancient Egyptian civilization, from the largest temples to the smallest amulets, have been much admired for their beauty and workmanship. Admiration soon leads to curiosity about the purpose or significance of certain themes and designs, many of which consist of ever-recurring religious symbols and images of gods in different guises. A knowledge of the more commonly represented deities allows the admirer to understand something of the purpose and motives which directed the skills of ancient Egyptian artisans.

In assembling this 'gazetteer' of the gods of ancient Egypt, I have aimed at introducing only the thirty or so more important members of a tribe numbered in hundreds, and in addition to more factual details of form, time and place have related the sometimes elaborate mythology pertaining to each. These mythologies are the ancient Egyptian version of the folklore and fairy stories which all societies produce. Throughout the book, references have been given to sources in which translations of the various myths and stories can be found; however, excerpts quoted in the book are from my own translations.

This book is not a study of ancient Egyptian religion as such, and the only purpose of the brief introductory chapters is to allow the reader to appreciate the theological context in which the gods were worshipped. No attempt has been made to make comparisons with the gods or beliefs of other cultures, although any description of a culture different from our own, especially one so far removed from us in time, inevitably incorporates implicit and sometimes very subjective comparisons with our own twentieth-century European tribal customs and beliefs.

The origins and chief places of worship of certain ancient Egyptian deities, and the beliefs associated with them, are set out in the following chapters, which are arranged more or less according to the importance of the gods discussed in them rather than in any historical or geographical order. The glossary found on pages 213–15 includes explanations of specialized words in the text; and an explanation of the way in which ancient Egyptian words (proper nouns, place-names, kings' names, etc.) have been written is given on page xii.

A NOTE ON TRANSLITERATION

From about 3100 BC, the Egyptian language was written in hieroglyphic script, a decorative and complex picture-writing that remained in use for over 3,000 years. In 30 BC, Egypt came under Roman rule. The Romans abolished the institution of monarchy in Egypt; and the dissolution of what had been the linchpin of Egyptian society, combined with the advent of Christianity, to which most of Egypt had been converted by the fourth century AD, meant that the use of hieroglyphs, and the alternative scripts, hieratic and demotic (see Glossary), fast deteriorated, to be replaced by Greek, and by Coptic, the last stage of the native language of Egypt, which employed the Greek alphabet as the basis of its written script.

The language of ancient Egypt, as expressed in hieroglyphs, hieratic and demotic, was lost for centuries until, in AD 1822, Jean-François Champollion became the first man of modern times to decipher hieroglyphs correctly. However, the pronunciation of ancient Egyptian is not known with a sufficient degree of certainty.

In order for an English-speaker, for example, to be able to read hieroglyphic script, the pictographs used in it have to be turned into an approximation of the English alphabet, that is, transliterated. Unfortunately, the Egyptians only used consonants in their written script; their language must have had vowels in it, but the position of these vowels in Egyptian-language words is not made clear in hieroglyphic script. It should perhaps be mentioned here that the official language of Egypt today is Arabic, and has been since the Arab Conquest of AD 640; and that Arabic is not the same language as ancient Egyptian, although the script of both has one thing in common: in neither language are the vowels written.

Thus, there are schools of transliteration for both languages with different traditions for inserting vowels: some write Idfu where we write Edfu (Arabic place-name); some write Ra where we write Re (name of ancient Egyptian Sun God), and so on. As a general rule of thumb, English-speaking readers of *Gods of Ancient Egypt* will find it convenient for pronunciation purposes to put an 'e' into ancient Egyptian words wherever it would otherwise be difficult to pronounce a string of consonants. Where this simple expedient of inserting an 'e' between consonants does not work, for example in *šn* (see Glossary), the word has been rendered into an approximation of English, *šn* being written *shen*.

CHRONOLOGICAL TABLE

It is customary to arrange ancient Egyptian history into dynasties, or groups, of kings, following the system first used by the third-century BC scholar-priest, Manetho, in his history of Egypt, written in Greek and entitled the *Aegyptiaca*. To the end of Manetho's original list have been added two dynasties to cover the years after his death. The thirty-two dynasties thus arrived at are divided into periods known as 'Old Kingdom', 'Middle Kingdom' and 'New Kingdom', interspersed with so-called 'Intermediate Periods'. The term 'Kingdom' is not a geographical description but is historical and refers to the times in ancient Egyptian history when the country was a unified state ruled by one king. The Intermediate Periods were times when there was no strong central government.

Since we are not certain of how ancient Egyptian was pronounced, many scholars prefer to use the Greek forms of royal names taken from Manetho. In the following table, both Greek and Egyptian forms are given where appropriate; in the book, the Egyptian form is used, so that it can be seen clearly which kings are named after gods.

PREHISTORY: i.e. Predynastic Egypt *c.* 5500–*c.* 3150 BC

Lower Egypt:	5500–4000 BC:
	Fayum and Merimde cultures
Upper Egypt:	5500–4000 BC:
	Badarian culture
Upper Egypt:	4000–3500 BC:
	Naqada I culture
Upper Egypt:	3500–3150 BC:
	Naqada II culture

PROTODYNASTIC PERIOD: *c.* 3200–*c.* 3050 BC

Naqada III culture

continued

HISTORY: i.e. Dynastic Egypt

	SELECTED KINGS NAMED IN BOOK	DEVELOPMENTS IN RELIGION AND HISTORY
Archaic Period: _c._ 3100–_c._ 2686 BC		
Dynasty I _c._ 3100–2890	Scorpion (predynastic?) Menes/Narmer Hor-aha	Union of Upper and Lower Egypt Capital city: Memphis
Dynasty II _c._ 2890–2686	Sekhemib/Peribsen Khasekemwy Sendji	Kings buried in _mastabas_ at Sakkara Beginning of writing Major gods: Horus and Seth
Old Kingdom: _c._ 2886–_c._ 2181 BC		
Dynasty III _c._ 2686–2613	Djoser	Development of step pyramids Major god: Atum
Dynasty IV _c._ 2613–2494	Khufu (Cheops) Khafre (Chephren) Menkaure (Mycerinus)	Peak of Old Kingdom achievements in art and architecture Kings buried in first true pyramids at Giza Royal power at peak Major gods: Atum and Re
Dynasty V _c._ 2494–2345	Unas	Decline of royal power Increase in power of Heliopolitan priesthood
Dynasty VI _c._ 2345–2181	Pepi I Pepi II	Spread of Osiris cult Kings buried in small pyramids at Sakkara and Abusir Pyramid Texts
First Intermediate Period: _c._ 2181–_c._ 2040 BC		
Dynasties VII, VIII _c._ 2181–2160		Early Coffin Texts
Dynasties IX, X _c._ 2160–2040		
Middle Kingdom: 2106–1633(?) BC		
Dynasty XI 2106–1963	Mentuhotep II (2033–1982)	State reunited

	Mentuhotep IV (1970–1963)	Capital city: Thebes
Dynasty XII 1963–1786	Amenemhat I (Amenemmes) (1963–1934) Senwosret III (Sesostris) (1862–1843)	Capital city: Lisht Kings buried in pyramids at Lisht, Lahun, Dahshur Major god: Amun
Dynasty XIII 1786–1633(?)		

Second Intermediate Period: 1786–1550 BC

Dynasties XIV–XVI	Hyksos Occupation	

New Kingdom: 1550–1069 BC

Dynasty XVIII 1550–1295	Ahmose (Amosis) (1550–1525)	Expulsion of Hyksos State reunited
	Thutmose II (Tuthmosis) (1492–1479) Thutmose III (1479–1425) Hatshepsut (1479–1457) Thuthmose IV (1393–1383)	Capital city: Thebes Kings of Dynasties XVIII–XX buried in rock-cut tombs at Thebes. Egypt becomes Imperial power and richest state in world Amun at height of power
	Amenhotep III (Amenophis) (1383–1345)	
	Amenhotep IV (Akhenaten) (1353–1337)	Amarna Period
	Smenkare (1338–1336)	Restoration of Amun
	Tutankhamun (1336–1327) Ay (1327–1323) Horemheb (1323–1295)	

continued

Dynasty XIX 1295–1186	Ramesses I (1295–1294)	
	Sety I (Sethos) (1294–1279)	Renewed interest in Empire
	Ramesses II (1279–1213)	
Dynasty XX 1186–1069	Ramesses III (1184–1153)	Invasion of Sea Peoples From Ramesses III, decline in Egyptian power
	Ramesses IV (1153–1147)	
	Ramesses V (1147–1143)	
	Ramesses XI (1099–1069)	

Third Intermediate Period: 1069–525 BC

Dynasty XXI (at Tanis: 1069–945) (at Thebes: 1080–945)	Psusennes II (959–945)	Capital city: Tanis Kings buried in sunken tombs at Tanis High Priests of Amun rule Upper Egypt from Thebes
Dynasty XXII 945–715	Sheshonq I (945–924)	Capital cities: Tanis and Bubastis Kings buried at Tanis
Dynasty XXIII 818–715		Capital city: Leontopolis
Dynasty XXIV 728–715	Tefnakhte (727–720)	Capital city: Sais
Dynasty XXV 716–664	Shabaka (716–702)	Egypt under Kushite (Sudanese) rule Capitals at Memphis, Thebes and Napata (Sudan) Kings buried at Kurru (Sudan)
Dynasty XXVI 664–525	Psammeticus I (664–610)	Saite Period: Renaissance in Egyptian culture Capital city: Sais Kings buried in Temple of Neit at Sais

The Late Period: 525–332 BC

Dynasty XXVII 525–404	Egypt under Persian rule	Capital city: Susa or Babylon
Dynasty XXVIII 404–399	Native kings	Capital city: Sais
Dynasty XXlX 399–380	Native kings	Capital city: Memphis
Dynasty XXX 380–343	Last native kings Nectanebo I (380–362) Nectanebo II (360–343)	Capital city: Sebennytos
Dynasty XXXI 343–332 332	Egypt once more under Persian rule Alexander the Great conquers Egypt	Capital city: Susa or Babylon

MACEDONIAN PERIOD: 332–304 BC

	Alexander (332–323)	
Dynasty XXXII 304–30 BC	Ptolemy V Epiphanes (205–180) Cleopatra VII (51–30) Caesarion (44–30)	The Ptolemaic era: Egypt ruled by the descendants of Ptolemy Lagides, one of Alexander's generals Capital city: Alexandria

ROMAN ERA: 30 BC–AD 395

	Egypt under Roman rule
	Roman Emperors:
	   Augustus (30 BC–AD 14)
	   Tiberius (14–37)
	   Claudius (41–54)
	   Vespasian (69–79)
	   Domitian (81–96)
	   Caracalla (198–217)
	   Decius (249–251)
	   Diocletian (284–305)
		Capital city: Alexandria

continued

BYZANTINE AND COPTIC ERA: AD 395–641

Byzantine Emperors

Capital city: Alexandria

State religion of Egypt:
Christianity (Orthodox),
believing Christ has both
divine and human nature

Native (Coptic) church
Monophysite, believing Christ
has one, divine, nature

ISLAMIC ERA: AD 641 TO PRESENT

Arab Conquest AD 640

Capital city: Cairo

State religion of Egypt: Islam

Khalifs (641–1258)

Mamelukes
(1258–1517)

Ottomans (1517–1882)

Mohammed Ali
(*c.* 1769–1849)

British Occupation
(1882–1914)

British Protectorate
(1914–1922)

Independent Kingdom
(1922–1953)

Republic: 1953 to present

EGYPTIAN PLACE-NAMES

On the map overleaf the place-names are those most commonly used today. It has become the custom for scholars to refer to many places by their Graeco-Roman names, following the practice of the early Egyptologists whose interest in Egypt was stimulated by the classical writers; however, this practice is not followed consistently. In the text of this book, the ancient Egyptian name has been used, except for particularly well-known places which have become familiar under their Greek or Arabic names: for example, Edfu, for which it would be perverse to use anything other than the name derived from Arabic.

In the following table, place-names are listed, roughly in geographical order from north to south, under 1) the modern Arabic name; 2) the name by which the place was known during the period of Graeco-Roman rule; 3) the ancient Egyptian name. Names used on the map are marked with an asterisk.

Modern name	Classical name	Ancient name
EL-ISKANDARIYA	Alexandria*	Raqote
ABUQIR	Kanopus*	
RASHID	Rosetta*	
DAMANHÛR*	Hermopolis Parva	Demit-en-Hor
SA EL-HAGAR	Sais*	Sau
TELL EL-FARA'UN	Buto*	Pe and Dep
BEHBEIT EL-HAGAR*	Iseum	Hebyt
ABUSIR	Busiris*	Djedu
SAMANNUD	Sebennytos*	Tjebnutjer
SAN EL-HAGAR	Tanis*	Dja'net
TELL ED-DAB'A	Avaris*	Hwt w'rt
QANTIR		Pi-Ramessu*
FAQUS	Phakussa*	
TELL ABU SEFAH*	Sile	Tjel
WADI EL-NATRUN*		
TELL ATRIB	Athribis*	Kem-wer
TELL BASTA	Bubastis*	Bast
WADI TUMILAT*		

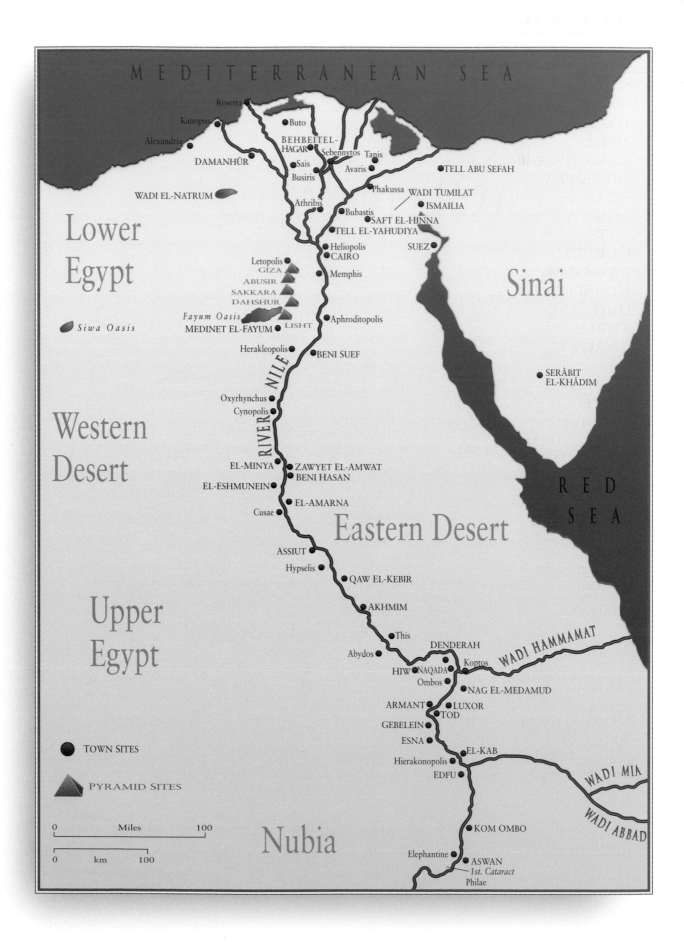

MEDITERRANEAN SEA

Lower
Egypt

Sinai

Western
Desert

RIVER NILE

Eastern Desert

RED
SEA

Upper
Egypt

WADI HAMMAMAT

WADI MIA

WADI ABBAD

Nubia

Rosetta
Kanopus
Alexandria
DAMANHÛR
Buto
BEHBEITEL-
HAGAR
Sebennytos
Tanis
Sais
Avaris
Busiris
Phakussa
WADI EL-NATRUM
Athribis
TELL ABU SEFAH
WADI TUMILAT
ISMAILIA
Bubastis
SAFT EL-HINNA
TELL EL-YAHUDIYA
Heliopolis
CAIRO
SUEZ
Letopolis
GIZA
ABUSIR
SAKKARA
DAHSHUR
Memphis
Siwa Oasis
Fayum Oasis
MEDINET EL-FAYUM
LISHT
Aphroditopolis
SERÂBIT
EL-KHÂDIM
Herakleopolis
BENI SUEF
Oxyrhynchus
Cynopolis
EL-MINYA
ZAWYET EL-AMWAT
BENI HASAN
EL-ESHMUNEIN
EL-AMARNA
Cusae
ASSIUT
Hypselis
QAW EL-KEBIR
AKHMIM
This
DENDERAH
Abydos
Koptos
HIW
NAQADA
Ombos
NAG EL-MEDAMUD
ARMANT
LUXOR
TOD
GEBELEIN
ESNA
EL-KAB
Hierakonopolis
EDFU
KOM OMBO
Elephantine
ASWAN
1st. Cataract
Philae

⬤ TOWN SITES

▲ PYRAMID SITES

0   Miles   100

0   km   100

SAFT EL-HINNA*		*Per-Soped*
ISMAILIA*		
SERÂBIT EL-KHÂDIM		
TELL EL-YAHUDIYA*	Leontopolis	*Nay-ta-hut*
AUSIM	Letopolis*	*Khem*
CAIRO (EL-QAHIRA)*		
MIT RAHINA	Memphis*	*Ineb-hedj*
GIZA*		*Rasetau*
ABUSIR*		
SAKKARA*		
DAHSHUR*		
FAYUM OASIS*	Moeris	*She-resy* (later *Mer-wer*)
MEDINET EL-FAYUM*	Krocodilopolis	
LISHT*		*Itje-tawy*
ATFIH	Aphroditopolis*	
IHNASYA EL-MEDINA	Herakleopolis*	*Henen-nesut*
BENI SUEF*		
EL-BAHNASA	Oxyrhynchus*	*Per-medjed*
EL-QEIS	Cynopolis*	
EL-MINYA*		
ZAWYET EL-AMWAT*		*Hebenu*
BENI HASAN*		
EL-AMARNA*		*Akhetaten*
EL-ESHMUNEIN*	Hermopolis Magna	*Khemenu*
EL-QUSIYA	Cusae*	*Qis*
ASSIUT*	Lykopolis	*Zawty*
SHUTB	Hypselis*	*Sha-sehetep*
QAW EL-KEBIR*	Antaeopolis	*Djew-Qa* (later *Tjebu*)
AKHMIM*	Panopolis	*Khent-Min*
MESHEIKH	This*	*Tjeny*
	Abydos*	*Aabdju*
DENDERAH*	Tentyris	*Iunet*
HIW*	Diopolis Parva	*Hoot-sekhem*
TUKH	Ombos*	*Nebet*
QIFT	Koptos*	*Gebtu*
WADI HAMMAMAT*		
NAQADA*		
LUXOR*	Diospolis Magna (Thebes)	*Waset*
NAG EL-MEDAMUD*		*Madu*
ARMANT*	Hermonthis	*Iuny*
TOD*	Tuphium	*Djerty*
GEBELEIN*	Aphroditopolis	*Per-Hathor*
ESNA*	Latopolis	*Ta-sny*
EL-KAB*	Eleithiapolis	*Nekheb*

KOM EL-AHMAR	Hierakonpolis*	*Nekhen*
EDFU*	Apollinopolis Magna	*Wetjeset-Hor*
WADI MIA*		
WADI ABBAD*		
KOM OMBO*	Ombos	*Nebet*
ASWAN*	Syene	
	Elephantine*	*Abu*
	Philae*	*Pi-lak*

For information on archaeological excavations at many of these sites
see the Bibliography on page 231 of the *Atlas of Ancient Egypt*
(Baines and Malek).

PRINCIPAL CULT-CENTRES

The list below gives the principal cult-centres of the major deities discussed in this book, using the names by which they are most likely to be referred to in other books. Modern Arabic place-names are in capital letters, Graeco-Roman names in lower case.

Abydos:	Osiris
AMARNA:	Aten
ARMANT:	Montu
Bubastis:	Bastet
Busiris:	Osiris
Buto:	Wadjet (Edjo)
Cynopolis:	Anubis
DENDERAH:	Hathor
EDFU:	Horus
Elephantine:	Khnum
EL-KAB:	Nekhbet
ESNA:	Khnum
Heliopolis:	Atum, Re, Geb, Nut, Khepri
Hermopolis:	Thoth
Hierakonpolis:	Horus the Elder
Koptos:	Min
Leontopolis:	Shu, Tefnut
Memphis:	Ptah
Ombos:	Seth
Philae:	Isis
Sais:	Neit
Sebennytos:	Onuris
Tanis:	Seth
Thebes:	Amun, Mut, Khonsu

PART

I

INTRODUCTION

eligion can be thought of as the recognition by human beings of a superhuman power that controls the universe and everything that is, was or shall be in it. Each individual human being can consider that the superhuman controlling power is a deity worthy of being loved; or capable of inspiring awe, obedience, and even fear. The effect of these feelings on individuals can lead to the setting-up of a system of worship of the deity, and to a drawing-up of a code of beliefs and conduct inspired by their religious faith.

Three of the major religions of the modern world, Judaism, Islam and Christianity, recognize a single god. Each is a revelation of one basic truth; its message, which in the case of Christianity and Islam, must be preached to the unconverted, is contained in a holy book, and the Torah, the Koran and the Gospels can all be used to teach the dogma of their faith. In ancient Egypt, religion was not like this. The Egyptians recognized many gods; they did not have one universal system of religious belief. They had no sacred books analogous to the Bible or the Koran, there were no theological commentaries or treatises, neither was there any dogma.

The polytheism of the ancient Egyptians led to tolerance. Apart from two brief periods in their history when there was an attempt to promote a solar monotheism, the Egyptians never suffered from persecutions carried out in the name of religion: there were no Egyptian saints, no martyrs. The Egyptians were a gentle people for whom the family was important. Hence, their religion was based on family life. The gods were given wives, goddesses given husbands; both had children.

Temples continued the domestic theme, being called 'mansions' of the gods (ḥwt nṯr), and architecturally they were based on the house form, with rooms in them for eating and sleeping. The innermost sanctuary was regarded as the bedroom of the god; and it was surrounded by 'guest bedrooms' for visiting deities. The daily ritual of the temple was domestic in form: the morning ritual gave the god his breakfast; the evening ritual gave him his dinner. Egyptian religion did not indulge in bloodbaths with animal or human sacrifices. Instead, each god lived in peace in his home, the temple, very often as part of a trinity of deities, a holy family consisting of father, mother and child.

For much of their history, the Egyptians were accommodating of other people's gods and always ready to receive additions to their own pantheon. They received but they did not feel any great need to give: hence there was no real attempt to persuade non-Egyptians to worship Egyptian gods. In ancient Egypt the basis of religion was not belief but cult, particularly the local cult which meant more to the individual. Thus, many deities flourished simultaneously and the Egyptians were seemingly ever-ready to adopt a new god or to change their views about the old.

The predominant characteristics of much of Egyptian religion were animism, fetishism and magic. There was also the belief that certain animals possessed divine powers – the cow, for example, represented fertility, the bull virility – which led to the cult of sacred animals, birds and reptiles, each of which was considered to be the manifestation on earth of a divine being. It was this aspect of Egyptian religion more than any other that the Greeks found curious and the Romans horrifying. Both Greeks and Romans were happy about the polytheism, being polytheistic themselves. However, their own gods, although they were celestial, immortal beings, were nevertheless recognizably human: they had human shapes, and were possessed of human emotions and frailties. But the Egyptian gods! The most cursory look at reliefs carved on temple walls showing representations of gods revealed one with the body of a man and the head of a hawk; another with the body of a man and the head of a jackal. Yet another man seemed to have a beetle in place of a head, while the woman standing next to him had the head of a lioness. They were all gods; and so were the vultures and cobras hovering in attendance on them.

Inside the temples, the Egyptians kept real live cats, bulls, ibises or hawks, and worshipped them as gods; and when they died, mummified and buried them as they did their kings. The Roman satirist, Juvenal, exclaimed:

> Who does not know, Volusius, what monsters are revered by demented Egyptians? One lot worships the crocodile; another goes in awe of the ibis that feeds on serpents. Elsewhere there shines the golden effigy of the sacred long-tailed monkey.[1]

Juvenal would perhaps have been even more scornful had he realized the number and diversity of the gods worshipped by Egyptians, who had created hundreds of deities, probably more than any people before or since.

If the Greeks and Romans found Egyptian religion difficult to comprehend, many modern Europeans have found it impossible. In the nineteenth century, several Egyptologists, themselves brought up in the Judaeo-Christian tradition, sought to prove that although the beliefs of the ancient Egyptians were complex, their religion was essentially monotheistic. Two great French Egyptologists, Jean-François Champollion (1790–1832) and Emmanuel de Rougé (1811–72), without whose work we would not know as much as we do, insufficient as that is, about Egyptian religion, subscribed to that belief. Champollion, the founder of Egyptology who deciphered the hieroglyphic script, and de Rougé, the founder of Egyptian Philology, the first man to lay down the correct rules for reading and translating hieroglyphic texts, were lauded by another great French Egyptologist,

Gaston Maspero (1846–1916), who declared that Champollion had deciphered the texts, and de Rougé given the method which allowed them to be utilized, thus bringing to perfection Champollion's discovery. The two men, however, read Egyptian texts and came to the conclusion that the Egyptians were monotheists. Champollion maintained that Egyptian religion was a pure monotheism which 'manifested itself externally by a symbolic polytheism'. And de Rougé, in the introduction to his edition of a hieratic text of the Book of the Dead, seemed to indicate that, in his opinion, the Egyptians believed in one supreme, eternal, almighty God, who had much in common with the God of both Hebrews and Christians.

A few years later, Wallis Budge, the doyen of British Egyptology, enlarged on the theories of the two Frenchmen, explaining that the Egyptians were monotheists, but different from Christian monotheists. The Egyptians had one god – the Sun God – and all other gods were but forms of the Sun God. Thus it can be seen that in modern times there has been reluctance to accept that the Egyptians, regarded as being advanced, intelligent and much to be admired in many ways, could yet be primitive enough to worship so many gods let alone so many peculiar gods.

Yet the desire to imagine the object of worship in tangible form is common to most people: god tends to be visualized in mankind's image. The Christian God, as depicted, for example, by Michelangelo, is a venerable old man with a beard; and Christian iconography reflects the conventions of the time in which a work was painted or sculpted. One supposes that the ancient Egyptians looked to their own surroundings for manifestations of divinity, as did other peoples in the early stages of development in their societies. Seen objectively, the Egyptians' worship of a falcon god, for example, is surely no more strange a manifestation of religious belief than was the image of the Angel Gabriel with his halo and enormous wings. And the Egyptians could daily watch the sweep of a falcon across the sky, whereas the number of people who have beheld the Angel Gabriel is not large!

CHAPTER ONE

THE LAND OF EGYPT AND ITS INFLUENCE UPON THE RELIGION OF THE ANCIENT EGYPTIANS

I t is a truism to say that the activities of people everywhere are influenced by the conditions under which they live, and religious thought is no exception to this. Before the days of mass communication, an Eskimo, living in a cold climate, had no experience of any great heat generated by the sun. His idea of hell, therefore, was of a place of extreme cold. Conversely, a man who had lived all his life in a hot climate could only visualize hell as an even hotter place than any with which he had ever had acquaintance.

Most ancient Egyptians lived in a river valley, 1,250 km long from ancient Egypt's southern border at Aswan to its northern boundary on the Mediterranean coast. For much of its length the Nile valley is hemmed in by ancient river terraces. The only naturally verdant land was that watered by the great river which flowed through the valley, the Nile; the rest was desert. In some places, the green strip of land was just over 1 km wide; in others, its width stretched up to 21 km. For the final 160 km or so, the Nile fanned out into the Delta, a triangular, flat area of tributaries, marshes and fields measuring some 240 km across at its widest point.

The land in which the Egyptians lived was 'the gift of the River',[1] according to the Greek traveller Herodotus, who visited Egypt in the middle of the fifth century BC. Every year, the Nile, swollen by the torrential rain that fell in Uganda and Ethiopia, where the river had its twin sources, and by melting snow from the Ethiopian mountains, flooded its banks. Herodotus noted that when the Nile inundated the land, 'the whole country is converted into a sea and the towns, which alone remain above water, look like the islands in the Aegean'.[2] The Inundation which came annually to Egypt was only halted at the end of the nineteenth century AD with the building of a dam at Aswan. After completion of this, the Old Aswan Dam, in 1902, the flood waters which had caused the Inundation were held back in a great 230 km long reservoir behind the dam and only allowed through its 180 sluices in a regulated flow.

The annual flood not only irrigated the narrow river valley of Egypt: it had another inestimable benefit. When the flood waters receded, they left behind them a rich alluvial silt, scoured from the soil of Uganda and Ethiopia as the White and Blue Niles flowed through their respective countries before joining together at Khartoum in the Sudan. This silt enabled the Egyptians to become a settled agricultural society rather than desert-dwelling nomads. The Nile brought prosperity to Egypt: the desert that bounded the area covered by the Inundation gave her security, for it was an effective barrier against attack from other countries.

The desert also isolated Egypt against outside influences. This and the narrowness of the land in which they lived, meant that the Egyptians had limited horizons both physically and metaphorically. They were an intensely inward-looking people, distrustful of foreigners. Indeed, they looked upon non-Egyptians as less than human: their word for mankind, *remeth*, was the same as that for Egyptians. Whenever they spoke of the inhabitants of other countries, they usually appended a derogatory epithet – 'that vile Kushite' or 'the wretched Beduin'. The phenomenon is not unknown to other peoples isolated from outside contacts: the Eskimos call themselves Inuit, 'the men', meaning human beings; to the Chinese, the term for 'foreign' and 'non-human' is the same.

The regularity of the Inundation and the security afforded by the desert not only moulded the mental attitudes of the Egyptians, they also determined the way in which they lived. Life in Egypt depended upon the vagaries of the Nile. If the annual flood was too high, havoc ensued. If the flood was too low, a smaller area of land was rendered fit for the sowing of crops and less food could be grown. If a low flood was repeated over several consecutive years, shortage of food was the inevitable outcome, sometimes reaching famine proportions.

The early Egyptians soon learned how important the Nile was to them. Over 5,000 years ago, the many separate tribes which then inhabited Egypt began to cooperate with each other. They banded together to make the best use of the Nile by harnessing and conserving the water, by building dykes, irrigation ditches and canals. In so doing, they became a unified society ruled by a central authority which was responsible for directing the control of the water, building and maintaining dykes and canals and storing the agricultural produce of the nation. They became, in fact, one of the earliest civilizations; and their conservatism, allied with their isolation behind natural barriers, ensured that they were to enjoy that civilization for over 3,000 years.

Many aspects of life in ancient Egypt were influenced by the Nile. The seasons of the year were determined by the behaviour of the River; there were three of them: Inundation (*akhet*, which means 'flooded'), the four months (July–October, provided the lunar and solar calendars were in step: see page 29) during which the land was covered by the flood waters of the Nile; Winter (*peret*, which means 'coming forth'), the four months (November–February) during which the fields emerged from the water and seed was sown; and Summer (*shomu*, which perhaps means 'deficiency of water'), the four months (March–June) during which the harvest was gathered.

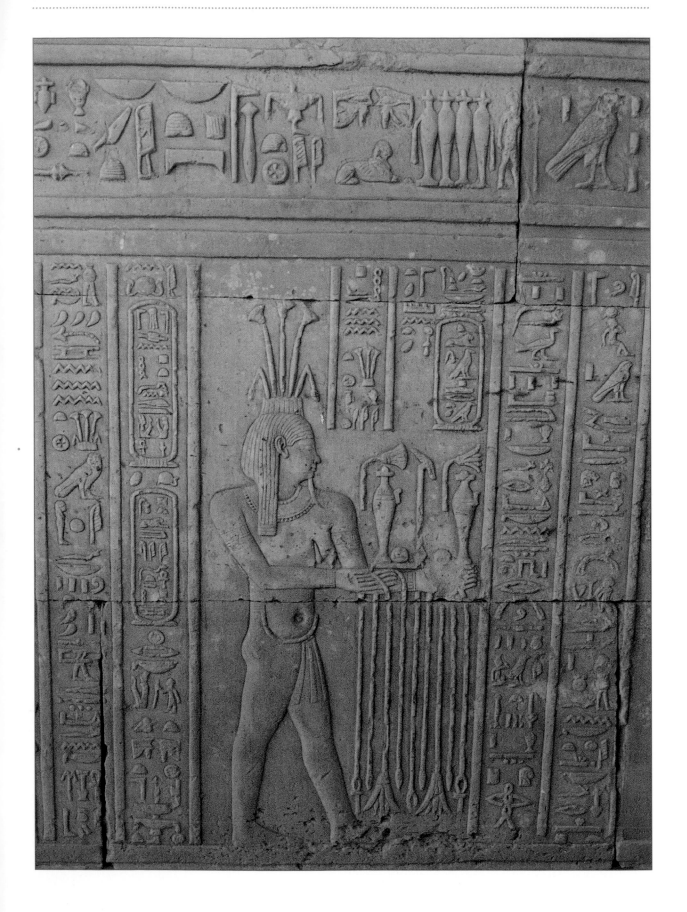

The Nile determined property values. Land in Egypt was divided into three categories: first, that which always received the benefit of the Inundation, second, that which sometimes did, and third, that which never did; and taxes were assessed accordingly. Even Justice was influenced by the Nile. There were incessant wrangles over rights to use water, or over boundaries that had been blurred during the Inundation, and many of these cases came to court. The importance of the Nile and its water was reflected in the accounts men gave of themselves in the Afterlife; or left as their records for posterity. The declaration that a man had not 'held up the water in its season' or 'built a dam against running water' or 'diverted his neighbour's water for his own use' was held to be of equal importance with the avowal of never having committed murder or robbery.

The Nile, which the Egyptians called the River (*itrw*), came, or so they thought, from the place where the world began. Accordingly, they oriented themselves southwards towards the cavern at Aswan where the Nile had its mythological source (see page 26). The mythological cause of the Inundation was the goddess Isis, weeping copious tears into the Nile in commemoration of her dear, dead husband, Osiris; and every year the Egyptians celebrated the event on the Night of Clouds (*Gerekh-en-Haty*), the great festival that marked the beginning of the Inundation, an event that modern Egyptians celebrated before the building of the Aswan Dam as the Night of the Tear Drop (*Leilet el-Nuktah*: 18 June).

Considering that the Nile was so vital to the Egyptians, it is surprising to discover that this great river was not elevated to the position of most important god in the land. In fact, the Nile as such was not deified at all. Instead, it was represented by Hapy, the Spirit or Essence of the Nile. Many are the figures of Hapy that can be seen in temples, carved on the dadoes that run along the bases of walls within the temple; he is depicted as a man with a pendulous belly (always a sign of a prosperous and well-fed man to the ancient Egyptians, a man to be respected) and the breasts of a woman, wearing on his head clusters of Nile plants.

Thus, the characteristics peculiar to the land of Egypt – a long, narrow valley surrounded and protected by desert, a river which ensured a plentiful supply of water and fertile soil, a climate which had little rainfall and no snow or fog, a land on which the sun shone constantly but which was prevented from turning into an arid waste by that plentiful supply of water – made the ancient Egyptians into a highly conservative, parochial, even complacent, society. They lived in a land that was productive but nevertheless demanded constant hard work, and forced its inhabitants to be practical. The Egyptians, therefore, tended to be people of little imagination, who did not indulge in any great flights of fancy. They were parochial: their eyes were turned on their own neighbourhood no matter how confined that neighbourhood might be. The ancient Egyptians had no real sense of nationalism, and they certainly did not have a sense of internationalism.

In spite of their narrow, inward-looking way of life, many Egyptians must have posed the eternal, universal questions – who created the world? and the sun

Opposite: Hapy: relief from Temple of Hathor, Denderah. Graeco-Roman period.

and the stars? who created life on earth, both animal and human? what happens when one dies? is there life after death? – and found acceptable answers to their questions by conceiving gods and a religion that were developed directly from their own experience of life as they lived it in the land of Egypt.

TWO

FORMS OF RELIGION IN ANCIENT EGYPT

he earliest Egyptians, in common with most primitive human beings, probably worshipped simple things such as oddly shaped stones and hills. This type of worship is called animism, that is, the attribution of a living soul to inanimate objects and natural phenomena. A 'rational' person might stub a toe against a stone and regard it as an accident. A primitive man is more likely to think that the stone has attacked him and consider it to be something unfriendly or even malevolent. If he were sufficiently in awe of it, he might turn the stone into an object of worship.

Animists believe that the souls attached to inanimate objects can detach themselves and become 'spirits'. Such a spirit is able to take any form it chooses. It thus poses a threat to human beings, for it is always looking for an opportunity to enter their bodies and those of animals. Once it does so, it changes the behaviour of its host whose death it can bring about through disease. Animists also believe that spirits can be disembodied and cause disasters and calamities, although, on the other hand, some spirits are beneficial and kindly. They also believe that the dead possess souls and must be propitiated by the living in case they try to do harm; hence, animists are often practitioners of ancestor worship.

The early Egyptians, like other animists, identified certain animals, birds, trees or stones as homes of spirits, both good and bad. Even geographical features could be venerated; thus the highest peak in the Theban area was worshipped as *Ta-Dehenet* (The Mountain Top) and became the goddess of the Theban necropolis. Gradually, the good spirits became 'gods' and were served by magicians who claimed to have power to influence their actions on behalf of their fellow beings; and to be able to avert the malevolence of the evil spirits.

Mankind has always had two basic needs: food and sex. In Egypt these needs, combined with a fear of the unknown and the inexplicable, gave the magician whose actions seemed to guarantee their continuance great power. In less primitive times, theories were promulgated that turned magic into religion.

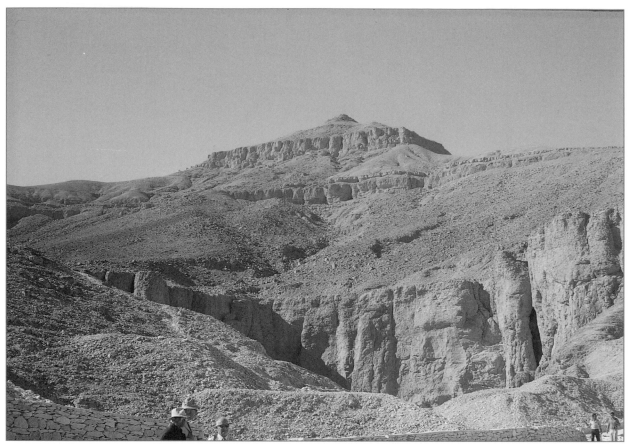

Ta-Dehenet (The Mountain Top), Luxor.

However, the Egyptians never entirely lost their primitive instincts; they remained a very superstitious people, and magic always played an important part in their religious beliefs.

The animism of the early Egyptians led to fetishism and the worship of animals. Fetishism endows an object with magical and mystical power. In many places in Egypt, different fetishes were worshipped. There often seems to be no clear reason why any particular object should be venerated, unless it is obvious that it had a close association with the district in which it was worshipped. But among the fetishes of ancient Egypt can be numbered a fossil belemnite, a shield and arrows, and a sceptre.

Being an agricultural people, the Egyptians were brought into daily contact with animals and birds; it was not surprising that they should turn such creatures into objects of worship, a worship that was localized according to the kind of animal found in a particular district. Animals were venerated at first because of the qualities they possessed – for their strength, their beauty, their virility or their swiftness; or because they were feared. The belief that certain animals possessed divine powers eventually led to these animals being linked with individual deities: such animals were considered to be imbued with the spirit of the deity, and to be his or her manifestation upon earth.

The Egyptians of the prehistoric era eventually began to give human form to their sacred animals and objects. They had discovered that there were inherent difficulties in having purely inanimate or animal gods: animal gods, for instance, were unable to speak and make their wishes known. The priests seem to have solved the problem by wearing masks, fashioned in imitation of the heads of the animal gods, from within which they themselves gave voice to the gods' wishes, a practice which resulted in the noted Egyptian custom of representing gods with human bodies and animal heads.

The third type of god worshipped by the ancient Egyptians was the cosmic god – moon, storm, wind, and, especially, the sun. This type of deity represents a higher order of divine being since it is difficult to personalize a cosmic god, with the result that this type of god is less easy to comprehend and therefore demands a greater degree of intellectual effort. Cosmic gods arrived on the scene much later than the fetish and local gods. It was not until the historic era that they were fully developed. At that time, the sun in particular became a universal god, worshipped throughout the land; and with the founding of the Egyptian state it was elevated to the status of state god.

The peculiar characteristics of the land in which the Egyptians lived influenced their religion by diversifying it. Until about 3000 BC, Egypt was divided into two distinct halves, each inhabited by tribes of different ethnic groups. The northern half, usually called Lower Egypt because the lower reaches of the Nile run through it, seems to have been inhabited by people of Semitic origins. It was cut up in all directions by arms of the Nile, marshes and canals. The southern half, or Upper Egypt, lay in the narrowest, least fertile part of the Nile valley, where the river often runs between high cliffs, thus denying the Inundation access to the land. It was inhabited by people of African origin.

Communication between the two halves of the country, and even within the two halves, was extremely difficult: the Nile was the only highway. Thus Egypt fell easily into provinces, each with differences in speech, ways of life, customs and religion. In the historic period, these provinces were called *separt*, later renamed *nomes* by the Greeks, the term that is now generally used. There were forty-two nomes, or administrative divisions, which were established early in Egyptian history: twenty-two in Upper Egypt and twenty in Lower Egypt. Their boundaries were shifted from time to time, but their number remained constant since forty-two was considered to be a magic number by the Egyptians.

Within each nome, towns and villages tended to be cut off from each other. The nomes themselves had characteristics of their own, since they were probably based on what had been tribal areas. Each nome had a capital city; a special deity which was given the name of the nome and could be impersonated by a human being during great national ceremonies in temples; and a nome standard which carried a representation of the chief deity or fetish worshipped in the nome. Thus in each province, town and village in Egypt, religion took on a special form peculiar to that particular place. Every locality had its own local deity, who was often worshipped in a way that was special to him or her, and who was often equipped with myths and legends of his or her own.

During periods of unrest, or when there was a weak central government, religious differences were intensified. However, when the country was united, a strange process commenced. The principal deity of the town or city which was the seat of the official royal residence – this varied from time to time according to the vicissitudes of history – became the state god. His temple was visited from all parts of the country, its god recognized by all. The fame that providing the state god for the country brought to his home town caused other towns to wish for a god of such distinction. And so they either introduced his worship into their own temples, or they 'discovered' that he was in reality one and the same god as their own local deity; and the two deities would be blended into one – for example, Amen-Re (see page 141).

As a uniform way of life developed in Egypt, this process of merging deities, called syncretism, should logically have led to the blending of all the gods and goddesses of Egypt into one god with a very long name made up of the syllables of the names of all the other gods. However, the Egyptians were not the most logical of people, and this 'happy' state was never attained! Thus, throughout their history, there were great numbers of deities. How many is impossible to establish, since some are merely names mentioned in hieroglyphic texts, and with each discovery or translation of a new text, more may be revealed. The number is enlarged, some estimate to over two thousand, because many gods have female counterparts; and because the hieroglyph denoting 'god', ⸏ or ⸎, is often added to the name of any unusual creature. Many gods, therefore, have more in common with fairies, pixies, goblins, trolls, demons and similar creatures than with anything that is generally accepted as a true deity.

The myriad gods worshipped by the ancient Egyptians fell into three main categories:

1) Local gods, which were the inanimate objects (fetishes) or animals, birds and other living creatures associated with a particular locality: the earliest type of deity worshipped by the Egyptians.
2) Universal gods, the cosmic deities who represented the forces of nature – the sun, the moon, the stars, wind and storm.
3) Personal gods, the objects or creatures chosen by individuals to receive their allegiance (see page 208).

Religion pervaded every aspect of life in ancient Egypt, apparently making the Egyptians into a very religion-ridden society. However, this does not mean that they were more pious than other people, or more devout, humble, godly, spiritual, pure in heart or worthy of being described by any other adjective listed in Roget's Thesaurus as synonymous with religion. It simply means that Egyptian history was the story of the interplay between gods and kings; that for much of that history the economy of Egypt was organized around the temples; that religious beliefs affected the way in which the Egyptians dealt with death.

At the same time, there was a private religion (see page 208). Because ordinary Egyptians had no admittance to the innermost areas of a temple, the only opportunity they were given to behold the deity to whom the temple was dedicated came when the cult statue, in which the spirit of the deity was thought to reside, and which was normally kept in his temple's innermost sanctuary, was brought out of its shrine on the occasion of one of the great festivals that took place at certain times of the year, and carried in procession around the town for the edification of the populace. Whereas the Egyptians erected official temples for local and universal gods, private individuals had their own beliefs, their own private god or gods, and were happy to construct with their own hands small shrines near their houses for their personal gods to whom they could turn for aid and comfort.

Meanwhile, the official state religion of Egypt concerned itself with promoting the well-being of the gods, which they reciprocated by maintaining the

Re and Maat: hieroglyphs from the memorial temple of Sety I at Abydos.

established order of the world. The vehicle through which the gods received favour, and in turn dispensed it, was the king, aided by a hierarchy of priests. One of the most important aspects of Egyptian religion was the fact that the king was regarded as a god. Tradition stated that in the beginning, kingship came to earth in the person of the god-king, Re, who brought his daughter, Maat, the embodiment of Truth and Justice, with him. Thus the beginning of the world was synchronous with the beginning of kingship and social order.

The kings of Egypt legitimized their claim to the throne in ways that were influenced by religious beliefs. The god-king Horus was the son of the god Osiris who had been king; and so every new king of Egypt became a Horus to his predecessor's Osiris. By acting as Horus had towards Osiris, in other words, by burying his predecessor, each new king made legal his claim to the throne (see page 87). Theogamy was another means through which this was accomplished. Here, the principal god of the time was said to have assumed the form of the reigning king in order to beget a child on his queen; that child later claimed to be the offspring of both his earthly and his heavenly father; and the earthly father was quite content to have been cuckolded by the god (see pages 126 and 141).

The king was the unifying factor in Egyptian religious life. In theory, he was chief priest in every temple; the only person entitled to officiate in the temple rituals, the only person entitled to enter the holy of holies within the temple. Obviously, this was a fiction: the king could not be in every temple at once. However, the fiction was maintained in the reliefs carved on the walls of temples, which always show the king making offerings to the gods. The king was the embodiment of the connection between the world of men and the world of gods, the linchpin of Egyptian society. It was his task to make the world go on functioning; it was his task to make the sun rise and set, the Nile to flood and ebb, the grain to grow; all of which could only be achieved by the performance of the proper rituals within the temples.

It is perhaps appropriate here to point out the vast differences between what the term 'temple' meant to the Egyptians and what it means to people today. Egyptian temples symbolized the earth: thus they were made of the most enduring materials that the Egyptians were capable of handling at any given period. The earliest temples were built of reeds and mud; in the early dynastic period most were constructed of mud-brick, only the lintels of their doors and windows, and the bases of columns, being made of stone. By the time of the Old Kingdom, the Egyptians were building their temples almost entirely in stone, although not many of these structures can be seen today due to the fact that it was the custom never to build a 'new' temple on a virgin site, but to 'renew' it on a site that had been in use since time immemorial. Thus, the great stone structures that can still be seen at Thebes, for instance, or at Edfu, have been built over much older temples. Inside, the ceilings of the temples were painted with stars to represent the firmament, and the walls decorated at the base with carvings of the marsh plants and reeds that grew on the banks of the Nile.

The Egyptians believed that the earth was constantly threatened by the forces of chaos that had existed before the world was created; they had been overcome but were an ever-present danger: only the gods could keep them at bay. These gods appeared in different guises in different places all over Egypt, where they had to be equipped with homes – temples, the mansions of the gods. Inside these houses, the gods could be protected and nourished so that they could perform their divine tasks.

From the beginning of the historical period, there were two distinct types of temple in Egypt: the memorial or funerary temple, dedicated to the worship of a dead king; and the cult temple, dedicated to the worship of one or more of the many deities of Egypt. Each type of temple owned property and estates, often in many parts of the country, and sometimes outside it, which not only rendered the temple self-supporting but also produced extra revenue so that temples could become owners of great wealth. The cult temple, especially, played an important part in the life of the community. However, for the ordinary person its role was not that of a place of worship. The Egyptian temple was nothing like a church, mosque or synagogue. It was not a place to which one might go for spiritual comfort, to praise god, to discuss theological points or to be instructed in religious matters. Although some temples were equipped with special areas where an ordinary person might speak to the god (see pages 146 and 169), normally cult temples were concerned with the religion of the state and the maintenance of the bureaucracy.

Ancient Egyptian temples were big business. The temple was a land-owner: the ordinary Egyptian could and did rent land from it. It was the repository for legal documents, the place where births and marriages were registered and contracts drawn up. Schools were centred on temples: scribes, artists and doctors were trained there. Most Egyptians were illiterate; temple scribes were therefore employed to draw up documents and write such letters as were necessary. Doctor-priests trained and based in temples tended the ailments of the Egyptians, and some temples even had rudimentary hospitals within their precincts where the sick could receive treatment, which often consisted of magical as well as medical methods.

Just as the Egyptian temple was unlike anything modern man understands by the word 'temple', so an Egyptian 'priest' was not like the spiritual leader that is the modern concept of a Christian priest or a Muslim imam; neither was he a recognized authority on religious law as for instance is a Jewish rabbi. The priests of ancient Egypt were not spiritual leaders or preachers; they did not have parishioners. They were not inspiring deliverers of sermons because congregations of worshippers did not feature in the life of an Egyptian temple. They were not expected to be authorities on general religious doctrine, for there was none. There was no central system of religious belief or organization; each town had its own, and so the priesthood of any temple followed the customs and practices peculiar to that temple. A majority of the priests in any temple were part-time laymen who, after their period of temple service, went back to their homes to carry on normal life.

In theory, the king appointed all priests; and in every temple in the land they served as his surrogates. A career in the priesthood was open to women, also.[1]

Important positions in certain temples, notably those of the goddess Hathor, were occupied by women, although most priestesses acted as musicians and chantresses. To become a priest, a man did not need to have any special calling or gift for religion. His task was that of administrator of temple property, estates and revenues; and within the temple his function was to act as a domestic servant to the god, ministering to his daily needs. This was the case whether the god was a living animal or bird kept in the temple as the representative on earth of a god, or a golden effigy of the deity. The one stipulation for entry to the temple was that a man, or a woman, be pure.

To achieve the required purity a priest (or priestess) had to purify himself for several days before entering a temple by chewing natron (carbonate or bicarbonate of soda) and fumigating himself with incense. On the day that he entered the temple, he had to wash himself, cut his finger and toe nails, and, in the case of a priest, be shaved and depilated of all body hair. Male priests had to be circumcised. Neither priests nor priestesses were required to lead celibate lives outside the temple. But they had to be prepared to observe the prohibitions observed by their particular temple – a taboo on eating fish, perhaps, or on certain gestures.

Although the priestly office was often hereditary, it was possible to be appointed priest by the king as a mark of favour, especially if he wanted to place his own man in office, or to purchase that office. Anyone prepared to make the sacrifice of, for instance, being circumcised, or refraining from sexual intercourse during his time of service, could become a priest; the essential qualification, at least for the lower ranks, was purity rather than a talent for the priesthood. The number of priests serving in a temple depended upon its size and importance, which in turn depended upon the importance of its god or of the town in which it was situated. Priests were divided into groups, called *s3* ('sa') in ancient Egyptian, often translated into the Greek word, *phyle*. There were four *s3* to each temple, and each served one lunar month in four.

Certain categories of priest were permanent members of the temple staff: the High Priest of the temple, whom the Egyptians called the 'First Servant of the God', was one such. The career structure that led to this position is well illustrated by one Bakenkhons, who served in the Temple of Amun at Thebes at the beginning of Dynasty XIX. Bakenkhons entered the service of the god at the age of fifteen, and served as a 'pure-priest' – the lowest category of priest – for four years. When he was nearly twenty years old, he was promoted to the rank of 'Father of the God', a second-rank priest. At thirty-two, he was made third 'Servant of the God'; at forty-seven, he became second 'Servant of the God'. Then, when he was fifty-nine years old, he became 'First Servant of the God' – in other words, High Priest of Amun, one of the most powerful men in the land at that time, a position he held for twenty-seven years until his death at the age of eighty-six.

The advantages of being a priest were many. Each priest received a share of the income from temple estates, and of the offerings which came into the temple every day, the share being greater or lesser according to the size of the temple and the rank of the priest. The wives and daughters of priests were entitled to certain allowances from temple revenue, and the priests themselves were exempted from certain taxes. They were often granted immunity from having to undertake state labour such as work on dykes and canals; and in certain temples, the priesthood was granted immunity from all such labour by special royal decree.

There was no rigid division between the sacred and the secular world in Egypt. The secular world viewed the temples that were to be found in every sizeable town more or less as places of business; the priests of those temples all worked, in their different ways and according to the beliefs and customs of their own temples, to maintain the equilibrium between the world of the gods and the world of men. The worship of gods, therefore, was just one of the many activities undertaken by the temple bureaucracy, which was also responsible for many of the functions that nowadays would come within the province of local government.

However, the worship of gods was the chief *raison d'être* for the existence of the temples. In some ways this worship bore a resemblance to, say, Christian worship, in that hymns of praise were sung to the gods. Other forms of extolling gods, such as dancing and clapping, were also employed. The most obvious difference between Egyptian and Christian worship can be seen in the prayers made to the god of each temple: Christian prayers tend to be supplications to the Almighty either for the general good or for the well-being of a person other than the supplicant. Christians are taught that it is not an acceptable way of praying to ask for things directly for oneself. The Egyptians adopted a much more business-like approach. Their 'prayers', as we know from the texts carved on the walls of their temples, are made in the spirit of *quid pro quo*. The priest/king makes an offering to the god, and the god reciprocates in kind. Thus, for example, if the king offers the god wine, the god in turn rewards the king with the gift of the vineyards that produce the wine; if the royal offering is incense, the god promises the king that he shall have dominion over the land whence the incense came. All this makes Egyptian religion sound less than spiritual. In many ways, it was. On the other hand, there is evidence from texts which exhort priests to live in accordance with high moral principles that spiritual ideals were not entirely absent from Egyptian religious life.

The number of gods worshipped in ancient Egypt meant that there was no one version of the answers to the questions posed at the end of Chapter One. For us, Egyptian religion seems to comprise many conflicting beliefs. One of the reasons for this is that the Egyptians, conservative as they were, never discarded any of their old beliefs in favour of new ones: they simply assimilated them. They were quite content to have several different explanations for the same thing, for each explanation might serve in different contexts. There were, for instance, several variations on the theme of the creation of the world, for the great creator gods such as Atum, Re, Ptah and Neit each had his or her own version. But whichever deity performed the act of creation, there was one underlying image: in the beginning, water covered the earth and all was dark and void. This primordial water was called the Nun, and it is a natural image for the Egyptians to have conjured up. They must have seen their land covered by water during the Inundation, and have seen, when the flood water began to recede, little islands of land begin to emerge. Just so did the first piece of earth emerge from the primordial waters of the Nun.

There were many ideas of what the universe was. The sky was visualized as a cow whose feet rested on the earth (Hathor); or as a woman who supported herself with hands and feet on the earth (Nut). The sky was said to be a sheet of water on which the stars sailed in boats, just as the Egyptians themselves sailed on the Nile. Or else the sky rested on four fabulous mountains situated at the four corners of the earth – the pillars of heaven. The sun was said to be the right eye of a great god whose left eye was the moon (Atum; Re). It was born every morning as the calf of the celestial cow (see above); or as the child of the Sky Goddess. It was rolled across the sky by a beetle (Khepri) until in the evening it became an old man (Atum). The sun, the moon and the stars were said to sail in ships over the heavenly ocean. There was said to be a second heaven under the earth; through this heaven a river ran just as the Nile runs through Egypt. Every night, the sun descended under the earth, where it traversed the underworld Nile. And every morning, it ascended to earth again through two whirlpools at Elephantine (Aswan).

The great gods were accompanied by their own retinues of lesser deities: thus, at Heliopolis (see page 23), Re is the head of a group of nine gods known to the Egyptians as the *pesdjet* and to us as the Great Ennead (from the Greek word *ennead* meaning 'group of nine'); at Hermopolis (see page 183), Thoth is the head of a group of eight gods, now known by the Greek term *Ogdoad*. When other towns wished to possess an ennead of their own, they displaced one of the original gods and inserted their own deity in his place. Sometimes, they simply added their own local god to the ennead, not a whit abashed that in so doing they made their 'group of nine' into a group containing ten members!

The Egyptians had a very relaxed attitude towards their gods, whether they were great state gods or lesser divinities. The stories told about Egyptian gods, often by their own adherents, show that the Egyptians regarded these deities as a class of being much like themselves: they had the same need for food and drink; they could suffer pain, age or death; they had the same vices and virtues, they were just as apt to commit acts of folly, treachery or trickery as a fallible human being. However, their lapses did not earn them scorn from their worshippers: instead, they merely moved the Egyptians to treat their gods in a tolerantly amused manner; and, as might be expected from an agricultural people, often to describe their activities in a frank and earthy way. In spite of this, the gods of ancient Egypt were beings to be respected, for it was only through their beneficence and goodwill that Egypt prospered, as she undoubtedly did, for over three thousand years.

PART
II

THE MAJOR GODS OF EGYPT

THE SUN GOD

· ·

The ancient Egyptians undoubtedly recognized that life was dependent upon the sun. In a land such as Egypt, where the sun shines every day, undimmed by rain or fog, winter and summer alike, it was perhaps inevitable that it should become an object of worship, reverenced for its beneficial qualities and at the same time feared for its potential for destruction.

The sun was worshipped in different forms, under several names. The most important sun gods were: Re, who was the sun's disk itself, the noonday sun; Khepri, who was thought of as a beetle (*Scarabaeus sacer*, the dung-beetle) and denoted the rising sun; Atum, who was thought of as an old man leaning on a stick and represented the setting sun; Horus, who usually took the form of a falcon; Horakhty, another falcon god, whose name means 'Horus-of-the-Two-Horizons', and who, when coalesced with Re as Re-Horakhty, became identified with the sun; Aten, who became especially popular during the reign of Amenhotep IV–Akhenaten (the Amarna Period) and was represented as the sun's disk with rays which terminated in hands.

The cult of the sun was established, probably long before dynastic times, at Iunu (On) in Lower Egypt, where it was worshipped in the forms of Atum, Khepri, Horakhty and, above all, Re. After the unification of Egypt into one kingdom, an event which took place around 3100 BC, Memphis was established as its capital city. However, the priesthood of Iunu continued to exert great influence, and this influence probably extended to the new Rulers of all Egypt. The Greeks later gave On the new name of Heliopolis (City of the Sun). Today, the site of the city which was once the spiritual centre of Egypt lies under the suburb of Matarieh on the north-east side of Cairo.

ATUM

Atum, whose name means 'The Complete One', was one of the great creator gods, possibly the oldest deity to be worshipped at Iunu, where, coalesced with Re to form Re-Atum, he became a sun god.

The ichneumon or Egyptian mongoose, which the Egyptians today call *kutt Fara'un* (Pharaoh's cat), is the great destroyer of snakes and crocodile eggs and was thought to be the incarnation of Atum. One legend says that the god was once attacked by a snake and had to transform himself into an ichneumon in order to destroy it. However, Atum is never depicted as an ichneumon but always as a man with a man's head.

Atum was held to be a self-created god who made the whole of creation out of himself. He first took shape as a serpent which came into being in the Primeval Waters of the Nun. Although eventually he took on human shape, the Egyptians believed that at the end of the world Atum would revert to his serpent form and return to the Nun, with which the earth would once more be covered.

The earliest written doctrine of Atum as procreator was set down about 2350 BC. At this time, the last king of Dynasty V, Unas, built a pyramid-tomb at Sakkara. Here, for the first time, inscriptions were carved inside a pyramid, in the burial chamber and its antechamber. These inscriptions are known as the Pyramid Texts. The Texts, which are found also in many of the Sixth-Dynasty pyramids, are a collection of so-called 'spells', arranged haphazardly and differing from pyramid to pyramid: Unas' selection, for example, has 228 spells out of a possible total of over seven hundred. The spells tell of the creation of the world according to the doctrine expounded at Iunu; they give the dead king all the information needed concerning the Afterlife and how to reach it; and they provide the magical means with which to ensure the well-being of the deceased.

By the end of Dynasty VI, exclusive royal power had waned. One result of this was the adaptation of the Pyramid Texts for use by those commoners who were accorded burial in a tomb. The tomb of a commoner was not a pyramid, a type of tomb reserved for kings and queens; and the magical texts which had originally decorated the walls of pyramids were, when used by commoners, painted on the wooden coffins in which they were buried. Hence, the Pyramid Texts became the Coffin Texts.

In one Coffin Text, Atum speaks about the Beginning: 'I [Atum] was still alone in the waters, in a state of inertness. I had not yet found anywhere to stand or sit, and Iunu had not yet been founded that I might be therein.' But before Atum arose from the Primeval Waters, he created the first creatures: Shu, a male, and Tefnut, a female. There are two versions of the act by which 'he who had been one became three'. One is told in Pyramid Text 527, which says that:

Atum was creative in that he proceeded to masturbate himself in Heliopolis. He took his penis in his hand so that he might obtain the pleasure of orgasm thereby. And brother and sister were born – that is, Shu and Tefnut.

This is obviously a late, Heliopolis-oriented version of the myth – several other Texts say that the masturbation took place not in Heliopolis but in the Primeval Waters.

Other myths concerning the creation of Shu and Tefnut maintain that Atum spat them forth from his mouth. This concept makes use of a play on two words which both mean 'to spit' or 'to expectorate' – *ishesh*, which has a sound similar to Shu; and *tef*, which forms the first syllable of the name Tefnut. The version of the birth of Shu and Tefnut through spitting from Atum's mouth rather than through the more crude but perhaps more logical method of masturbation is the forerunner of the idea that the world was created through God's word (see page 40).

Atum's mouth contained spittle and the breath of life. Tefnut was formed from the spittle and therefore became the Goddess of Moisture. Shu, being formed from Atum's breath, became the God of Air; and, because air is essentially the breath of life, he became Life itself. After their birth, the two newly formed deities became separated from their father, Atum, and were lost in the dark immensity of the Nun. Atum sent his Eye to look for them. When they were found, he named his son, Shu, as Life, and his daughter, Tefnut, as Order, the personification of what we would call the forces of nature; and lay entwined with them in the Nun, keeping them safe.

Spell 80 of the Coffin Texts tells us what happened next. Atum, tired of lying inert in the Nun, asks how he can create a resting place for himself. Nun tells him, 'Kiss your daughter, Order, put her to your nose; so will your heart live. Never let her leave you, let Order, who is your daughter, be with your son, Shu, who is Life.' Atum then asks Shu to support him while he holds Tefnut to his nose, by which the Egyptians meant that he kissed her. And so Iunu came into being as the first mound which rose out of the waters of the Nun. And Atum was able to rest upon it. According to Pyramid Text 600, Atum was this mound, which was called the High Hill in Iunu. Only when Atum appeared as or on the High Hill did light break over the hitherto dark Nun.

Other accounts of the first dawn tell of a heron, known to the Egyptians as the Benu Bird, skimming over the waters of the Nun until it came to rest on a rock. As it did so, it opened its beak and a cry echoed over the unutterable silence of the Nun. The world was filled with 'that which it had not known'; the cry of the Benu Bird 'determined what is and is not to be'. Thus, the Benu Bird, as an

The Benu Bird: tomb of the workman, Iry-nefer,
Deir el-Medina, Dynasty XIX.

aspect of Atum, the god who created himself, brought light and life to the world.

The rocky perch upon which the Benu Bird alighted was worshipped at Iunu in the form of the Benben-stone, a pillar topped by a pyramid-shaped stone, the pyramidion, the sides of which reflected the sun's light at dawn. This stone was the most sacred fetish worshipped at Heliopolis. The capstone of every pyramid, if not the pyramid itself, was thought to be a representation of the Benben-stone and the dead king buried under it was thought to be under the direct protection of the Sun God himself.

The Benu Bird's cry began the cycles of time which the Egyptians believed to be divinely appointed: the twenty-four hour day with twelve hours allotted to daytime and twelve to night-time; the cycle of ten days which made up the Egyptian week; the thirty-day month; the year of twelve months but 365 days (see page 29); the periods of 1,460 years during which the civil and astronomical calendars diverged and then coincided again due to the fact that the astronomical year has 365 days plus one quarter of a day. The Benu Bird became the deity connected with the division of time, and its temple at Iunu, where the chief title of its High Priest was 'Overseer of Observers', was primarily concerned with the regulation of the calendar by solar and astral means. The priests of Heliopolis (Iunu) were the most learned of all, according to Herodotus.

Herodotus recounted the legend of the Benu Bird, which the Greeks called the *phoinix*, as follows:

> I have not seen a phoenix myself, except in paintings, for it is very rare and visits the country (so at least they say in Heliopolis) only at intervals of 500 years, on the occasion of the death of the parent bird. To judge by the paintings, its plumage is partly golden, partly red, and in shape and size it is exactly like an eagle. There is a story about the phoenix: it brings its parent in a lump of myrrh all the way from Arabia and buries the body in the Temple of the Sun. To perform this feat, the bird first shapes some myrrh into a sort of egg as big as it finds, by testing, that it can carry; then it hollows the lump out, puts its father inside and smears some more myrrh over the hole. The egg-shaped lump is then just of the same weight as it was originally. Finally, it is carried by the bird to the Temple of the Sun in Egypt. I pass on the story as it was told to me – but I don't believe it.[1]

Herodotus did not believe the story, but other Greeks did and enlarged upon the myth until eventually the phoenix became a fabulous bird that consumed itself in flames only to be reborn from the ashes. The Greeks thought of the phoenix as a herald of important events, while to the Egyptians, a heron flying out of the sunlight was a sign of joy and hope.

The Benu Bird depicted in Egyptian paintings, or on the papyrus rolls placed in the coffins of the dead to help them find their way to the Afterlife, is undoubtedly a gigantic heron, usually said to be an enlarged version of the grey heron, *Ardea cinerea*, which is common in Egypt. However, there is a possibility that it is based on the Goliath heron, *Ardea goliath*, now found, among other places, on the coast of the Red Sea but which may have been more widespread in ancient times. Recent excavations at Umm an-Nar (Trucial Oman) uncovered bird bones which, when reconstructed, proved to be from a species of heron much larger than any now living. It seems certain that a heron considerably larger than the Goliath heron lived in the region of the Persian Gulf some 5,000 years ago. Accordingly, the ornithologist Ella Hoch has proposed that a new species be erected for this heron under the name *Ardea bennuides*, the Benu-bird heron. She points out that although many thousands of ibises, baboons, cats and other creatures have been found mummified in Egypt, no example of a mummified heron has yet come to light, and she makes a very persuasive case for the Egyptians having seen her *Ardea bennuides* only as an extremely rare visitor to Egypt.[2] The Benu Bird may, in fact, be based on travellers' tales of the enormous heron seen on their trading expeditions to the Arabian Seas.

In the Heliopolitan myths, Shu and Tefnut produced two children, Geb, the earth, and Nut, the sky. Thus were created, step by step, air and moisture, earth and sky. Only when these elements were put together did the physical world come into being – an intellectual concept of the creation. In Egyptian representations of the universe, Shu is depicted standing with arms upraised supporting above his head the outstretched body of a woman wearing a long dress, with a man lying prone at his feet. The woman is Nut, the man is Geb; and thus was earth separated from sky by air. How this separation came about is a problem which exercised the minds of many early cultures. A complete Egyptian version of the solution to the problem is lost, but the story can be pieced together through allusions in the Pyramid Texts, and through inscriptions and pictures on coffins dating from the New Kingdom.

It seems that even in the womb Nut, the Sky Goddess, was at odds with her mother, Tefnut, and freed herself violently. She lay with her brother, the Earth God Geb, placing herself on top of him. But when Nut became pregnant by Geb, her father, Shu, the God of Air, was jealous. He tore the lovers apart and, placing one foot on Geb, pinning him down on his back, he held Nut aloft in his arms. Thus Earth became separated from Sky by Air.

Nut eventually gave birth to Geb's children – they became the sun, the stars and the planets and were placed on Nut's belly. According to a legend retold by Plutarch, Shu was so enraged by his beloved daughter bearing these children to Geb that he cursed her with a peculiar form of barrenness. He declared that she should never again be delivered of a child in any month of any year. Nut determined to evade her father's curse. She had a lover, the God of Time, Thoth, whom she challenged to a game of dice, and she succeeded in winning from him five days. The Egyptians used this myth to account for the five extra or epagomenal days which they had to add on to their regular calendar of 360 days, divided into twelve thirty-day months, in an attempt to bring lunar and solar time into balance. They never made allowance for the extra quarter of a day which is now accounted for in our Leap Year; hence the astronomical year gradually fell behind the civil calendar, so that the real winter fell in the summer of the civil calendar.

Because the five extra days Nut won from Thoth lay outside the normal year, the curse of her father, Shu, did not apply to them. Nut was therefore able to bring forth children on these days. On the first day, her son, Osiris, was born; on the second she delivered her son, Horus, later known as Haroeris or Horus the Elder. On the third day she gave birth to her son, Seth; on the fourth day, her daughter, Isis, was born; and on the fifth, her daughter, Nephthys. In due course, Osiris married Isis and Seth married Nephthys. They, together with their parents, Geb and Nut, their grandparents, Shu and Tefnut, and their brother, Haroeris, formed the group of gods which, with Atum at its head, was the Great Ennead of Iunu.

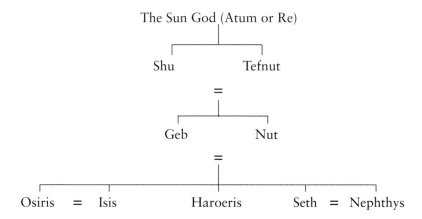

SHU

● ●

Shu, the son of Atum, was one of the oldest cosmic deities: the God of Air and Light. Since these were qualities difficult to portray, he was usually represented as a man wearing on his head the feather which is the hieroglyphic symbol for his name. His main function was to support the heavens, which he accomplished by kneeling on the earth with his arms raised above his head holding up the Sky Goddess, Nut. Apart from the feather, his other symbol was ▭, which depicts the four supports of heaven that supposedly stood at the four corners of the earth and helped Shu with his task.

Shu's chief sanctuary, which he shared with Tefnut, was some 20 km to the north-east of Heliopolis, at *Nay-ta-hut*, now known as Tell el-Yahudiya (Mound of the Jews). The Greeks named the city Leontopolis (City of the Lion), since here Shu was worshipped in the form of a lion and Tefnut in the form of a lioness. The explanation for this is to be found in the local version of the Heliopolitan creation legend which says that Shu and Tefnut first took shape as a pair of lion cubs who grew into the Two Lions who guard the eastern and western horizons. It is easy to understand why lions should be connected with the sun on the horizon: they lived in the deserts where the Egyptians thought that the sun died each evening and was born again each morning; and they were also thought to be able to see as well in the dark as in the light. Hence, the Lion of the Western Horizon guarded the sun by night while the Lion of the Eastern Horizon supervised the rising of the sun each morning.

The belief that man needed to be guarded while he slept at night so that he might rise like the sun next day led the Egyptians to decorate their beds with lion motifs. Headrests were treated in similar fashion, one of the finest examples being that found in the tomb of Tutankhamun in the Valley of the Kings at Luxor. It is made of ivory, with a carved figure of Shu kneeling on the base, holding the neck-support in his outstretched arms and flanked by the Lions of the Eastern and Western Horizons.

Legend says that Shu reigned as King of Egypt for many years. A late version of his story was inscribed during the Ptolemaic Period on a black granite shrine[3] which was erected in Phakussa (Faqus), the capital of the 20th Nome of Lower Egypt. In the nineteenth century AD, this shrine was removed to nearby Ismailia, where it was placed in the museum of the Suez Canal Company. According to the

Phakussa inscription, Shu was a good king who reigned upon the throne of his father – Re-Harmakhis in the Phakussa version of the legend – in his palace at Memphis. When his son, Geb, asked the gods what his father, Shu, had accomplished during his reign, he was told that Shu had slain all the enemies of Atum and Re, and had irrigated the towns, the settlements and the nomes of Egypt, erected walls to protect her, and built temples throughout the Two Lands (i.e. Egypt).

After many years of unchallenged rule, Shu became weak in body and diseased in his eyes. His followers quarrelled among themselves. Even his son, Geb, was disaffected, partly because he was envious of his father's position as king and partly because of Shu's action in separating him from Nut (see page 29). At last, Shu went up into heaven together with his followers. Darkness fell upon the land and the wind howled. For nine days neither god nor man could see the face of his fellow; and then the wind died down, the darkness receded and Geb appeared upon the throne of his father with all those who were in the palace making obeisance to him. Geb became King of Egypt while Shu took a place in the Company of Gods who attended upon Re, the Sun God.

Opposite, above: Shu holding Nut aloft: vignette from a Twenty-first-Dynasty Book of the Dead. (Now in the British Museum and known as the Greenfield Papyrus after its donor)

Below: Headrest from the tomb of Tutankhamun showing Shu and Tefnut as the Two Lions. (Cairo Museum)

TEFNUT

· ·

Tefnut took her place in the Heliopolitan Ennead as the daughter of the Sun God and the wife of his son, Shu. She personified the element of moisture and was usually depicted in human form wearing a sun's disk encircled by a cobra on her head. Like other goddesses, notably Hathor and Sekhmet, she was often called the Eye of Re.

A very ancient legend, set in the time when Re lived on earth as King of Egypt, tells of how Tefnut became estranged from her father and fled into Nubia. The cause of the rift between father and daughter is not known; however, once Tefnut reached Nubia, she transformed herself into a lioness and raged throughout the land emitting flames from her eyes and nostrils, drinking blood and feeding on flesh, both animal and human. Re missed his Eye, Tefnut, and longed to see her again. He sent for Shu, and for Thoth, the messenger of the gods, famed for his eloquence, and commanded them to go to Nubia and bring back his daughter. Shu and Thoth, having first disguised themselves as baboons, set off for Nubia.

Thoth found Tefnut in Bugem, and tried to persuade her to return to Egypt. At first, she refused: she had begun to enjoy herself hunting in the desert. Thoth persevered and painted for her a picture of the gloom that had descended on Egypt because of her absence. He promised her that the game that she now had to hunt for herself would be piled high on the altar that the Egyptians would build for her in gratitude if only she would return to them. At last, Tefnut agreed to accompany Thoth and Shu back to Egypt, and the two baboons led her home amidst great rejoicing. Attended by a great throng of Nubian musicians, dancers and baboons, Tefnut made a triumphant progress from one city to another until finally she was welcomed home by Re himself and restored to her rightful position as his Eye.

In some versions of this story, Tefnut is replaced by Hathor, who retreats to Nubia in high dudgeon because she has been prevented from destroying mankind (see page 43), and Shu takes over Thoth's role as chief pacifier of the angry goddess. However, the original version of the story seems to have belonged to the god Anhur, perhaps better known by the Greek version of his name, Onuris. Anhur – whose very name, which in ancient Egyptian means 'He-who-brought-back-the-Distant-One', links him with the estranged goddess, the Distant One, Tefnut – was the essential warrior god, a manifestation of the universal theme of the legendary hunter who returns to his people after subduing some monstrous beast. He was usually represented as a man wearing four tall plumes on his head, grasping a long spear in his hands, and poised on the balls of his feet ready to thrust down with the spear at some foe lying prone on the ground.

Onuris had two great sanctuaries, one at This, near Abydos, the town from which the first king of a united Egypt, Menes, originated; the other at Sebennytos (modern name, Samannud) which lies some 90 km north of Heliopolis, and which was the capital of the 12th Nome of Lower Egypt, the city from which the kings of the Thirtieth Dynasty originated. The most famous of Sebennytos' sons was Manetho, the historian who first divided Egyptian history into dynasties of kings. He was born at the beginning of the third century BC, and was probably a priest in the temple at Sebennytos.

At Sebennytos, Onuris had a mate, a lioness goddess called Mehit, a name which means 'She-who-has-been-completed'. The word *mehit* was also used by the Egyptians to refer to the Eye of Horus, which was gouged out by Seth and healed (or completed) by Hathor (see page 86). Thus, the legend of Onuris and the bringing back of the angry goddess from Nubia is inextricably mixed up with the symbolism of the Eye.

The Eye in the Onuris legend and its derivatives is sometimes said to be the Moon, the Eye of Horus which was taken from him. However, more often it is Tefnut as the personification of the Eye of the Sun. For the Egyptians, as for many ancient peoples, the absence of the sun was a time of fear and uncertainty. They were frightened of the dark when the sun was absent from the sky at night; they were uneasy during the winter when the sun lost its warmth, apprehensive lest the crops that lay dormant would never spring into life again. Thus, the return of Tefnut symbolized the return of the sun, bringing light after a period of darkness and life after the season of lifelessness, blessings which Tefnut offered to the Egyptians in addition to the boon that she, Order, had brought to them at the very beginning when her father, Atum, lifted her up in his arms and kissed her, thereby bringing the Mound of Creation into being.

GEB

· ·

Geb, the grandson of Atum, was the Earth God; his sister, Nut, was his counterpart as the Sky Goddess. He was often depicted as a recumbent male figure lying beneath a woman, who is Nut. Sometimes he appears as a goose; at other times, as a goose-headed man, or a man carrying a goose on his head. In predynastic times, he was probably worshipped in the form of a sacred goose.

It is perhaps surprising that Geb, the Earth God *par excellence*, should be male in gender. In most cultures, the earth, the bringer-forth of vegetation and living things, is regarded as female: Mother Earth. In at least one place, his shrine at Bata in Iunu, Geb was worshipped as a bisexual god and credited with having laid the Great Egg from which the sun emerged at the dawn of time in the form of the Benu Bird (see page 25). One of Geb's epithets was 'The Great Cackler', a reference to the cackle he gave as he produced this egg.

The Phakussa Stele (see page 31) tells of how Geb fell in love with his mother, Tefnut. He yearned for her and wandered about the land in great distress until the day that his father, Shu, departed the earth. On that day, Geb came upon his mother in the palace of Shu at Memphis. He seized hold of her with great violence and raped her. Geb does not seem to have been punished for the rape of his mother. Instead, he became King of Egypt in his father's place, and reigned successfully for many years. He was given the title, unique to him, of *Iry-paat-neteru* or 'Heir of the Gods'. Geb named as his heir his eldest son, Osiris, who thus became the first of many kings, both mythological and human, to sit upon the Egyptian throne known as 'The Seat of Geb', and the first to hold the title 'Heir of Geb', which was later borne by the mortal kings of Egypt.

There was another earth god worshipped by the Egyptians: he was Aker, whom they sometimes depicted as a strip of land with a human head, and at other times as a double-headed lion or sphinx. This fabulous sphinx was supposed to guard the Two Gates, one on the east, the other on the west, which were the only entrances to the Underworld. Aker was a fearsome deity, greatly feared by all who had to pass by him on their way to the Underworld. However, Geb was regarded as a god who was at all times benevolently disposed towards the world and mankind.

NUT

• •

Nut was the personification of the vault of heaven. She often appears in the form of a woman carrying on her head what was probably her old fetish – a water pot. She can be depicted as a woman stretched out over the earth with her feet resting on the eastern horizon and her head or her hands touching the western horizon. Her body, or her dress, which is long and blue, is spangled with stars and heavenly bodies. Nut can also be depicted as a cow straddling the earth with her underbelly studded with stars.

The sky itself was represented by ⇔ which shows a flat plate supported by two projections on its lower side. The two projections are the Two Pillars of Heaven: Mount Bakhau on the east and Mount Manu on the west, with Mount Manu providing a pillow for Nut's head and Mount Bakhau a footstool for the goddess's feet.

In the Heliopolitan creation myth, Nut was the granddaughter of the Sun God, the wife of Geb, the mother of Osiris, Isis, Horus the Elder, Seth and Nephthys, the five children whom she was able to bring into the world only after winning five days in the game of dice that she played with her lover, Thoth (see page 29). In addition, Nut was also believed to be the mother of the sun. Each evening, when the sun reached Mount Manu on the western horizon, Nut, the Sky Goddess, raised her head from her pillow and swallowed it; and each morning, she gave birth to it anew.

Nut was sometimes depicted as a cow, for this was the form she assumed when she carried the Sun God, Re, on his journey to heaven after he had decided to abdicate his throne on earth (see page 43). Since Hathor, also, was a cow goddess, the roles of these two female deities were frequently interchanged, with Hathor playing Nut's role as Sky Goddess, and Nut taking over from Hathor as a goddess of the dead. Thus Nut sometimes takes Hathor's place in the sacred sycamore tree (see page 121) from which she offers succour to the deceased.

Nut's links with the dead were further enhanced thanks to the Egyptian convention of decorating the ceilings of tombs with stars, thereby turning them into representations of the heaven that the dead man aspired to reach. This theme was taken up in the decoration of the undersides of the lids of

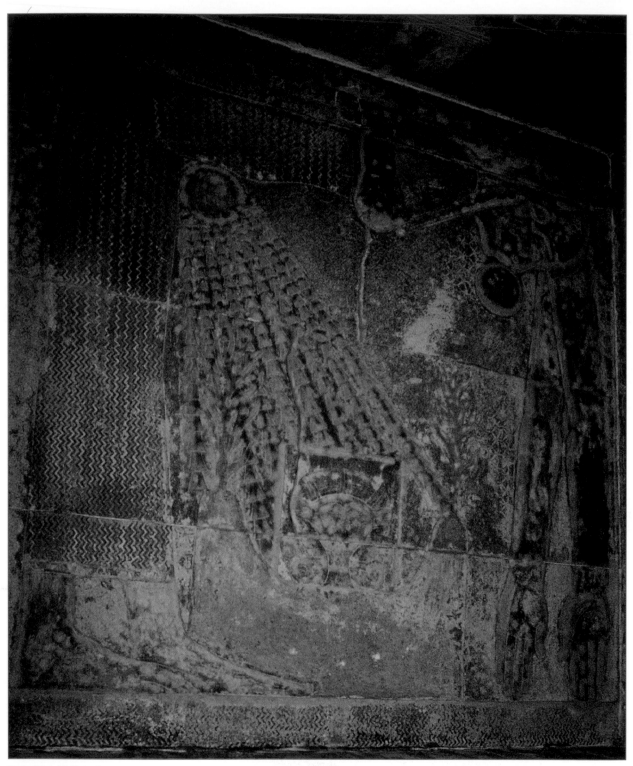

Nut giving birth to the sun:
relief on the ceiling of 'The
Pure Place', a chapel to the
west of the innermost
sanctuary, Temple of
Hathor, Denderah.

sarcophagi which were embellished with stars and, often, with figures of Nut as a naked woman standing on tiptoe with her arms stretched above her head. Once the lid of the sarcophagus was closed, Nut therefore came face to face with the dead person inside, in which position she was able to protect him throughout eternity.

Nut: interior of a New Kingdom mummy-case lid. (Cairo Museum)

RE

Re was the self-engendered Eternal Spirit who first appeared on the waters of the Nun as a beautiful child floating on a great blue lotus. To the Egyptians, the water-lily, called lotus by the Greeks, was the most perfect type of flower. In contrast to the white lotus (*Nymphaea lotus*) the sacred blue lotus (*Nymphaea cerulea*) had a delightful perfume which suggested to the Egyptians the perfume of Re's sweat, the divine essence. Re, having created himself by means of magic, turned his attention to the creation of the world. He made the four winds, and the Inundation waters. From his sweat, he created gods; from his tears, he created mankind (in Egyptian, the word for tears is *remyt*, that for mankind *remeth*, the sort of pun the ancient Egyptians loved to make).

The magic used by Re in his creation of the world and everything in it was the Word. The method of creating things by naming them was used by the Great God of the Babylonians, and by the God of the Hebrews – in the New Testament of the Bible, we read: 'In the beginning was the Word, and the Word was with God, and the Word was God' (John 1: 1). Re spoke the Word, and by speaking the name of things, he created them. To the Egyptians, as indeed to all ancient and primitive peoples, the name of a thing was a magical concept. A man's name is as vital to him as his eyes, his heart, his tongue, or any other part of his person. A Native American, for instance, takes care of his name in the belief that he can be injured by its misuse just as much as by a wound inflicted on his body. Native Australians believe that if an enemy knows your name he can make use of it magically in order to harm you. Thus, they have a name which is used from day to day and a secret name which is known only to fully initiated members of their tribal group.

Having created the world by naming all its parts, Re became king of both gods and men, ruling with his daughter, Maat, at his side. Maat was the personification of Truth and Justice. She was depicted by Egyptian artists as a woman wearing an ostrich plume on her head. A picture of this feather was often used as the hieroglyphic symbol both for her name and for the noun 'truth'. The feather was used in the Judgement of the Dead, when it was weighed in a balance against the heart of the deceased person undergoing the Judgement to see if he were 'maaty', that is, had lived his life in conformity with truth and justice. The concept of Maat stood for much more than Truth and Justice: it represented the divinely appointed order of things, the equilibrium of the universe with the world, the regular movements of the stars, the sun, the moon, the seasons and the sequence of time. Within the world which Re created according to his divine plan, Maat stood for social and religious order, the relationship between one human being and another, between mankind and the gods, and between mankind and the dead.

Kingship, in the person of Re, and Order, in the person of Maat, came to earth at the very beginning. Thus, the creation of the world was synchronous with the creation of kingship and social order. However, Chaos was an ever-present threat to the existence of this divinely created order. Only by practising Maat could the Egyptians preserve the harmony of the universe. This belief was the basis of Egyptian religion; and the cult practised in temples was designed to uphold Maat so that Egypt might prosper.

Re ruled the world as king of men and gods only while he was in full possession of his powers. However, at last the time came when the god-king began to grow old: according to Egyptian legend, 'his bones were silver, his flesh was gold and his hair was real lapis-lazuli' – the Egyptian way of describing old age. And his subjects became rebellious. Chief among these rebellious subjects was the goddess Isis. She, like Re, was omniscient. She was also, according to legend, 'a woman skilled in words', a great magician. Her ambition was to reign like Re in heaven and earth. But the only way she could achieve her ambition was by learning the Great Name of Re, his secret name. The way in which she did this is recounted in two papyri, one of which is now in the British Museum and the other in the Turin Museum.

Re had many names, but his Great Name was the one which gave him power over gods and men. It had remained hidden in his body since his birth so that no magician might gain power over him. Isis plotted in her heart the means by which she could learn it. Because Re had grown old, he was inclined to slobber at the mouth and shoot his spittle onto the ground. Isis took some of this spittle, kneaded it with soil and made it into a serpent in the form of a dart, which she laid on the path where Re was accustomed to stroll every day. When Re, accompanied by his retinue of gods, passed by the dart it took shape as a serpent from which issued a living fire. The serpent stung Re. The god opened his mouth and his cry of pain echoed round the sky. His companions rushed up to him, exclaiming, 'What is the matter?'; gods everywhere asked, 'What has happened?'

Re could not find the strength to answer them. His jaws shook, his limbs trembled as the poison seized hold of his flesh even as the Nile in flood seizes hold of the land of Egypt. At last, he managed to still the racing of his heart and summon his followers, calling out, 'Come to me, you who were created from my limbs, who came forth from me!' When his followers had gathered round him Re told them what had happened: 'I know in my heart that something deadly has bitten me, but I did not see what it was. I only know that it was not something that I myself have made. I have never experienced suffering like this. I am sure it would not be possible to endure more severe pain.'

Re was profoundly shocked that he should have suffered such an attack. His Great Name ought to have ensured that such a thing could never happen. In desperation, the stricken god summoned his children, especially those gods who were skilled in magic and healing words. Not one of them was able to help their father. At last, Isis came, she who could give the breath of life with her mouth, who could drive away pain with her spells, who could bring the dead back to life with her magic words. She said, 'What is it, divine Father?' And Re told her what had happened to him. He continued: 'I am colder than water, I am hotter than fire. All my limbs sweat yet I am shivering. My eyes are dim, I cannot see the sky. My face is bathed in perspiration just as if it were summertime.'

Then Isis said, 'Tell me your Name, divine Father, for he who is called by his Name is he who shall live.' Re cast round in his mind for a name that he could give her that would prove efficacious enough for her magic spells. He did not, of course, intend to give her his Great Name, his secret name. He played for time by listing his achievements, and then, with a great show of reluctance, revealed three of his names: 'At dawn, I am called Khepri; at midday, Re; and in the evening, Atum.' The wily Isis was not impressed. She waited implacably while the poison worked its way deeper and deeper into the body of the great god until he could no longer walk. Then she said, 'You have not told me your Name. Tell me your Name so that the poison will go away. For he who is called by his Name is he who shall live.'

The poison burned like fire. Re cried out, 'Swear that no one will ever know my Great Name except for yourself and your son, Horus, whom you shall bear to Osiris and who shall reign over the land of Egypt when Osiris has passed to the West, the Land of the Dead.' Whereupon Isis swore an oath, and the secret of Re's Great Name passed from his heart to hers. Immediately, Isis bade the poison leave his body; the poison died and Re lived.

Isis was not the only one to scheme against the ageing Re. It came to his notice one day that mankind was plotting against him. The story of how Re dealt with the plotters is told in the Book of the Divine Cow. The earliest-known version of this book so far found is on the largest of the four great shrines of gilded wood which protected the sarcophagus of Tutankhamun in the burial chamber of his tomb. The text of the story is on the inside back panel of the shrine and is illustrated by the image modelled in sunk relief of a gigantic cow – the goddess Nut – whose belly is decorated with stars and who is supported by Shu. Unfortunately, the text is incomplete, although it can be filled in from later versions of the story. The best of these occur in the royal tombs of the late New Kingdom, especially those of the Nineteenth-Dynasty rulers, Sety I and his son, Ramesses II, with the best-preserved version surviving in a small antechamber deep inside the tomb of Sety.

Unsure of what to do about those who were plotting against him, Re summoned Hathor, whom he called his 'Eye', Shu, Tefnut, Geb and Nut, as well as the fathers and mothers who had been with him in the Primeval Waters, and even the god Nun himself, the personification of the waters, so that they might give him advice. Re commanded that they meet him secretly: he did not wish mankind to realize what they were doing. So the gods were brought before Re, and, having touched the ground at his feet with their foreheads in token of respect, they listened to what he had to say.

Then Nun spoke: 'My son, Re, the god greater than I from whom you came forth and mightier than those whom you have created, sit on your throne with confidence, for great would be the fear of you if your Eye were turned against those who are plotting against you.' Re then told them that many men had fled into the desert because they were afraid of what he would say to them. And the gods recommended that Re should send someone in pursuit of them but not his Eye since mankind had been made from the tears of Re's Eye and the Eye might feel sorry for its 'children'. Instead, Hathor should go in the form of a fierce lioness, who would devour the evil ones in the desert.

Hathor performed her task with such gusto that Re became alarmed. Having tasted blood, she was loath to give up her slaughter. She told Re how pleasant it was to her to have prevailed over mankind and to have earned a new name – Sekhmet or 'She-who-prevails'. But Re did not want her to prevail over all of mankind, for he had wished only to teach them a lesson, not to destroy them utterly. And so he sent his swiftest messengers to Elephantine to bring him quantities of the red ochre that was found in that region. When the red ochre had been brought to him, Re ordered his High Priest in Heliopolis to grind it up. Meanwhile, barley beer had been prepared by maidservants. The red ochre was added to the beer so that it looked like human blood, and seven thousand jars of the mixture were made ready for inspection by Re and his entourage.

On the morning of the day upon which Hathor intended to complete her destruction of mankind, Re inspected the beer and deemed it excellent. He announced: 'I will save mankind with it!' and ordered that it should be carried to the place where Hathor intended to slay the remainder of mankind. There, the blood-red beer was poured over the land until the fields were flooded elbow-deep with this soporific. When Hathor arrived, she found the land covered with what she thought was human blood. Her face glowed in its reflection as she drank deeply, and became so drunk that she forgot all about destroying mankind.

Re came to meet Hathor in the city of Yamit, and welcomed her not as Sekhmet nor as Hathor, the terrible slayer of mankind, but as the Beautiful One, his Eye. And from thenceforward, Yamit became famous for its beautiful women and 'The Beautiful One' became one of Hathor's names. Hathor became the Goddess of Drunkenness, and a great annual festival was initiated which was celebrated by drinking the intoxicating liquid that Re decreed should be brewed in honour of Hathor.

Unfortunately, Re was still dissatisfied with mankind and with exercising his power on earth. He was weary; he wished for rest. And so Nun commanded the goddess Nut to change herself into a cow, so that Re might rest himself upon her back. When mankind saw the sun's disk riding on the back of a cow, they were astonished. Some of them were angry with their fellows for having plotted against Re so causing him to remove himself from them. They took up their bows and shot arrows at the enemies of Re, who warned them that from henceforward men would always be prepared to slaughter each other. And thus did war come into the world.

Re commanded Nut to ascend high above the earth, and she became the sky. Because in her womanly form she wore a blue dress, the sky became the colour of this dress. From his vantage point on Nut's back, Re was able to observe the earth from a distance, something which he found very peaceful. He created the Field of Abundance for the cow, Nut, to stand and browse in, and planted it with green plants. He brought into being the Field of Reeds, in which men would be able to pass to their Afterlife. He began to create the stars and the planets. Eventually, Nut became dizzy through standing so far above the earth and she began to shake. Re commanded the God of Air, Shu, to stand beneath Nut and support her with his hands. Nut's husband, Geb, was put in charge of the earth.

And so Re had created the earth and all that was in it; the air that men and beasts breathed; the sky and the firmament with its planets and stars; the divine places of the Afterlife. Having abandoned mankind on earth, Re made himself responsible for the Afterlife, where he became the Great Judge of the Dead. He also created night and day. During the twelve hours of the night, he sailed through the Netherworld in his Night Barque. At dawn, he emerged on the eastern horizon where a choir of baboons danced and sang with joy at his appearance. He then boarded his Day Barque and for the twelve hours of the day he sailed across the sky illuminating the earth with his bright rays.

This daily journey across the sky made the Egyptians very happy. However, every night Re disappeared over the western horizon and mankind was left in the dark, deprived of the light of Re's Eye, the sun. Re decided to provide a substitute. He sent for the god Thoth, and commanded that he provide light for mankind at night. Re created the moon and gave it into the keeping of Thoth. From thenceforward, the earth was illumined during the day by the Sun God, Re, and during the night by the Moon God, Thoth, acting as Re's representative.

During the New Kingdom, if not before, the Egyptians believed that the powers of darkness, in the guise of fiends led by the monster serpent Apophis, posed an ever-present threat to the sun. During the night, they lay in wait for Re; and in the darkest hour before the dawn, they attacked his Barque in an endeavour to prevent the sun rising. Every morning, Re fended off the attack, aided by the deities who made up the crew of his Barque. Re himself, in the guise of a cat, the Great Cat of Heliopolis, cut off the head of Apophis with a knife. He never vanquished Apophis utterly because at the end of every night, the serpent was found waiting for him again, eager to renew his assault.

During the Old Kingdom, the cult of Re spread from Heliopolis to the rest of Egypt until he achieved nationwide recognition, enabling his priesthood to exert great political power. From Dynasty III onwards, the building of pyramids shows that Re had become a powerful influence in funerary beliefs and practices. The origin of the pyramid form of tomb can probably be traced back to predynastic times. Prehistoric Egyptians normally buried their dead in pits dug in the desert – at no time in Egyptian history did the Egyptians willingly waste good agricultural land by burying their dead in it. The grave was marked by a mound of sand piled over the pit.

In Dynasty I, a more elaborate tomb was evolved for the burial of kings and their relatives. This was the *mastaba*, which consisted of a deep burial-shaft

The Cat of Heliopolis: tomb of Inherkhau, foreman of the gang (of workers), Deir el-Medina, in the reigns of Ramessess III and IV, Dynasty XX.

surmounted by a superstructure made of mud-brick arranged in a rectangular shape with slightly inclined walls (see Glossary). Excavations at Sakkara, the necropolis of the ancient capital city of Egypt, Memphis, have revealed the presence, inside the superstructures of several *mastabas*, of mounds, the earliest examples of which are simply cores of sand overlaid with mud-brick. Later examples consist of a solid brick construction with four sides rising in steps. Since the mounds have no architectural function, their purpose must have had a magico-religious significance. They were probably meant to represent the hill which emerged from the Primeval Waters when the earth was created, and to act as a potent magic symbol to counteract death.

The stepped mounds inside *mastabas* perhaps influenced the next development in the architecture of royal tombs. In Dynasty III, King Djoser's architect, Imhotep, designed a tomb at Sakkara which consists of six *mastaba* shapes of ever-decreasing base measurements placed one on top of the other until the monument reaches a height of over 60 metres, forming a stepped pyramid. The Step Pyramid of Djoser, as this monument is called today, is built entirely of limestone and is the earliest monumental building in dressed stone known to history (see page 165).

The stepped mounds inside *mastabas*, and the step pyramids of Djoser and at least three of his successors, were natural developments from the pit graves of the predynastic period. However, the priests of Re at Heliopolis found a magico-religious explanation for them, an explanation which associated the king with their god, Re. It was believed that Re sailed through the sky every day in his Day Barque. What more natural ambition could a dead king have than to join the Sun God on his daily journey and thus spend his Afterlife with him. But how to reach the Barque? Why, by means of a staircase up to heaven. The step pyramids, with the aid of magic spells, provided a stairway to the sky (see page 48) by means of which a dead king could join Re in the heavens.

At the end of the Third Dynasty, a straight-sided pyramid was built at Meidum, and two more straight-sided pyramids were built at Dahshur for the Fourth-Dynasty king, Sneferu. The earliest geometrically true pyramid is that constructed at Giza for Sneferu's son, Khufu, and geometrically true pyramids were built at Giza for Khufu's successors, Khafre and Menkaure. Khafre's tomb is comparable in size with that of his father, Khufu, whose Great Pyramid is over 146 metres high and covers an area of more than 50,000 square metres. Menkaure's pyramid is less than half that size. Together, these three pyramids formed one of the Seven Wonders of the ancient world.

The Giza pyramids were built during one of the most powerful dynasties in Egyptian history, and have been described as an exercise in nationalism. Their straight-sided form had probably occurred through natural architectural progression, but doubtless the priesthood of Re found a religious significance for it, perhaps one that was inspired by the sight of the sun's rays shining down to earth through a gap in the clouds, producing a straight-sided, pyramidal effect.

The Step Pyramid of Djoser, Sakkara, showing enclosure wall.

Giza: the pyramids of Khufu (right) and Khafre (left), with the Sphinx (see page 98) in the foreground. (Lithograph by David Roberts (1796–1864))

The pyramid form of royal tomb persisted in Egypt for over a thousand years, until Re was superseded by Amun (see page 139) as the country's most powerful god. Many of the pyramids built during this time were equipped with stone-lined pits, lying outside the pyramid, either at its base or a short distance away. Some pits are merely shaped like boats; others contain actual examples. Three cedarwood boats were found at Dahshur, on the south side of the pyramid of the Twelfth-Dynasty king, Senwosret III. In AD 1954, two pits at the foot of the southern face of the Great Pyramid at Giza were discovered. In one of them, a cedarwood boat, over 40 metres long, lay dismantled but complete from its keel to the canopied cabin on its deck. This magnificent boat, which has become famous as the oldest in the world, was part of the funerary equipment of Khufu, who ruled Egypt over four and a half thousand years ago. It has been reassembled and is now on display at Giza. The second boat pit also contains a dismantled boat, but it has been left undisturbed in its pit. Some of the boats may have been used to ferry the dead king and his funerary equipment to his pyramid; however, their most important function would have been a mythological one: to carry the dead king on his funerary journey to the sky.

The Giza pyramids are the greatest ever built; all later pyramids – and there are over eighty of them – are very much smaller. However, the kings of Dynasties V and VI endeavoured to make up for the smallness of their tombs through the magic of the Pyramid Texts (see page 24) carved within them. Judged on subject matter and language, these Texts are based on very old rituals and customs. One

Spell says: 'A brick is drawn for you out of the great tomb' – a reference to mud-brick *mastabas*, a type of tomb no longer used by the kings of Dynasty V. Another Spell alludes to predynastic sand burials: 'Throw off the sand from your face'.

The early Pyramid Texts are obviously Heliopolitan in origin, for there are many references in them to the Sun God. The death of the king, for example, is described in one Spell thus: 'The king departs life in the West . . . he shines forth anew in the East', just as the sun sets [or dies] in the west and rises again in the east. The king's journey to the sky can be accomplished in two ways, either by means of a boat, or by ladder: 'The two celestial reed-floats [rafts] have been set in place for the king so that he might journey in them to the horizon, to Re'; and 'A stairway to the sky has been set up for him so that he might ascend to heaven thereby'; and 'The king ascends upon this ladder which his father [Re] made for him'. Having reached the Afterlife, the king must undergo the Judgement of the Dead before he can take his place as one of the gods, acclaimed and recognized by them. In the early Pyramid Texts, it is Re who is the Great Judge, who sits at the head of the Tribunal of the Gods. After his Judgement, the king is acclaimed and accepted as a member of Re's retinue: 'Oh pure one! Assume your throne in the Barque of Re and sail upon the way.'

By Dynasty V, Re had become State God, officially recognized as leader of the pantheon of Egyptian gods. His greatest political success was achieved in Dynasty IV. Until this time, the King of Egypt had been deemed a god. However, in Dynasty IV, Khafre took as one of his royal titles the epithet 'Son of Re', indicating a diminution in the importance of the king since he was now not a god in his own right but merely the son of a god. This royal link with Re was maintained for the remaining two and a half thousand years or so of Pharaonic Egypt. Reference to Re is implicit in the way two of the five names borne by a reigning king were written on monuments and official documents. 'Son of Re' and 'King of Upper and Lower Egypt' were the prefixes to the two most important names in the royal titulary. The names themselves were written inside cartouches. A cartouche is an elongated version of the hieroglyphic sign Q, which represents a loop of rope with a knot at its base. It is pronounced *shen* and means 'that which the sun encircles'. A king's name written inside a cartouche, Q, was intended to show that he ruled the world – a world illuminated by Re.

The political success of Re was further enhanced in Dynasty V by several kings of that Dynasty who built their pyramids at Abusir. Every pyramid had attached to it a memorial temple in which the dead king was supposed to be worshipped forever; at Abusir, for the first time, each pyramid had another sort of temple built near it – a solar temple, in which the god, Re, was destined to be worshipped in the very place that was most sacred to the king.

The most outstanding feature of a solar temple was the giant obelisk that provided a focal point in the temple. Obelisks were cult symbols of the Sun God, and date back to predynastic times when they were worshipped as models of the miraculous shaft of stone upon which the sun was thought to place itself on first rising. The use of obelisks was especially popular in the New Kingdom. Today,

Cartouche of Ramesses II:
from his memorial temple
at Abydos.

less than half a dozen remain standing in Egypt. Many have been removed by the conquerors of Egypt, from Ashurbanipal, who removed two to Nineveh, to the Roman Emperors, who carried off many of them to Rome and Constantinople. The Viceroy of Egypt, Mohammed Ali, presented an obelisk to the French in AD 1830, although it was the French themselves who had to pay for its removal from Luxor to Paris, where it now graces the Place de la Concorde. Eleven years previously, Mohammed Ali had given an obelisk to the British; but it was not until 1878 that it was taken from Alexandria to London, where it was named Cleopatra's Needle. There are over fifty obelisks in public squares and parks throughout Europe and Northern America.

By the end of Dynasty VI, the ordinary Egyptian had turned to Osiris for spiritual comfort. The cult of Re had always been a royal cult, concerned with the well-being of the king. It held no direct appeal for the common man. The cult of Osiris, on the other hand, was found to be sympathetic by all levels of Egyptian society. Re was never again to achieve the heights he attained during the Old Kingdom. However, as early as Dynasty II he had been worshipped at Heliopolis in the form of a great black or piebald bull. This animal – the *Mer-Wer* or Mnevis Bull – was thought to be the living soul of the Sun God, and was provided with two wives, the cow goddesses Hathor and Iusas. The lavish endowments provided for him by Ptolemy V Epiphanes (205–180 BC), which are recorded on the Rosetta Stone, demonstrate that Re retained an important place in the Egyptian pantheon to the end of the pharaonic period and beyond into Graeco-Roman times.

KHEPRI

· ·

At Heliopolis, the god Khepri was believed to be a manifestation of the Creator God taking shape as the rising sun. His name is derived from the Egyptian word *kheprer*, which means 'to become' or 'to come into existence', an abstract idea which might have been very difficult to illustrate in hieroglyphs. However, the Egyptian language makes great use of puns; and in this case, the verb *kheprer* has the same sound as the word for the *scarabaeus* or dung-beetle, hence a picture of such a beetle could be used as the hieroglyphic sign denoting both the beetle itself and the verb 'to come into existence'.

The Creator God was believed to have come into existence through his own actions. So, according to Egyptian belief, did the *scarabaeus* beetle. Thus, the word for beetle, *kheprer*, became the name of the god of spontaneous creation, Khepri. Plutarch explained this in the following way:

> As for the scarab-beetle, it is held that there are no females of this species; they are all males. They place their seed in a round pellet of material which they roll up into a sphere and roll along, pushing it with their hind legs, imitating by their action the course of the sun from east to west.

The ball of material, usually dung, is then buried in the sand until the 'seed' is hatched. This idea is reflected in tomb paintings in the Valley of the Kings at Luxor which show the scarab-beetle emerging backwards from the sand dragging the sun with it.

The god Khepri normally appears in Egyptian paintings as a human being with the head of a scarab-beetle. The scarab-beetle itself became one of the most popular motives in Egyptian art. Egyptian scarabs were made in various sizes from many different materials – stone such as limestone or steatite, as well as semi-precious stones such as carnelian, amethyst, green felspar, and faience. They could be almost exact replicas of a dung-beetle or merely stylized versions of it. They could be covered with decorative designs, magical signs, hieroglyphic inscriptions, or pictures of gods and kings.

When set in a ring as a bezel or hung on a necklace as a pendant, the scarab was often used as a personal seal. Its flat underside, inscribed with the name and titles of its owner, could be pressed against the clay sealings which were

Scarab-beetle pushing ball of dung. (Photograph: Paul Warburton)

appended to letters and official documents, or attached to bolts on the doors of rooms or to the lids of chests and containers such as wine jars. Mounted on a plaque in a bracelet or necklace, the scarab was used as a protective amulet. The insect was the symbol of the perpetual renewal of life, and its popularity as a means of protection led to many thousands of scarabs being made of cheap materials with little care taken over their decoration. Hence it is often difficult to distinguish ancient scarabs of inferior quality from the modern, sometimes well-made, versions which are the most popular souvenirs for visitors to Egypt. No such difficulty is encountered with the scarabs used in some of the items of jewellery found, for example, in the tomb of Tutankhamun.

Scarabs were used as funerary talismans. As such, they were usually made of hard stone, faience or gold, and equipped with replicas of a falcon's wings. They were placed over the heart of a dead person inside the bandages in which the mummified body was wrapped; or mounted in a pectoral or ornamental collar and placed on the mummy's breast. In this position, the wings of the scarab could take the body of the dead person in a protective embrace. Heart scarabs were often inscribed with Chapter 30 of the Book of the Dead, the Spell that instructed the heart on how it should behave at the Judgement of the Dead: 'Oh my heart, the most intimate part of my being! Do not stand up against me as a witness before the Tribunal' – so that the dead person might emerge triumphant from the Judgement.

Large stone scarabs were made to commemorate historical events, an early exercise in the art of issuing public relations bulletins! The less important historical scarabs bear the name of a king plus an epithet referring to his achievements – the building of a temple, for example. Other scarab bulletins contain more information. The most famous series of such commemorative scarabs was issued in Dynasty XVIII by Amenhotep III: in them he registered in permanent form some of the outstanding events of his reign.

One series of scarabs records the two-day hunt, which took place in the second year of Amenhotep III's reign, in which ninety-six wild cattle were captured; another series, of which over forty examples survive, registers the fact that in his first ten years as king, he shot 102 'fierce lions'. The first series of scarab bulletins issued by Amenhotep III were those that were sent out at the beginning of his reign to announce his marriage to Tiy, daughter of the High Priest of Min, Yuya, and his wife, Thuya (see page 194), although another series, dated to Year 10 of his reign, announced his marriage to a foreign princess as 'a miracle brought to his Majesty, namely the daughter of the ruler of Naharin, Shuttarna – Kirgipa and persons of her harem, 317 women'. Inevitably, the construction of a pleasure lake that Amenhotep III had made for his beloved wife, Tiy, was recorded on a scarab:

Regnal year 11, First day of Inundation, under the Majesty of Amenhotep, Ruler of Southern Iunu, long may he live. The great royal wife, Tiy, long may she live: his Majesty commanded that a lake be constructed for the great royal wife, Tiy, in the city of Djarukha, 3,700 cubits long and 700 cubits wide. His

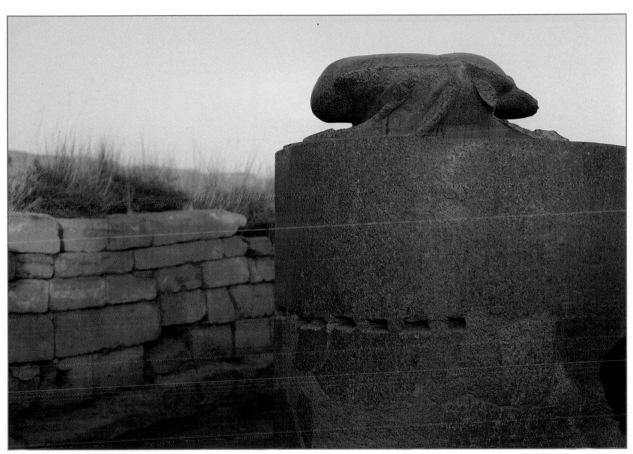

Scarab of Amenhotep III,
Karnak.

Majesty celebrated the feast of the inauguration of the lake on the 16th day of
Inundation when his Majesty was rowed in the royal barge, Splendour of the
Aten.[4]

Perhaps the most impressive scarab to be seen in Egypt is the large granite
sculpture erected in the reign of Amenhotep III that can still be seen standing on
its plinth near the north-west corner of the sacred lake of the Temple of Amun at
Karnak. However, Khepri is to be found in paintings and reliefs in many a temple
or tomb of ancient Egypt, for he was a pervasive and ever-popular god.

OSIRIS

· ·

The myth of Osiris tells how he once ruled Egypt as king until he was betrayed and murdered. He died but was resurrected thanks to his wife, Isis, whose love and loyalty made this resurrection possible. Their son, Horus, avenged his father's wrongs and in his turn became King of Egypt. The story of Osiris, with its emphasis on the ideal family, and the hope that it holds out of immortality through resurrection, had a universal appeal. Osiris thus became one of the most popular Egyptian gods, not only in Egypt itself but throughout the Near East.

Osiris' beginnings are obscure. The hieroglyphic symbols in which his name is written, 𓊨, a seat, and 𓁹, an eye, are simply phonetic signs, 𓊨 being transliterated as *ws*, and 𓁹 as *ir*, making *wsir*, pronounced Osiris by the Greeks. The earliest written references to Osiris are found in the Pyramid Texts. How he was worshipped in prehistoric times, or where his original cult-centre was situated is not known. However, by the time he appears in the Pyramid Texts he is a fully developed deity with his own theology and mythology. Undoubtedly, Osiris was first worshipped as a fertility god. But as his cult spread throughout Egypt, he displaced indigenous gods in several places, notably in *Djedu*, where he replaced Andjety; and at Abydos, where he superseded Khentyamentiu. At Heliopolis, he became a member of the Great Ennead, and in Memphis he was assimilated to Sokar.

As gods gave way to Osiris, he absorbed their functions and attributes. This process led to the standard depiction of Osiris which shows him as a human male whose body is covered by a tight-fitting white garment that allows only his hands and head to be seen. In his hands, he grasps a crook and a flail. He wears a beard, and on his head he bears either the White Crown of Upper Egypt or the Atef Crown, a form of the White Crown in which the top has been cut off and replaced by a small sun's disk, the whole being flanked by two ostrich plumes. Osiris' flesh is usually coloured black or green; to the Egyptians, black, being the colour of the rich, alluvial soil from which their crops sprang up year after year, was the colour of resurrection and eternal life. Hence, Osiris' black flesh indicates that he has died and risen again. Green, being the colour of plant life, is symbolic of vegetation and youth.

The crown, the crook and the flail infer that Osiris is a king; the white shroud that he is a dead king, for the shroud represents the bandages that were used in mummification. The beard he wears is the ritual false beard as worn by kings that, throughout the dynastic period, was regarded as an emblem of the supernatural thanks to its association with Osiris. In shape, this beard is unlike beards as they were normally depicted by the Egyptians, which are straight; Osiris' beard is long and curved, and is perhaps a stylized version of the beard of a goat, which possibly indicates that Osiris was worshipped at one time in the form of a goat or ram.

Ram gods were extremely popular with the Egyptians from predynastic times onwards, for rams were considered to be symbols of strength and virility. To name but three: there was Herishef (in Greek, Arsaphes), the ram god of Herakleopolis, whose name means 'He-who-is-on-his-Lake' and whose city, which lies some 15 km west of Beni Suef, provided the kings of Dynasties IX and X; the Ram of Mendes (see below); and Khnum, the best-known ram god of all (see page 189). All of these deities were originally manifest in the ram of the species *palaeoaegypticus*; in dynastic times, this species became ever more rare until it disappeared altogether (*c.* 2000 BC). Long before this happened, the Egyptians had substituted *palaeoaegypticus* rams with rams of other species, and often with the male specimens of the mountain-goats that abounded in Egypt.

In dynastic times, the soul of Osiris was thought to be lodged in the sacred ram that was worshipped in the Western Delta town of *Djedet*, and was known as *Ba-neb-Djedet* (Ram-lord-of-Djedet), who remained a popular deity down to the Ptolemaic period. The Greeks garbled the last three syllables of *Ba-neb-Djedet*'s name into Mendes, and two Greeks in particular, the geographer Strabo, and the poet Pindar, not to mention the Roman historian Diodorus of Sicily, made the Ram of Mendes famous. Pindar insisted that this Ram was permitted to have intercourse with women. Less sensationally, the Ram of Mendes was allotted a consort in the shape of the dolphin goddess *Hat-Mehit* (The-First-of-the-Fish), whose figure was found on the standard of the 16th Nome of Lower Egypt, of which *Djedet* was the capital.

The Egyptian word for ram was *ba*; *ba* also meant soul. Hence, although it was as a *ba*/ram that the god of *Djedet* was worshipped in predynastic times, this persona was later refined. In dynastic times, the *ba*/soul aspect was emphasized, and the Ram of Mendes was syncretized with Osiris as his soul. In the Late Period, the Ram of Mendes was allotted four heads and was then supposed to be the soul not only of Osiris but also of Re, Shu and Geb.

A few miles to the west of *Djedet* lay the similarly named town of *Djedu*, which seems to have been the oldest centre of the cult of Osiris. *Djedu* became known as *per-wsir*, which the Greeks later translated as Busiris, and which means 'The House of Osiris'. Long before Osiris arrived there, the cult symbol of *Djedu* had been the *Djed*-pillar. This prehistoric fetish gave its name to the city, and since the Egyptian word for the pillar, *djedu*, was homophonous with the word *djedu* meaning 'stability' or 'endurance', the *Djed*-pillar became a popular motif in jewellery and decoration as the embodiment of these qualities.

The precise significance of the *Djed*-pillar is uncertain. It may have been a representation of the sheaf of corn which played an important part in agricultural rites. In many parts of the world, the last sheaf of corn to be cut at harvest-time is treated in a special way, since it is thought to contain the spirit of the corn, and the *Djed*-pillar is possibly a stylized version of this last sheaf of corn. As such, it is an appropriate cult-symbol for Osiris in one of his aspects, that of corn god. However, once Osiris had become established at *Djedu* whatever the original symbolism of the *Djed*-pillar had been it became merged with a new belief: that the backbone of Osiris was buried at *Djedu*, and the *Djed*-pillar, which bears a resemblance to a backbone, became the embodiment of this sacred relic.

At *Djedu*, Osiris supplanted a more ancient god, Andjety, who may actually have been a king who once had ruled the city, since representations of him show an old man holding a crook in one hand and a flail in the other, and wearing on his head a double-plumed crown. Osiris took from him these items of royal regalia and incorporated into his own legend the story that he had once been a king who ruled Egypt.

As King of Egypt, Osiris brought the arts of civilization and agriculture to his subjects. He taught them to worship the gods and to obey the laws which he gave them. Before his reign, the Egyptians had been cannibals. However, when Isis, the sister-wife of Osiris, discovered wheat and barley growing wild, Osiris persuaded the Egyptians to give up cannibalism and learn how to cultivate these valuable cereals. He was believed to have been the first to pick fruit from trees and to train vines to grow on poles. He discovered how to tread the grapes picked from the vines in order to make wine. In areas where the vine could not be cultivated, he taught the inhabitants how to brew beer from barley instead.

The Egyptians were not the only people to whom Osiris brought the blessings of civilization and agriculture. Having installed his wife, Isis, as regent in Egypt, he travelled the world conveying these discoveries to the whole of mankind. Everywhere Osiris went he earned the gratitude of people for the benefits he bestowed on them, and was worshipped as a deity. He was given the epithet Wennefer, 'the perpetually good being', in recognition of his beneficence.

In one of his aspects, Osiris was worshipped as a god of vegetation, and more particularly as a corn god, who made the earth bring forth its produce in due season. Annually, at the beginning of the fourth month of the Egyptian year, at the time when the Inundation waters were beginning to recede and the fields to re-emerge from the flood ready to receive seed, Egyptians made little clay figures shaped to look like Osiris, and pressed seeds into them. Within a short time, the seeds germinated and a miniature corn-field appeared, shaped like Osiris. Just as, every year, the soil of Egypt 'died' under the blistering summer sun, only to be reborn after the Inundation had made it fertile again, so these 'corn-Osiris' figures symbolized the rebirth and regeneration that Osiris, as God of Resurrection (see page 58), promised.

Corn-Osiris figures were placed in Egyptian tombs as symbols of the resurrection that the tomb owner hoped for. For king and commoner alike corn-Osirises were designed to show that just as grain, a seemingly dead substance, can sprout into life, so also could a dead body come to life again. Perhaps the most famous corn-Osiris belonged to Tutankhamun. In the store chamber that leads off the burial chamber of his tomb was found a hollow wooden figure, about a metre long, shaped to look like Osiris and lined with linen. It had been filled with Nile silt and planted with corn-seed, which had been kept moist until the grain germinated. The figure was wrapped in linen and housed in a large wooden box. Other corn-Osiris figures were found in the tomb of Yuya and Thuya (see page 194), and in the tomb of the king who came to the throne four years after Tutankhamun's death, Horemheb. They have been found in non-royal tombs also, often placed between the legs of mummies, or occasionally, as at Cynopolis, in small pottery or wooden coffins placed in bricked-up recesses in the wall of the tomb.

The concept of corn-Osiris figures as symbols of rebirth and regeneration was closely allied to the identification of Osiris with the corn itself as a corn god, turning him into a deity of joy and sorrow. Harvest-time everywhere, especially in a year that yields good crops, is a joyful time. To the ancient Egyptians, as to many peoples, it was also a time of regret, for, with every stroke of his sickle, the Egyptian farmer believed that he was not only reaping the grain but that he was killing it. Symbolically, he was cutting the body of the corn god before trampling it to pieces on the threshing-floor. It was, accordingly, the custom in Egypt, and elsewhere, for the corn-reapers to lament over the first sheaf to be cut.

The yearly death of the corn, and indeed of other forms of vegetation, was part of the natural cycle of decay and revival of life. In the ancient Near East, the phenomenon was personified as a god who died annually only to rise again from the dead. This god had many names. In Babylonia and Syria, he was called Tammuz, a form of whom was found outside the Near East, in Greece, where he was known as Adonis. The Phrygians called him Attis and the Egyptians, Osiris.

Tammuz was the lover of the Babylonian mother goddess Ishtar, who was carried off to the Underworld by his enemies. Ishtar followed her lover and remained in the Underworld with him, thus removing from mankind and beasts the urge for sexual intercourse. The great god Ea, realizing that the world was thereby threatened with extinction, persuaded the Queen of the Underworld, Allatu, to sprinkle the lovers with the water of life, thus enabling them to return to the world bringing life and procreation with them.

The Greeks borrowed this myth from the Babylonians, turning the Semitic term *adon*, which means 'lord', the honorific title by which Tammuz's worshippers addressed him, into the appellation Adonis. In Greek mythology Adonis was a beautiful child beloved by the Goddess of Love, Aphrodite, who gave him into the safe-keeping of Persephone, Queen of the Dead. When Adonis grew up, he became Persephone's lover. Aphrodite, jealous and wanting Adonis as her own lover, quarrelled with Persephone and appealed to Zeus to settle the issue. Zeus entrusted the case to the muse Calliope, who decreed that Adonis should spend one third of the year with Aphrodite, one third with Persephone, and have one third to himself in which to recuperate from the amorous attentions of the two goddesses.

Aphrodite cheated, and persuaded Adonis to spend his third of the year with her. Enraged at this, Persephone incited the god Ares to change himself into a boar and attack Adonis, which he did while the lovers were out hunting on Mount Lebanon. Adonis, gored before Aphrodite's horrified eyes, bled to death; and wherever drops of his blood fell, anemones sprang up. The distraught Aphrodite pleaded with Zeus to allow Adonis to come back to her. Finally, Zeus agreed that Adonis should spend the winter months in the Underworld, but return to earth every spring to spend the summer months with Aphrodite.

Attis was a youth who was loved by the Phrygian mother of the gods Cybele. One version of his story says that he, like Adonis, was killed by a boar; another that he castrated himself and bled to death, whereupon he was turned into a pine tree. In both versions, Attis was said to return from the dead every year. The essential difference between Osiris and Attis, and other gods of resurrection who were supposed to die and rise again, is that they returned to earth for at least part of the year. Osiris never did, but remained in the Underworld; he lived forever, but not on this earth.

The myth of Osiris as a god of resurrection had its origins in the ancient custom of killing the king, a practice known to many countries other than Egypt. In primitive societies, a king was expected to be fit and virile, able to demonstrate his own fertility and his prowess as a hunter. When he became old, or unfit through injury or illness, it was feared that his failing capacity to produce human 'seed' would bring a blight on the crops; and that the impairment of his ability to track animals and bring them down by his speed and strength in the chase would affect the well-being of the tribe.

In many ancient societies and, until comparatively recently, in tribes such as the Shilluk of the Sudan, an old or sick chieftain or king was ritually put to death and a new king chosen to replace him. Other societies did not wait for their king to show signs of infirmity; instead, they appointed him for a fixed term of years, at the end of which either the king or a substitute for him was killed. The dead king was often buried in the ground as an encouragement for the crops to grow. In less primitive times, the substitute took the form of a statue that was buried while the king was allowed to renew his powers by magical means. The Egyptians of dynastic times adopted this practice as one of the rites that made up the ritual of the so-called Heb-Sed ceremony, during which the Egyptian king renewed his power and virility by means of magic (see page 165).

The legendary Osiris was not old but a king in the prime of life when he died. There is no full account told by the Egyptians themselves of the story of Osiris' death, which may have been based on an Egyptian tradition of a real king who once was sacrificed for the good of his people. There are only incomplete references to it in religious and magical texts on papyri and in inscriptions on temple walls which refer to the rites practised in the rituals of Osiris-worship. The most complete version of the Osiris legend is that told by the first-century AD Greek writer Plutarch, in *De Iside et Osiride*. The sources mentioned above indicate that Plutarch's account, although an extremely late version, is substantially correct.

Having brought civilization to Egypt, and then to the rest of the world, Osiris enjoyed an enviable fame and the reputation of being a good king. Such was his popularity that his brother Seth became unbearably jealous. The culmination of Seth's envy came when Osiris made his wife, Isis, regent in his absence from Egypt during his mission to bring civilization to the rest of the world. Seth considered that he himself should have been entrusted with the governance of Egypt; and in any case he lusted after Isis. And so the resentful Seth plotted against his brother, the king. By the time Osiris returned to Egypt, Seth had gathered together seventy-two accomplices. He intended to kill Osiris and take for himself their sister, Isis.

Accordingly, Seth invited Osiris to a banquet that he was holding in a place called Nedyt to celebrate the twenty-eighth year of Osiris' reign. At the end of the banquet, Seth had a beautiful chest made of cedarwood inlaid with ebony and ivory brought before the assembled guests. Immediately, the chest became the object of everyone's admiration and envy, so beautiful was it, so fine the workmanship. Seth laughingly promised to give it to the person whom it fitted most exactly when he got into it and lay down. One by one, the seventy-two accomplices tried on the chest for size. But, like the feet that Cinderella's ugly step-sisters tried to squeeze into the glass slipper, to no avail, they were all too tall or too short, too fat or too thin. Finally, the only person left at the banquet who had not tried on the chest for size was Osiris.

Osiris had hung back from the competition thinking it rather unbecoming for the King of Egypt to participate in such a contest. However, even a king of Egypt was not averse to a free gift, especially one as handsome as this chest. With great dignity, Osiris advanced to the chest, stepped in and lay down. Since Seth had taken the precaution of obtaining the precise measurements of his brother's body and having the chest made to the same size, it was not surprising that the chest fitted Osiris exactly.

Before Osiris could savour the pleasure of ownership of the magnificent chest, the conspirators rushed up to it, slammed down the lid and nailed it shut. Not content with trapping Osiris inside the chest, they lapped it round with molten lead; and even before Osiris had had time to suffocate, the chest had been thrown into the Nile. The current carried it down to the Great Green, the name by which the Mediterranean was known to the Egyptians. Many days later, the chest was washed up on the coast of the Lebanon, near Byblos. At once, a tamarisk tree sprang up on the very spot where the chest lay, enclosing both coffer and the dead Osiris within its trunk.

Eventually, the tamarisk grew to such a tremendous size that it attracted the attention of the King of Byblos, who ordered it to be cut down and carried to his palace, where it was trimmed and set up as a pillar in the main hall. And there Osiris stayed until eventually his wife, Isis, reached Byblos and persuaded the king to give her the pillar. She cut the body of her husband free from its imprisoning wood and carried it back to Egypt. As soon as Isis reached Egypt, she hid Osiris' body in a thicket of papyrus and journeyed alone to the island of Khemmis in the Delta where, according to some versions of the story, she gave

Ramesses II as Osiris:
columns from his memorial
temple (the Ramesseum) at
Luxor.

birth to Osiris' son, Horus, whom she had conceived by magical means on the journey from Byblos. Other accounts say that Isis was pregnant before Osiris was murdered and that she gave birth to their son before she set out on the quest to find her husband's body.

In these versions, Isis left her son, Horus, in the care of the goddess Wadjet, while she journeyed to Byblos. On her return, she left the body of Osiris unattended while she went to collect Horus. All versions of the Osiris story agree that, for whatever reason, Isis left his body unattended for a while; and that during this time, Seth, who happened to be out hunting in the Delta marshes, came upon the body of the brother he had murdered. This time, Seth determined that Isis should never find the body again. And so he cut it into pieces – some say fourteen, others sixteen – and scattered the pieces up and down the length of Egypt. Poor Isis had to begin her quest again, her task made so much more difficult by Seth's butchery. Her sister, Nephthys, who was also Seth's wife, offered to help her and together they wandered through Egypt, seeking the parts of Osiris' dismembered body.

They found the body, piece by piece. At each place where a part of Osiris' body was found, Isis fashioned a wax model of that particular member, and left it with the local priests with the injunction that they place it in their temple and worship it. Some say that Isis pretended to the priests that the relics she gave them were not wax models but really were parts of Osiris' body. She also commanded that the priests choose an animal commonly found in their locality and honour it as a representative of Osiris. Thus the bull called Apis, which was already worshipped at Memphis as an animal sacred to the god Ptah, was thenceforward worshipped also as a representative of Osiris; and the priests of Memphis rejoiced because they thought that they had been entrusted with the head of Osiris.

By distributing parts of Osiris' body to different places in Egypt, Isis ensured that the worship of her husband became widespread throughout the land, from Busiris in the north, which was held to be the last resting-place of his backbone, to Elephantine in the south, where his leg was said to be buried in a cavern on the island of Biga. The waters of decomposition which issued from this leg were supposed to be the source of the Nile. In later times, the tomb of Osiris' leg on Biga was called 'Abaton' and was regarded as a particularly sacred shrine.

Occasionally, parts of Osiris' body are claimed by several places: his head was buried at Memphis, according to the Memphite priesthood, but the same member was claimed by Abydos! The phenomenon of miraculous multiplication is not unknown today – there are extant enough pieces of the True Cross to make up a veritable forest.

At last, Isis and Nephthys had collected all the pieces of Osiris' dismembered body, with the exception, according to Plutarch, of his penis, which Seth had thrown into the Nile where it was swallowed by a *Mormyrus-* or *Oxyrhynchus-*fish. The two sisters sat down beside the assembled parts of the body and wept. They wept so loudly that the Great God Re took pity on them and sent the jackal-headed god Anubis, and the ibis-headed god Thoth to help them. Anubis embalmed the members of Osiris' body with costly unguents, and wrapped them in bandages. Then he, and Thoth, with the aid of Isis, Horus and Nephthys, pieced together the parts of the body until it was reassembled in its former shape. The whole body was then swathed in linen bandages and placed on a lion-headed bier inside a pavilion – the first mummy had been made.

Isis changed herself into a kite and used her wings to fan the breath of life into Osiris. He was partially revived, but not enough to be able to take his place upon the throne of Egypt ever again. Instead, he was conveyed to the Underworld, a dark and menacing place. There, he remonstrated with the Great God Atum, saying:

> Oh Atum, what is this desolate place into which I have come? It is without water; it is without air; its depth is unfathomable; its darkness is black as night. Must I wander hopelessly here where one cannot live in peace of heart or satisfy the longings of love?[5]

Atum replied to this cry of despair with the assurance that in the Underworld contentment and peace render unnecessary air and water and love. When Osiris asked if he would ever see the light of day again, Atum told him that he would remain in the Underworld, ruling as king but seeing no other god, while his son, Horus, took his place on the throne of Egypt and in the Company of Gods in the Barque of the Sun God. And when, with foreboding, Osiris asked Atum how many were to be the years of his existence in this dreadful place, he was told that he would live for millions of years until the day came when Atum would destroy what he had created and be united with Osiris in the Primeval Waters of the Nun. Thus, reluctantly, did Osiris become King of the Underworld.

During his rise from an obscure prehistoric fertility god to the Egyptian God of the Dead *par excellence*, Osiris was incorporated into the mythologies of the two deities who were paramount at the beginning of the historic period in Egypt: Ptah of Memphis and Re of Heliopolis. At Heliopolis, as we have seen (page 30), Osiris became part of the Great Ennead as the son of Nut and Geb, born on one of the five epagomenal days, the brother of Isis, Nephthys, Horus the Elder and Seth, the husband of Isis, destined to become King of Egypt after Geb. At Heliopolis, Osiris was regarded as a sky god. Sometimes, he was said to be the moon; at other times, the constellation Orion. When, eventually, he supplanted the Sun God as Ruler of the Underworld, he was thought of as the shadowed half of Re, with Re being the sun by day to Osiris' 'dark sun' at night. Osiris took on his first funerary associations at Memphis, where he was identified with Sokar, the ancient Memphite deity of the dead who had been coalesced with Ptah.

Osiris found his true home, his final and best-known resting-place, at *Aabdju*, now usually known by the Greek form of the name, Abydos. This most sacred site in Egypt lies between Assiut and Luxor, near the predynastic city of This, which, by late predynastic times, had become the capital of Upper Egypt. The cult of Anhur (Onuris), the divine huntsman (see page 34), was celebrated at

This (or Thinis), which may have been sited at Mesheikh, on the east bank of the Nile opposite Abydos. Abydos was the Thinite necropolis. When, around 3100 BC, the greatest of the Thinite kings, Menes, united both Upper and Lower Egypt under his rule, he and his successors, the kings of the First and Second Dynasties, chose to be buried at Sakkara, the necropolis of the newly built capital, Memphis. However, they commemorated the fact that their origins were at This by building cenotaphs at Abydos.[6]

At this time, the local god of Abydos was Khentyamentiu. His name means 'Foremost-of-the-Westerners', a reference to the belief that, just as the sun rose or was 'born' in the east, and set or 'died' in the west, so men when they died followed the sun into the west, where the dead had their abode and where Khentyamentiu was the foremost or most important god. He himself had supplanted the oldest-known god of Abydos, Wepwawet.

Wepwawet, whose name means 'The-Opener-of-the-Ways', was believed to usher the dead on the paths of the Underworld. He was usually represented as a jackal, an appropriate totem animal for a god of the dead since the jackal, then as now, at night frequents the edge of the desert where cemeteries are situated. Unlike the other jackal-headed funerary deity Anubis, who is always depicted with a black head, Wepwawet is portrayed with a grey or white head, an indication that he was originally a wolf god. As well as being the oldest deity of Abydos, Wepwawet was worshipped some 120 km to the north in the 13th Nome of Upper Egypt. The Greek name of the nome capital, Lykopolis (Wolf City) confirms that Wepwawet was originally worshipped as a wolf. Today, Lykopolis is called Assiut, and is an important provincial capital.

The god who ousted Wepwawet from Abydos, Khentyamentiu, was represented in human form, his arms folded across his chest, his body entirely swathed in bandages; on his head, the White Crown of Upper Egypt. The bandages indicate that he was a god of the dead, albeit a relatively obscure one. He was local to Abydos where he was worshipped for a very long time, right down to Dynasty XIII, even though Osiris had by then long since divested him of his attributes and functions and replaced him as the chief god of Abydos.

Osiris arrived at Abydos during Dynasty V. Although the city had enjoyed considerable prestige as the necropolis of This for a long time before the advent of Osiris, his ever-increasing popularity was to ensure that, by Dynasty XII, Abydos had become one of the most famous religious centres in Egypt. Under the patronage of the kings of Dynasty XII, Osiris enjoyed more power and importance than ever before.

Through his resurrection, Osiris held out the hope of eternal life at first to the King of Egypt alone, but eventually to every Egyptian, for the Egyptians believed that if their friends acted towards them as the gods had acted towards Osiris, they, too, would achieve eternal life. Thus, when an Egyptian died, his body was mummified and wrapped in bandages in imitation of the body of the dead Osiris. The priests attending his burial performed their parts as the gods had performed theirs; the chief female mourners enacted the roles of Isis and Nephthys, and the burial rites were conducted by a priest impersonating Anubis. By the end of the

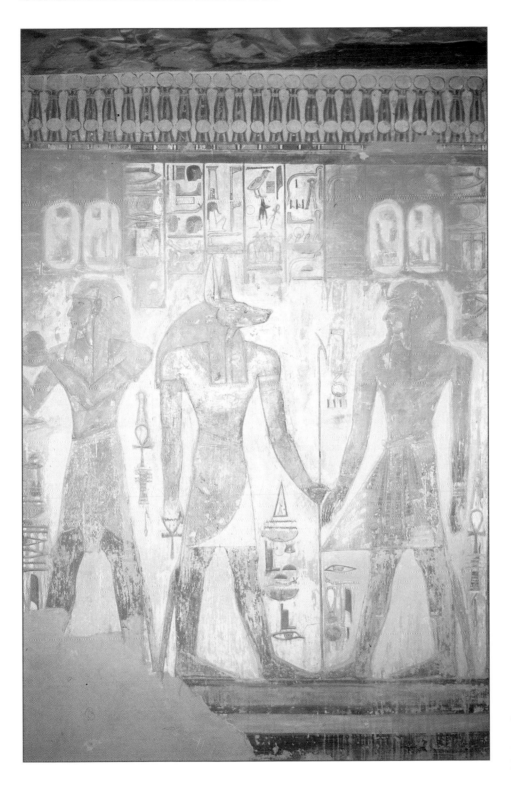

Wepwawet: relief from the memorial temple of Sety I at Abydos.

Old Kingdom, every dead Egyptian was identified with Osiris and addressed as 'The Osiris [such-and-such a name]'.

In the Old Kingdom, when Re held sway, the Solar religion as expressed in the Pyramid Texts represents Heaven as an essentially royal domain to which the ordinary person could not aspire. By the end of the Sixth Dynasty, the Pyramid Texts had been edited and rewritten to accommodate Osiris. The Old Kingdom belief in a Solar Hereafter was gradually fading as the Osirian beliefs became increasingly popular. By Dynasty XI, the Pyramid Texts had been adapted for use by those who were not entitled to be buried in pyramids, and selections from the Texts were written inside coffins, usually on the walls, sometimes on the base. The Pyramid Texts became the Coffin Texts, a collection of magic spells that enabled the Egyptians to cope with death and what comes after it.

The Coffin Texts reveal that the Egyptians went in terror of death and the next world; it was indeed 'the undiscover'd country from whose bourn no traveller returns', and an obsessive fear of the unknown is the hallmark of the Coffin Texts. The Egyptian conception of the Underworld was that it was a nightmarish place – dark, dismal, unsafe, peopled with monsters, genii and all kinds of carnivorous animal. The Coffin Texts provide spells for escaping from such creatures, and spells for the prevention of suffering from evils such as walking upside down or eating excrement.

Everything necessary for life upon earth was thought to be just as necessary for life after death: hence, many spells in the Coffin Texts are for enabling the dead person to breathe pure air; to conserve his sexual powers; to help him find his family again so that they can serve him with funerary offerings of clothing, ointments, drink and, above all, food – a fear of lack of food was uppermost in the minds of the Egyptians.

The obsession with food found in the Coffin Texts is matched only by an obsession concerning the preservation of the body. Therefore, many spells refer to the care of the body, especially the head and the heart; other spells confer the ability to move about with ease. The Coffin Texts are concerned with the problem of survival after death, and in the final analysis, this means the preservation of the body. The theory of what happens to the soul and to the dead in the Afterlife, although referred to in the Coffin Texts, is not fully developed until the New Kingdom.

The New Kingdom saw the final triumph of Osiris. In the middle of the sixteenth century BC, the princes of Thebes succeeded in uniting the whole of Egypt under their own rule. During the period of civil war which led up to this event, Osiris' chief shrine, Abydos, was captured by the Theban rulers who were to found the New Kingdom. They used Osiris in their political struggle, and persuaded their subjects that a pilgrimage to Abydos was something that every Egyptian should aspire to make.

In the Middle Kingdom, the Egyptians had often arranged for funerary stelae to be deposited on their behalf at Abydos in place of actually making the journey there. In the New Kingdom, the Journey to Abydos became an essential part of funerary belief: accordingly, Egyptians decorated their tombs with painted pictures of this journey, which they may or may not have actually undertaken, but which could be accomplished by magical means by the expedient of having it depicted on the walls of their tombs. The best examples of these paintings are at Thebes, where many tombs have on one wall a depiction of the boat used for the Journey to Abydos, its sail furled for the journey downstream; and on the opposite wall, the boat with its sail set for the triumphal return journey upstream.

It was the wish of every Egyptian to be buried at Abydos, as near as possible to the place where Osiris was said to be buried. Since this was clearly an impossibility in the majority of cases, those who made a pilgrimage to Abydos were content to leave votive messages to Osiris, written on pieces of broken pot. The vast number of potsherds to be seen today strewn across the site of Abydos give the locality its Arabic name, *Umm el Ga'ab*, (Mother of Pots), and bear testimony to the number of Egyptians who must have visited Abydos over the centuries.

The Theban doctrine of Osiris, which was fully developed by Dynasty XVIII, saw the democratization of the Afterlife. From then on, the Afterlife was available to every follower of Osiris, king or commoner, male or female. It would not be true to say 'rich or poor', since the poor could not normally afford to make the preparations deemed necessary to make absolutely sure of gaining the Afterlife, but it seems that even the poor had some hope of reaching it. The secret of the enormous popularity enjoyed by Osiris from the New Kingdom to the end of the Pharaonic period lay in the hope of eternal life that he held out to everyone who had made at least some preparations for death.

These preparations included a safe burial place for the body, in which, it was thought, an entity called the *Ba* resided. According to Egyptian belief every person was made up of three parts: the *Ka* ⊔, the *Ba* 🐦 and the *Akh* 🦅. Although it is difficult to find modern concepts which faithfully convey the Egyptian idea of what the *Ka*, the *Ba* and the *Akh* were, the *Ba* is often described as the soul of a man or woman, the *Ka* as his or her double and the *Akh* as a glorified spirit. The Egyptians believed that when human beings were conceived, the god Khnum, or his deputy, made their bodies on a potter's turntable and at the same time made their *Kas* or doubles. The *Ka* lived in the body until the moment of death, when it divided into two – into a bird (the *Akh*) which flew to the Afterlife where it turned back into the *Ka*; and into a human-headed bird, the *Ba*, which stayed behind on earth living in the dead body left behind by the *Akh*.

Although the Egyptians did not look forward to death, their acceptance of the inevitable end to life was made easier if they had made the correct preparations for burial. It is sometimes said that the ancient Egyptians spent so much of their wealth on funerary preparations that they must have been an extremely morbid people. However, judging solely from the decorations on the walls of their tombs, many of which show the daily activities of the Egyptians, they enjoyed life to the full; and it would seem that their preparations for death owed much to their wish to perpetuate that enjoyment. Even the poorest Egyptians, who could afford little for their burial, looked forward to eternal life as souls sailing through the sky in little boats – a peaceful eternity as stars in the quiet heavens in contrast to their life of toil on earth.

The places in which bodies were laid so that the *Bas* that they housed could live on in safety, sustained by regular offerings of food and drink, were called 'houses of eternity' (*pr nḥḥ*). In early times, the dead were buried in pits dug in desert sand through which the fluids of decomposition drained away quickly, thus preventing the body from rotting. In addition, the heat of the sun penetrated through the sand to the body in the pit below, accelerating the rate of desiccation. Thus bodies were preserved by natural means. However, once the Egyptians began to construct tombs of brick and stone the elaborate superstructures of these buildings prevented the natural desiccation of the body, causing it to rot, thereby destroying the 'home' of the *Ba*. The Egyptians were forced to find a way of preserving the body by artificial means, and the means they found, probably sometime during the early Old Kingdom, was mummification.

The whole purpose of tomb-building and mummification was to protect the *Ba*. However, if, in spite of everything, a body was destroyed after burial, the Egyptians believed that the *Ba* could take up residence in a statue or relief of the dead tomb owner. Hence, at an early date, they learned how to carve statues and reliefs – not as decorations but as substitutes for the body. As long as the *Ba* continued to live on earth, so the dead person could go on living in the Afterlife. It was only if the *Ba* were destroyed that the dead person would suffer the second death, the death that really did come as the end: he was annihilated, made as if he had never come into existence.

In order to reach the Afterlife, the dead had to face a perilous journey through the Duat. The Duat is sometimes translated as 'Hell' or 'Hades', but these terms convey ideas that were alien to the Egyptians, and it is perhaps safer to translate Duat simply as the Underworld. The Underworld was thought to be a narrow valley with a river running through it – not unlike Egypt itself! It seems to have been separated from this world – and to the Egyptians, that meant Egypt – by a range of mountains. At the eastern end of this range was a mountain called *Manu*, at the western end another, called *Bakhau*, and it was through openings near these mountains that the sun entered and left the Underworld each night. The dead used the same passes. Just as Egypt was divided into provinces, so the Underworld was divided into regions which the dead entered via gates guarded by demons. The dead were only allowed to pass through the gates if they gave the demons the correct passwords; and every dead person should have taken care to have these passwords, together with a map of the Underworld, written on papyrus rolls such as the Book of the Dead, or the Book of What-is-in-the-Underworld, and buried with him!

A dead person could only remain in the Afterlife, which was conceived of as being exactly like this life on earth, by undergoing the Judgement of the Dead. From the New Kingdom onwards, it was Osiris who was supreme Judge of the Dead; and he, together with forty-two Assessor Gods, each Assessor representing one of the nomes of Egypt, sat in the Hall of Judgement waiting for the deceased to appear before them. In front of Osiris, a balance was set up. In one pan of the balance was placed the Feather of Truth; in the other, the heart of the dead person. The god Anubis waited to release the balance, and the god Thoth stood by to register the verdict. Close to the balance sat the monster Ammit: a composite animal with the head of a crocodile, the forequarters of a lion and the hindquarters of a hippopotamus. Ammit waited to eat the heart of anyone found guilty.

A man, or woman, undergoing the Judgement of the Dead stood in front of Osiris, accompanied by his or her *Ba*, and made confession. This confession, which was written down in Chapter 125 of the Book of the Dead, is not an admission of sins as we would understand it. The dead person lists the things that he has not done: he denies, among other things, that he has stolen, killed, cheated, blasphemed, lied, spoken slanderously, gossiped, committed sodomy, masturbated or committed adultery. The words 'I have not' preface every 'sin', a fact that has led Egyptologists to call this list the 'Negative Confession'.

Having made his 'confession', the dead man waited while his heart was weighed in the balance against the Feather of Truth. If the feather weighed down the heart, or if the balance did not move, the man had made a true 'confession'. If the heart, heavy with guilt, weighed down the feather, then the man was found 'guilty'. Since he had taken the precaution of placing a papyrus in his tomb with the Negative Confession written on it, the Egyptian believed that no matter what sins he had committed, the Negative Confession wiped them out: what was set down on the papyrus became fact. There is no record that Ammit, the 'Eater-of-hearts', ever had to perform his task since no Egyptian appearing in the Hall of Judgement was ever found 'guilty'. Thus, although the ancient Egyptians seem to have had a strong sense of ethics, they nullified it by the use of magic. Everyone was declared '*maa heroo*' ('true of voice') in the Hall of Judgement, and in hieroglyphic inscriptions in his tomb, every tomb owner confidently adds these words after his name. They came to mean, in effect, 'the late' or 'the deceased'.

Throughout the centuries, Abydos maintained its position as the most important religious centre in Egypt. Many shrines and temples were erected there, the earliest of which was probably a simple edifice built of mud-brick, or even of reeds, and dedicated to Khentyamentiu, later to be displaced by Osiris. In Dynasty XII, Senwosret III had a memorial temple built at Abydos in addition to the memorial temple connected to his pyramid at Dahshur. The first king of Dynasty XVIII, Ahmose, built a cenotaph at Abydos for his grandmother, Tetisheri, and several other temples are known to have been built there by kings of Dynasties XVII and XVIII, although their sites have not yet been located. In Dynasty XIX, Ramesses II added to their number.

The most famous temple at Abydos, indeed one of the most renowned temples in Egypt, largely because of the beauty of the reliefs within the building, is the memorial temple of Ramesses II's father, Sety I. This temple has an unusual L-shaped plan, and seven sanctuaries: one dedicated to Sety himself, the others to Ptah, Re-Horakhty, Amun, Isis, Horus and Osiris. Throughout the temple, the hieroglyphs in which King Sety's name is written spell it out alphabetically rather than write it using a pictograph of the god Seth, a tactful admission of the fact that Osiris had been murdered by Seth. Behind the temple is the building known as the Osireion, which was designed to be a recreation of the Island of Creation set in the waters of the Nun. It was a cenotaph for Sety, who was actually buried in the Valley of the Kings at Thebes, and it is possible that the king lay in state in it before being taken on his last journey to Thebes. The Osireion is constructed from massive granite blocks in a style reminiscent of the Old Kingdom. Its central part is open to the sky, and it was here, probably, that barley was germinated as a symbol of the resurrection of Osiris.

At Abydos, the Osiris Mysteries were enacted every year during the last month of Inundation (October) when the flood waters were receding. In the New Kingdom, the Mysteries lasted for eight days, and began when a statue of Osiris was carried on the shoulders of his priests towards his tomb, which was traditionally situated at the site of the tomb of the First-Dynasty king, Djer. The procession, which was led by a priest wearing a jackal-mask who represented Wepwawet, the Opener of the Ways, consisted of priests and priestesses impersonating the chief actors in the Osiris legend. The following three days and nights were filled with lamentations; having buried the statue of Osiris, the mourners, led by 'Isis' and 'Nephthys', grieved for the god. Next came the re-enactment of the trial of Seth before the Tribunal of the Gods, and a mock battle between the followers of Seth and those of Osiris. Eventually, Osiris made a triumphant reappearance in his sacred Barque, the *Neshmet*, and, finally, the most sacred act in the Mysteries was carried out – the erection of the *Djed*-pillar, the ancient representation of the backbone of Osiris, an act which symbolized the resurrection of the god.

The cult of Osiris lasted for over two thousand years. His final transmogrification came in the reign of Ptolemy I Soter, who introduced a new god into Egypt in an attempt to provide all his subjects, both Greek and Egyptian, with a divinity whom both cultures would find sympathetic. The new god, called Serapis, was a combination of Osiris and Apis, the sacred bull of Memphis (see page 167), but with many Hellenistic elements also. He borrowed some of his attributes from Zeus, Asklepios and Dionysus: hence he was a god of fertility and of the Underworld who was also a physician. The cult of Serapis was centred on Alexandria, where his temple, the Serapeum, was regarded as a place of pilgrimage throughout the Greek and Roman world until its destruction on the orders of the Emperor Theodosius in AD 389. The old burial place of the Apis Bulls at Sakkara (also called the Serapeum) was granted a new lease of life because of the introduction of Serapis. However, the Egyptians never fully accepted this hybrid deity with his Hellenistic overtones.

Osiris is probably the best known of all Egyptian gods. His appeal lay in the belief that he had lived on earth as a man who brought nothing but good to mankind but who was betrayed and murdered. His resurrection and the hope of eternal life that he held out to everyone further enhanced his popularity, which was unrivalled until Roman times when the popularity of his wife, Isis, gained ground. Only the advent of Jesus Christ, who brought the same message to mankind, eclipsed the fame of this, the most sympathetic of all the deities in the Egyptian pantheon.

Osiris has found new followers in modern times in the shape of Freemasons, some of whom identify the god with Hiram, the supposed architect of Solomon's temple in Jerusalem. Masonic myth tells of how Hiram, like Osiris, was murdered but rose from the dead.[7] Curiously, a further manifestation of Freemasonry's fascination with ancient Egypt is the obelisk, which nineteenth-century Masons believed to be associated, not with Re (see page 48), but with Osiris, considering the obelisk to be a representation of the god's missing penis (see page 62). Hence the predilection in the last century, when Freemasonry flourished in affluent and governing circles, for erecting obelisks in town squares, gardens and graveyards. In the United States, one obelisk in particular is worthy of note – that of the Washington Memorial, built to honour America's first president, George Washington, himself a Mason. Masonic symbols are still to be seen on United States one dollar bills, on which the 'eye' of Osiris, set within the Benben-stone of a pyramid, steadfastly gazes out.

ISIS

. . . .

Isis was more popular than any other goddess in the Egyptian pantheon. Nothing is known of her origins, although it is more than probable that at the outset she was a fetish goddess who was worshipped in a locality in the Delta situated close to Busiris, the oldest-known centre of the cult of Osiris. Isis was a universal goddess who took her place in the sky as Sirius (the Dog Star), but there was no town or city in Egypt that claimed recognition as her place of origin or her burial place. For many years, therefore, Isis was not exclusively connected with any one town or temple. Instead, a part of every temple in the land was reserved for her worship.

The standard depiction of Isis shows her as a woman wearing on her head the hieroglyphic sign 𓊹, which represents a seat or throne. It is possible that originally Isis wore on her head her fetish object, which later became confused with the hieroglyph 𓊹, thus connecting Isis with the royal throne, perhaps as a personification of it. She was known as 'The Goddess of Many Names' and indeed she is found as a form of every great female deity from Nut and Hathor (from whom she borrowed the cow's horns that she is sometimes depicted wearing) to the Greek moon goddess Astarte. The Greeks also equated her with their corn goddess, Demeter.

The first great shrine built specifically in honour of Isis was begun in Dynasty XXX in the reign of Nectanebo II. This is the Temple of Isis at Behbeit el-Hagar, which lies between Tanta and Damietta in the Eastern Delta. The temple, which was known to the Greeks as the Iseum, was completed in the reign of Ptolemy III Euergetes I, and in it Isis, together with Osiris and Horus, was worshipped until the sixth century AD. At Denderah, the Emperor Augustus had a small temple – another Iseum – built for Isis to the south of the main temple, which was dedicated to Hathor; in this small temple, the birth of Isis was recorded and celebrated.

Perhaps the most famous temple dedicated to Isis is that on the island of Philae. The southern border of ancient Egypt was set at Elephantine (Aswan), which means that as Philae lies upstream of Elephantine it lay beyond the borders of ancient Egypt. The earliest parts of the temple were erected by Nectanebo I but Ptolemaic kings and Roman emperors built there also. The great hall of the temple was turned into a church under the Byzantine Emperor,

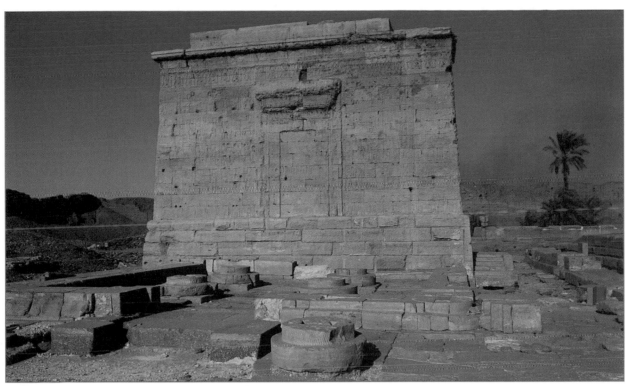

Temple of Isis (Iseum),
Denderah.

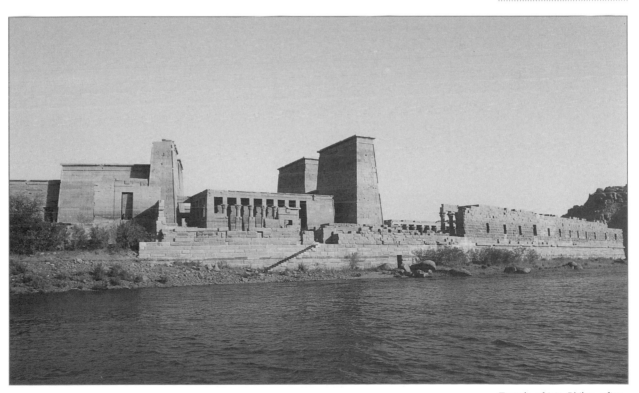

Temple of Isis, Philae, after
its removal to Agilkia island.

Justinian. Philae has come into prominence once again in the last few years due to the building of the High Dam at Aswan. In order to save the temples and shrines on Philae Island from drowning under the waters of Lake Nasser, they have been dismantled and re-erected on the nearby island of Agilkia.

Originally, Isis was significant because of her relationship to other divinities: she took her place in the Heliopolitan Ennead as the daughter of Geb and Nut, the wife of Osiris and the sister of Seth and Nephthys. She was allotted a role as protector goddess: Isis, together with Nephthys, Neith and Selkis, guarded the four corners of royal sarcophagi; the mummified liver of a dead man was set under her protection; she and Nephthys were regarded as the chief divine mourners. Isis' role as mourner and protector of the dead arises from her association with Osiris and with her quest to find his body after his murder by Seth (see page 59).

Isis was often depicted as a female figure with arms outstretched and placed around the figure of Osiris; or as a mother suckling her son, Horus, making her the prototype of the faithful wife and devoted mother. On more than one occasion, Isis changed herself into a kite in order to breathe life into Osiris; and it is her propensity for achieving her purposes by changing herself into this bird of prey so familiar throughout Egypt that gave rise to the depictions of Isis as a human female with wings, most notably when she is protecting the royal sarcophagus (see page 112). Her reputation as a great magician, as exemplified by the story of Re and his Great Name (see page 41), would have done her no harm in the esteem of the Egyptians, who were great respecters of magic. But it is as the faithful wife and, more especially, as the devoted mother, that she was most revered.

The fullest account of how Isis kept faith with Osiris is found in Plutarch's *De Iside et Osiride*. After the murder of Osiris, the grief-stricken Isis set out to find his body, which Seth had thrown into the Nile. She journeyed up and down the land of Egypt and beyond, enquiring of everyone she met whether they had seen her beloved husband. At last, the goddess came across a group of children playing on the shore of the Great Green (the Mediterranean). They told her of the beautiful chest that they had seen floating in the sea being carried eastwards on the waves. And so Isis followed the shoreline of the Great Green until she came to Byblos in the Lebanon. There, she used her magic arts to learn the whereabouts of her husband's body and discovered that it had been enclosed in the trunk of the great tamarisk tree that was now a pillar in the main hall of the royal palace.

Isis disguised herself as an old woman and sat down by a well. She spoke to no one until, one day, the handmaidens of the Queen of Byblos passed by. To them, she spoke beguilingly and showed them how to braid their hair in new ways, and as she bent over them dressing their locks, she impregnated the tresses with the divine perfume of her own body. When the queen saw her maidservants' hair and smelled the sweet smell that emanated from it, she asked her women who had taught them to dress their hair in this new way, and they told her of the old woman who sat by the well. The queen sent for the old woman, and,

Isis suckling the infant
Horus: relief from the
mammisi, Temple of Isis,
Philae.

realizing that she was an Egyptian, thought that she might be one who knew the
magical arts for which Egypt was famous; and so she asked her to be the nurse of
her baby son. And Isis agreed.

The little prince of Byblos was ailing and was not expected to live long. The
queen hoped that the old Egyptian woman would have a knowledge of magic
that would save him. Her hope proved well founded, for, under Isis' care, the
prince grew better every day. Indeed, he improved so quickly that the queen was
curious to know what magic the old woman was using. One night, she hid
herself outside the baby's room. For a long time, she waited in vain for
something to happen. Then she saw the old woman leave the nursery, and
followed her until she reached the main hall of the palace. There, the old woman
changed into a swallow and flew round and round the great pillar that had been
made from the tamarisk tree, twittering mournfully. The queen watched for a
while and then, realizing that her son had been left alone, ran back to his room.

To her horror, the baby was standing in the middle of the floor engulfed in
flames. The queen uttered a loud shriek and rushed forward to snatch her son
from the fire. Before she had had time to comprehend that the baby was quite
unharmed, she was confronted by Isis, not in the guise of an old woman or a
swallow, but in her full splendour as a goddess. The queen fell to her knees

before her as she said, 'I was burning away the mortal parts of your child so that he might live forever. Now, however, you have broken the spell and he will die as all men must die.'

When the King of Byblos learned what had happened, he begged Isis to forgive his wife. Isis agreed, providing that he would give her the magnificent tamarisk pillar in his hall. Only too glad to appease the goddess so easily, the king had the pillar cut down. Isis cut open the pillar and drew forth the chest which contained the body of Osiris. She threw herself onto the chest and lamented so loudly that one of the king's children died of fright. Then Isis wrapped the tree-trunk in fine linen and poured costly ointments over it. She gave it to the King of Byblos, who built a temple for it in which the people of Byblos could worship the tree-trunk: the temple stands to this day.

Isis took the chest with its precious contents and placed it in a boat. Maneros, the king's eldest son, went with her to sail the vessel. As soon as they had put to sea, Isis opened the chest and gazed sorrowfully upon the face of her dead husband. As she leaned forward to kiss him, Maneros approached the divine couple, and Isis turned to look at him, her face filled with such grief that the prince backed away in horror and fell over the side of the boat. Maneros was drowned, and for many years the Egyptians commemorated him by calling upon him in their harvest songs as they lamented over the cutting of the first sheaf of corn.

And so Isis brought the body of her husband home to Egypt. She grieved that she had no son to inherit the throne of his father which would now fall to the murderer, Seth; and she determined that her husband, Osiris, should have a son to avenge him and claim his rightful inheritance. One version of her story says that she changed herself into a kite and produced light from her feathers and air from her wings. By this means she made Osiris' penis rise up from his inert body. She drew from him his essence and with this she made for him a son and heir whom she carried within her body. Osiris became King of the Underworld and Isis was left alone to protect his seed with which she was pregnant and bring it to fruition; to guard her unborn child from Seth. She tried to hide herself from Seth but he caught her and imprisoned her in a spinning-mill.

What happened next is told on a stele made for King Nectanebo II in the fourth century BC, a late version of what is clearly a very old legend. The stele was found in AD 1828 at Alexandria and is now known as the Metternich Stele.[8] The god Thoth realized that Isis was in grave danger from Seth, and was fearful of what might happen to her when Seth discovered that she was pregnant. And so he rescued her from the spinning-mill. Thoth advised Isis to go into hiding until her little boy grew to the age at which he could claim his inheritance. After her escape, Isis waited until evening before setting out for the Delta where she intended to hide herself in the papyrus thickets and marshes which covered the area. She was accompanied on her perilous journey by seven scorpions, the leader of which was called Tefen.

On the journey to the Delta, the weary Isis and her companions came to the town of *Per-sui* and decided to ask for refuge for the night at the house of a certain rich lady named Usert. Usert shut her door in Isis' face, an act that so vexed the scorpions that they put all their venom into the sting of Tefen, who crept under the double doors of Usert's house and bit her son. Meanwhile, a little fisher-girl had offered shelter to Isis and her companions in her own humble home.

The venom of Tefen, enriched as it was by his fellow scorpions, caused Usert's little boy extreme agony. His frantic mother rushed into the town calling for help, but everyone ignored her. However, Isis found that she was sorry for the child, who was, after all, innocent. She decided to cure him and called to his mother, telling her to bring the little boy to her, for she was one who knew how to expel poison with her magic spell. Isis put her hand on the child, who lay panting for breath, and recited, 'Oh poison of Tefen, come forth and drip onto the ground. May the child live and the poison die.' Usert was overcome with remorse for her callous treatment of Isis. Filled with gratitude, she sought to make amends by filling the hut of the little fisher-girl who had sheltered the goddess with valuable possessions from her own house.

Isis went on with her journey and eventually came to Khemmis in the Delta. There she gave birth to her son, Horus, whom she named Horus-Avenger-of-his-Father. She took off her girdle and tied it round the baby for his protection. It is the knot of this magic girdle that was used to form the amulet *Tyt*, which became a symbol of protection to the Egyptians.

Although Isis was a goddess, her divine status availed her not at all in Khemmis. She was a fugitive, terrified lest Seth find her and her baby son; and she was hungry – there was no one to feed her and care for her. Eventually, she was forced to leave Horus alone and, disguised as a beggar-woman, go in search of food. All day she wandered, seeking things to eat, longing all the while to be with her little boy. For some reason Isis must have removed her protective girdle from her son before she set out to find food because when, at the end of the day, she returned to the place where she had left him, she found the child lying on the ground, water streaming from his eyes and saliva dribbling from his mouth. Isis rushed to her son, her innocent, fatherless child. She picked him up and cradled him in her arms. Sobbing, she cried out, 'Here I am, here I am'. But the child lay still as a stone. Thinking that her son was in distress because he had been left all day without food, Isis tried to suckle him. But even the smell of his mother's milk and the sensation of her nipple pressed against his mouth failed to rouse the baby.

Isis did not know where to turn for help. She dared not call out to the gods, for fear of Seth. Instead, she appealed to the marsh-dwellers, who left their huts and came hurrying to exclaim over Isis in her sorrow. None of them knew how to cure Horus, who lay rigid on the ground showing no signs of life. Isis began to fear that Seth had attacked her child. Eventually, a woman came to Isis, a great lady in her town with a reputation for learning. She assured Isis that Horus' malady was no trick of Seth's devising because Atum had decreed that Seth should not enter Khemmis. She advised Isis to seek another reason for the sickness and suggested that Horus had been bitten by a snake or a scorpion.

Isis laid her nose to her child's mouth and sniffed 'to find out whether there was any smell in his skull'. There was and it told her that Horus had been poisoned by a scorpion. Ironically, it seems that she had no power to cure her own son as she had the child stung by Tefen; and the cries of anguish that she uttered when she found herself unable to heal her child brought Nephthys and Selkis to her side. Their combined voices reached Re in his Barque of Millions of Years and caused the boat to come to a standstill, whereat darkness descended on the earth.

Thoth alighted from the boat and recited the spell by which Horus would be restored to health:

> Come back, Oh Poison. You are exorcised by the spell of Re himself . . . the Barque of the Sun God will stand still . . . until Horus recovers – to his mother's delight. Fall onto the earth, Oh Poison . . . darkness will cover everything . . . wells will be dry, crops will wither . . . until Horus recovers – to his mother's delight.

At last, the poison was overcome. Thoth, with a final injunction to those who dwelt in Khemmis that they should guard the child, Horus, until he grew up, returned to the Barque of Re to report to the Sun God that Horus was alive and well – to his mother's delight.

And so Isis waited patiently during the years when Horus was growing up in Khemmis, guarded according to Thoth's decree. Eventually, the day came when he was old enough for her to take him before the Tribunal of the Gods to claim his inheritance. There, Horus found that the sympathies of Re were with Seth: Re preferred that the kingship should be in the hands of an experienced man rather than in those of a youth scarcely out of childhood. The story of what happened next is told in a papyrus written in the reign of Ramesses V and now kept in the Chester Beatty Library in Dublin (see page 86). After much arguing among the gods in the Tribunal, Re decreed that the Company of Gods should be ferried across to an island in the middle of the water, there to decide the fate of Horus and Seth. He gave instructions to Anty, the ferryman, not to let any woman who resembled Isis cross over to the island, for he intended that the gods should settle the issue without interference from the wily goddess.

But Isis was determined to avenge her husband's murder and uphold her son's rights by ensuring that Seth should never sit upon the throne of Egypt. She disguised herself as an old woman and, approaching Anty the ferryman as he was sitting near his boat, she succeeded in bribing him with the gold ring that she wore on her finger to ferry her across to the island in the middle of the water. The Ennead was sitting down eating bread when Isis reached the island. Seth looked up and saw her while she was still some way off, and before he could see her more clearly, Isis recited one of her magic spells and changed herself into a shapely young woman. Whereupon Seth loved her to distraction. He sprang up from where he was sitting eating bread and went to meet the beautiful girl before any of the other gods had had a chance to see her. The besotted Seth stood behind a tree and called out, 'Yoo-hoo, pretty maid! Here I am!' But the 'pretty maid' repulsed Seth's advances while she wrung his heart with the following tale:

> I was married to a cattle herdsman. I bore him a male child and the lad grew up, tending his father's cattle. But then a foreigner came. He sat down in my byre and said this, speaking to my little boy, 'I will beat you and take away the cattle which belonged to your father and throw you out'. And now . . . I should like you to act as my little boy's champion.

The lovelorn Seth, realizing that the only way to gain the affections of this shapely young woman for whom he had fallen at first sight, immediately offered his services, declaring indignantly that it was outrageous that the cattle belonging to her husband should be given to a stranger while her son was still alive. Poor Seth. He had not noticed that when his 'pretty maid' spoke of 'cattle' she was using a word that meant not only cattle but was also used as a synonym for 'Egyptians'. His answer, therefore, meant that the Egyptians belonging to Isis' husband, Osiris, should be given to their son, Horus.

With a loud shriek, Isis changed herself into a kite and flew up to perch on top of an acacia tree, calling out to the discomforted Seth, 'Now it's your turn to weep! You have condemned yourself out of your own mouth, so what are you complaining about?' Realizing how he had been tricked, Seth began to cry. Still crying, he ran to Re-Horakhty, who enquired in a resigned tone of voice what was the matter with him. Seth recounted the way in which Isis had beguiled him by changing herself into a shapely young girl and telling him the sad story of how her husband had died and how a stranger had stolen the cattle that had been left to her little boy.

Re asked Seth what his reply had been. He was told: 'I said to her, "Is it to the foreigner that the cattle should be given while the child of your good man is still alive?" So said I to her. "The face of the stranger should be beaten with a stick. He should be thrown out and your little boy be put in his father's place." So said I to her.'

And Re said to him, 'Well, you have passed judgement on yourself. So what are you complaining of?' Seth was furious. He had the ferryman, Anty, bastinadoed until the soles of his feet were entirely removed for disobeying orders just for the sake of a little gold ring. But his rivalry with Horus went on.

Isis is sometimes represented as a headless goddess. The reason for this is also to be found in the story of Horus' struggles against Seth as related in the Chester Beatty Papyrus. Seth was determined that the incidents that took place on the island in the middle of the water should not be the end of the matter. He challenged Horus to a race, a race which ended with the contestants fighting each other with harpoons. When Seth's harpoon struck Horus, he cried out to his mother to use her magic spells to make the harpoon drop from him. This she did. But when Seth was in his turn struck with Horus' harpoon, Isis felt sorry for her brother. Once again she used her magic, this time to make the harpoon drop from the body of Seth.

At this, Horus became very angry. With his face as savage as a panther's, he took hold of his axe and chopped off his mother's head, and, clasping the head to his bosom, stalked off to the mountains. Meanwhile Isis had changed herself into a headless statue made of flint until a new head could be made for her. Re was angry at what Horus had done, but Isis forgave her son. She continued with her struggle to ensure that he inherited the throne of Egypt and, eventually, she triumphed.

During the Late Period especially, Isis was universally worshipped by virtue of her assimilation with deities such as Astarte, Hathor, Bastet, Nut, Sothis (with whom she merged and was worshipped under the name of Isisothis), and Renenutet. Renenutet (sometimes called Ernutet or Thermuthis), whose name means 'The-Provider-of-Nourishment', was the goddess of fertility and the harvest. She was personified as a cobra and was much respected during harvest-time when the Egyptian peasant was apt to encounter manifestations of her as he cut his wheat or barley. Renenutet was the mother of Nepri, the personification of corn, who was equated with Osiris, the corn god. The obvious parallel between Renenutet and her son, and Isis and the child Horus, led to a merging of the two goddesses during the Late Period when they were worshipped as Isermithis.

The cult of Isis was widespread in the Egypt of the dynastic period. From Egypt, it spread northwards to Phoenicia, Syria and Palestine; to Asia Minor; to Cyprus, Rhodes, Crete, Samos and other islands in the Aegean; to many parts of mainland Greece – Corinth, Argos and Thessaly among them; to Malta and Sicily; and, finally, to Rome. In the first century BC, Isis was perhaps the most popular goddess in the Eternal City. Just as in Egypt she was identified with many other Egyptian goddesses, so in foreign lands was she worshipped as a form of many native goddesses. In *The Golden Ass*, Apuleius lists some of her names: in Phrygia, she was 'The Mother of the Gods'; to the Athenians, she was Minerva; in Cyprus, she was Venus of Paphos; the Cretans called her Diana; the Sicilians, Proserpine. Only the Egyptians, Apuleius noted, called her by her true name: 'Isis the Queen'.

The cult of Isis spread to the furthest limits of the Roman Empire, including Britain; her only rival was Mithras. Had the Emperor Constantine not forsaken Mithras in favour of Christ, and, together with the Emperor Licinius, issued the Edict of Milan in AD 313, granting everyone freedom of worship, Mithras and Isis might still be supreme deities. The cult of Isis, in Egypt and elsewhere, was superseded only by that of the Virgin Mary and the Infant Jesus; and even then, she was not forgotten. The iconography of Mary and the Christ Child owes much to that of Isis and the infant Horus, who was often depicted sitting on his mother's knee. Today, the memory of Isis, Queen of the Gods, is evoked in the aria 'O Isis und Osiris', which Mozart wrote for *Die Zauberflote*; thereby ensuring that the goddess's name is remembered whenever the opera is performed.

HORUS

. . . .

Falcons were more numerous in ancient Egypt than they are in that country today. These impressive birds, with their fine plumage and their ability to hover motionless above the earth before swooping on the prey that they have seen from afar, or to swerve upwards into the sky, higher and higher until they disappear from sight, appealed to the ancient Egyptians' sense of awe at the mysteries of nature. Thus, falcons were worshipped at many places, under many different names. Several gods took on the form of a falcon from time to time – Re, Montu and Sokar among them; but the most famous of the falcon gods were those called Horus. There were several deities bearing this name, each with his own cult-centre and legends. However, over the years their cults and legends became inextricably mixed until finally all falcon gods were eclipsed by the most popular falcon of all, Horus of Edfu, who manifested himself in the shape of a peregrine.

Who was Horus and what was his place of origin, his attributes and legends, that he could displace so many indigenous gods? In the beginning, Horus was a sky god. His Egyptian name, *Hor*, can mean either 'face' or 'distant'; slightly modified to *horet* it means 'sky'. 'The Distant One' is an appropriate name for a falcon since this is a bird that seems to fly further and higher than any other as it ranges widely over the heavens; thus Horus was visualized as the face of the sky. In this face, the left eye was the moon and the right eye was the sun; and the deity to whom the face belonged was worshipped as 'The Great Horus' or 'Horus the Elder', whom the Greeks called Haroeris, the sky god who had come into existence before mankind and who manifested himself on earth in the form of a falcon. This falcon could also represent a moonless night: as *Hor-Khenty-en-Irty* (Horus-Foremost-one-without-Eyes) he was worshipped as the face of the sky at the time when neither sun nor moon could be seen.

There is some argument as to whether Horus was originally a god of Lower Egypt or of Upper Egypt: two places, *Behdet* and *Nekhen*, are rival claimants for the distinction of having been the first to establish his cult. The exact location of *Behdet* is uncertain: it undoubtedly lay in the Western Delta, close to the ancient town of *Imarut* (Town of the Trees), the predynastic centre of the cult of a tree goddess, Sekhet-Hor, who, according to legend, changed herself into a cow, a form of the goddess Hathor, in order to protect Horus when he was a child. *Imarut* lay in what eventually became the 3rd Nome of Lower Egypt, and in the

New Kingdom, it became nome capital. In later years it was called *Demit-en-Hor* (Town of Horus), which is preserved today in the Arabic name of the modern town that stands near the site, Damanhûr. At *Behdet* Horus came to be worshipped not in purely falcon-form but as a hawk-headed man equipped with bow and arrows, and a spear whose point was triangular and backed by the head of a hawk; Horus of *Behdet* was a warlike god.

One of the earliest Upper Egyptian centres of a falcon-cult was at *Nekhen* (modern name, Kom el-Ahmar), on the west bank of the Nile some 80 km south of Luxor (Thebes), a very important predynastic settlement that became the capital city of the 3rd Upper Egyptian Nome in the dynastic period, a position that it held until the New Kingdom. The jackal-headed figures depicted in reliefs and known as 'The Souls of *Nekhen*' probably represent the early rulers of the city, analogous to 'The Souls of *Pe*' (see page 129); and just as *Pe* was linked with *Dep*, so *Nekhen* became the twin town of *Nekheb* (see page 132).

The chief god of predynastic *Nekhen* was not Horus but *Nekheny* or 'The Nekhenite', a falcon who wore two tall plumes on his head. The finest portrait of the falcon of *Nekhen* is the gold head found at the site in AD 1898 by the English Egyptologist, James Quibell, and now in Cairo Museum. By the time this head was made – Dynasty VI – *Nekheny* had long been assimilated with Horus who thus became Horus the Nekhenite. The Greeks acknowledged that *Nekhen* was truly 'The City of the Hawk' and called it Hierakonpolis.

The Souls of *Pe* and *Nekhen*: inner side of rear enclosure wall, Temple of Horus, Edfu. (See also page 129)

Some of the authorities who maintain that the cult of Horus originated in the Delta suggest that it made its way into Upper Egypt when the inhabitants of the North sailed as far south as *Nbt* (modern name, Tukh) and conquered the followers of the local god, Seth. Certainly, this was a tradition enshrined in inscriptions in the temple that was built at Edfu (see page 87) in Ptolemaic times. Some even go so far as to say that all the legends concerning Horus' struggles with his great enemy, Seth, are based on fact and symbolize the conquest of the South by Horus' followers from the North.

However, other authorities suggest that Horus originated in Upper Egypt, and that his cult spread northwards as the Upper Egyptian kings Scorpion and Narmer/Menes subjugated that part of the land. This theory might account for the monogram on the famous Narmer Palette (see page 115), which shows a falcon perched on a papyrus plant from which a human head protrudes. A rope tied through the nose on the head is held by a hand projecting from the falcon's breast. The monogram is thought to depict Horus bringing the people of the North, symbolized by the papyrus of Lower Egypt, as captives to the King of Upper Egypt – an act, perhaps, that he would be more likely to perform as an Upper Egyptian god.

Long before the Unification, Horus had achieved the status of royal god *par excellence*. This was due to the fact that he had important sanctuaries in both halves of the country, in cities that were seats of power for the native rulers – *Pe* in Lower Egypt and *Nekhen* in Upper Egypt – by virtue of which he became patron deity of both lines of kings. Horus was the earliest state god of Egypt. In both halves of the country, the reigning king was considered to be the earthly embodiment of the god and was called 'The Living Horus'. After the Unification, the King of Upper and Lower Egypt adopted as part of his official titulary the Horus Name, symbolic of his role as Horus incarnate. This name was inscribed in the top half of the *serekh*, a rectangular frame at the bottom of which is a design that imitates the recessed or panelled façade of the royal palace, and on top of which Horus, often wearing the Double Crown of Egypt, is perched.

Another of the names in the king's titulary was the Golden Horus Name, which was written as a monogram showing a falcon sitting on the hieroglyphic sign for gold, ▲. It has been suggested that the sign for gold, read *nbw*, symbolizes Seth, whose cult-centre was in the city called *Nbt* (Gold Town; see above) and commemorates the victory of Horus over Seth. On the other hand, the Golden Horus Name may simply indicate a concept of the king as a falcon made of gold, although whether this falcon is Horus or some other god remains a mystery.

Although Horus was the earliest state god of Egypt, it was not long before Re of Heliopolis made a bid for that position. However, the priests of both deities seem to have come to an amicable arrangement: at an early date, the character of Horus had changed from that of a sky god to that, more specifically, of a sun god; and it was in this guise that he was received at Heliopolis, the oldest centre of the cult of the sun. There he was coalesced with Re and became Re-Hor-Akhty or Re-and-Horus-of-the-Two-Horizons, that is, the two horizons of sunrise and

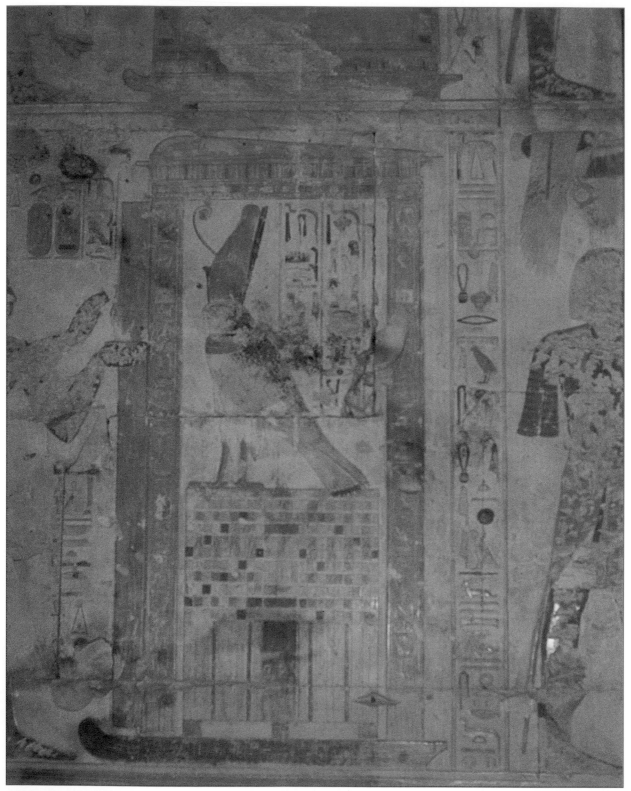

Horus on *serekh*: Osiris
Chapel, memorial temple of
Sety I, Abydos.

sunset, and represented as a man with the head of a hawk surmounted by a sun's disk.

Horus was fitted into Heliopolitan theology not in his own form of sun god but as the son of Osiris and Isis, born after his father's death, in the Delta where Isis protected him from his father's murderer, Seth, until he was old enough to claim his inheritance, the throne of Egypt. This Horus was called variously *Hor-sa-Isis* (Horus-son-of-Isis; in Greek, Harsiesis); *Hor-nedj-her-itef* (Horus-avenger-of-his-father; in Greek, Harendotes); and *Hor-pa-khred* (Horus-the-child (of Isis); in Greek, Harpocrates). Harpocrates, who was represented as a young boy sucking the forefinger of his right hand and wearing the long, curled side-lock of hair that denoted youth, was especially popular during the Late Period.

Horus-son-of-Isis (Harsiesis) was thought to be a friend of the dead, concerned to protect them. He was helped in his task by the four genii known as 'The Four Sons of Horus', whose mother was said to be Isis, Horus' own mother. They were: Imset, who was man-headed; Haapy, baboon-headed; Duamutef, jackal-headed; and Qebehsenuf, hawk-headed. They in turn were aided by four goddesses: Isis and her sister, Nephthys; Neit, the great creator goddess of Sais; and Selkis (sometimes known as Selket or Serquet), the scorpion goddess who was a manifestation of the scorching heat of the sun. Their role was to guard the viscera that had been removed from the body during mummification and placed in the vessels known today as Canopic jars.

The Greeks gave the name Kanopus to the port in the Western Delta, near Alexandria, that is now called Abukir, where tradition had it that Kanopus, the pilot who guided Menelaus and Helen to Egypt after the fall of Troy, was buried. Osiris had been worshipped in this place since predynastic times in the form of a jar with the head of a god, and so when modern Egyptologists found jars in tombs which contained the viscera of the tomb owner and had stoppers shaped, in some cases, like human heads (actually the head of Imset, see above), they called such vessels Canopic jars.

From Ramesside times, the stoppers of Canopic jars were fashioned in the form of the head of the particular Son of Horus whose task it was to guard that jar's contents. The jar containing the liver was set under the protection of Isis and Imset, its stopper, therefore, was carved in the shape of a man's head. That containing the lungs was protected by Nephthys and Haapy, its stopper was shaped like the head of a baboon; that containing the stomach was guarded by Neit and Duamutef, its stopper was jackal-headed; and that containing the intestines was protected by Selkis and Qebehsenuf and topped by a hawk-headed stopper.

At first, the priests of Heliopolis made a distinction between Horus the Sun God and Horus-son-of-Isis; but eventually the two gods merged and Horus the Sun God was absorbed to a great extent by Horus-son-of-Isis, who achieved great popularity throughout Egypt, not merely because of his compassion for the dead when he interceded for them with his father, Osiris, at their Judgement before the Assessors (see page 68), but also because of the heroic role he played in the stories told of his fight against Seth, a contest which lasted for eighty years.

The tale of this contest is told in the Chester Beatty Papyrus. This papyrus, which was written, in hieratic, in the reign of Ramesses V, was found in the nineteenth century AD in Luxor; and the story it contains is today usually called *The Contendings of Horus and Seth*.[9] The tale of 'How judgement came to be passed on Horus and Seth', the opening line of the papyrus, is recounted by the story-teller in a series of episodes in which the gods, from Re downwards, do not appear in an awe-inspiring light, but rather as indecisive, fickle and easily persuaded to back each of the contestants in turn.

The Papyrus relates how Horus and Seth came before the Tribunal of the Gods whose task it was to decide which one should have the throne of Egypt. After much discussion, the gods awarded the throne to Horus, whereupon Seth sprang up and threatened to kill one god per day with his sceptre, which he claimed weighed 4,500 lb – more than two tons! Immediately, Re decreed that they should cross over to the island in the middle of the water to debate the matter further (see page 78). Again, the Crown was awarded to Horus, but Seth insisted on a trial of strength. He suggested that he and Horus should change themselves into hippopotami and jump into the waters of the Great Green (the Mediterranean), and whoever emerged first within the space of three whole months should lose the Crown of Egypt.

The two gods duly turned into hippopotami and plunged into the water. Whereupon Isis decided to take a hand: she made a rope and a copper harpoon and threw them into the water at the place where Horus and Seth had jumped in. Unfortunately, the harpoon hit her son, who yelled to his mother for help. Isis commanded the harpoon to leave the body of her son, retrieved it and threw it into the water again. This time it hit her intended target, Seth, who yelled in his turn, 'What have I done to you, Isis? Call to your blade to let go of me, Isis, for I am your maternal brother!' Then Isis was sorry for him and made her blade loose him. This not unnaturally angered Horus, who jumped out of the water holding his great axe in his hand. He chopped off his mother's head, tucked it into his bosom, and stalked off into the mountains in high dudgeon.

Re was angry with Horus for what he had done to Isis, and, after restoring her head by magic, he commanded the gods to go in search of her errant son and bring him before him to account for his actions. Seth was the first to find Horus, who lay asleep on a mountain-side. He threw him over onto his back, straddled him and gouged out his eyes. And then he buried the eyeballs in the mountain-side, where they turned into two bulbs which grew into lotuses.

Seth, meanwhile, had returned to Re to report that he could not find Horus. But Hathor did not believe him and went in search of Horus herself. She discovered him lying weeping in the desert, terribly injured by the loss of his eyes. Immediately, she caught a female gazelle, milked her, and said to Horus, 'Open your eyes so that I may put this milk into their sockets'. She did so, and Horus' eyes were restored to him. From then on they were called his *Wadjet-* or healed-eyes.

Isis forgave her son for beheading her, and the struggle went on; but eventually the gods settled the dispute over the throne of Egypt by dispatching a letter to

Pectoral (3.8 cm high × 5.7 cm long) from a Dynasty XII necklace reputed to have come from Dahshur and now in Eton College, Windsor. In the centre is a representation of the goddess Bat (the personification of the sistrum of Hathor), supporting on her head a sun's disk flanked by two cobras (Wadjet and Nekhbet as uraei). To the left and right of the disk are Wadjet Eyes (symbols of Horus). To the left of Bat is Horus as a sphinx, to her right the Seth-animal: they are confronting each other not as enemies but as allies in the protection of the royal wearer of the pectoral.

Osiris in the Underworld asking for his opinion on the matter; to which he replied, 'Why should my son, Horus, be cheated since it was I who made you strong. It was I who made the barley and the emmer-wheat to feed gods and men – no other god found himself able to do so!' The letter elicited a rash response from Re, who declared, 'Even if you had never come into existence, even if you had never been born, the barley and the emmer would still have come into being.' This claim brought forth such an angry letter from Osiris that Re was persuaded that it would be wise to give the Crown of Egypt to Osiris' son, Horus. He did so, and before all the gods, Horus was placed upon the throne as King of Upper and Lower Egypt.

In due course, Horus handed on the throne of Egypt, from thenceforward called the Horus Throne, to a human successor. From that time on, every reigning King of Egypt was 'The Horus', and every dead king, 'The Osiris'. One of the ways in which a king legitimized his claim to the throne was by acting as a Horus to his predecessor's Osiris. The dead king need not necessarily have been the new king's father: by the act of burying his predecessor, the new king became in effect his 'son' and heir. Thus, it was possible for a Crown Prince to lose his throne if he were abroad at the time of his father's death and unable to get back to Egypt within the seventy days ritually allotted for the preparations for the dead king's burial. Sometimes, a king died before producing a male child to succeed him: Tutankhamun was one such king, and in this case, the dead king was succeeded by Ay, a relative by marriage and not of the royal blood. However, Ay could legitimately claim the throne and become king because he acted as Horus to Tutankhamun's Osiris by virtue of the act of burying him.

The myths concerning Horus' struggles against Seth are made much of in the temple that was the Upper Egyptian centre of the cult of Horus – Edfu – where he was worshipped both as Horus the Behdetite, the great Sky God and as

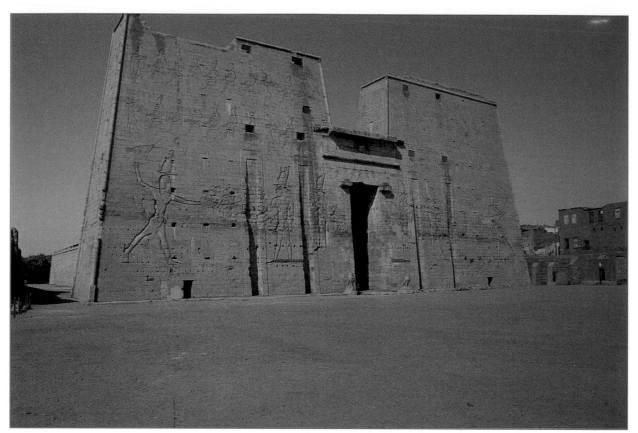

Temple of Horus, Edfu.

Horus-son-of-Isis; thus Horus of Edfu, as a combination of these two powerful deities, could take shape as a hawk-headed man or as a falcon, and his temple at Edfu contained statues and reliefs of Horus in both forms.

Edfu, or to give it the name by which it was known to the ancient Egyptians, *Wetjeset-Hor*, which means 'The-Place-where-Horus-is-Extolled', lies on the west bank of the Nile some 100 km south of Luxor, and was the capital of the 2nd Nome of Upper Egypt. From an early date, Edfu was the site of a shrine dedicated to Horus, and according to tradition the first stone temple at Edfu was built by the famous Imhotep (see page 168) in Dynasty III using a plan that, it was claimed, 'fell from heaven'. The great stone temple that stands there today in a remarkable state of preservation was built during the Ptolemaic period. It was begun in 237 BC by Ptolemy III Euergetes I and finished in 57 BC, and was the only Ptolemaic temple to be completed and that within a comparatively short space of time. The Ptolemaic structure, the last temple to be built at Edfu, was, like its predecessors, erected over older temples, obliterating them. However, the base of an entrance pylon dating to the reign of Ramesses III is still to be seen on the eastern side of the temple, and remains of the earlier building have been uncovered from beneath the paving stones of the temple forecourt.

The Temple of Horus at Edfu, the best preserved of all Egyptian temples, had two names, one sacred, the other secular. The sacred name was *Behdet*, which means 'throne' or 'seat', and seems to have been used since Dynasty III, probably adopted because by that time the true origins of Horus had become obscured and he was thought to have transferred his home from *Behdet* in the Delta to *Wetjeset-Hor* in Upper Egypt, from then onwards also called *Behdet*. The official secular name of the temple was *Djeba*, which means 'Retribution Town', a reference to the fact that the enemies of Horus, notably Seth and his confederates, were brought to justice there. The word *Djeba* became Etbo in Coptic, and hence was the origin of the modern, Arabic name of the town, Edfu. The Greeks, who identified Horus with their own sun god, Apollo, called the place Apollinopolis Magna.

Because Ptolemaic temples were built during a period when Egypt was ruled by foreigners, namely Macedonian Greeks, and many of its old customs and beliefs were under threat, the priests of these temples inscribed on their walls as much information as they could concerning temple ritual and festivals, information which in former times they had either carried in their heads, to be passed on from generation to generation by word of mouth, or written on scrolls of papyrus which they had found to their cost could be removed from their safekeeping, destroyed and their precious contents lost. The priests of the Ptolemaic Period took care to write the inscriptions on the walls of the temples in a complicated script deliberately designed to ensure that even those few who could read would have great difficulty in understanding it: temple secrets were to be maintained!

In the huge Temple of Edfu, seemingly every wall and pillar is covered with hieroglyphs. The enormous amount of inscription, not all of which is as yet translated, although the inscriptions themselves were transcribed and published over a period of forty years by the French Egyptologist Emile Chassinat, gives us, among other things, some idea of the history of the construction of the temple; descriptions of the building, with each part, large or small, being named and its dimensions and purpose given, its decorations described. The great ceremonial occasions such as the Foundation of the Temple, the Consecration of the Temple, and the annual New Year Festival, are recorded in the inscriptions and reliefs on the walls of the building. The daily rituals are listed; even the route taken by the processions of priests taking part in festivals, and the doors through which they passed in and out of the temple, can often be traced.

The most important of the daily rituals at Edfu as at any other temple was the Morning Service,[10] which took place at dawn. The priests would have been up and about long before dawn, making preparations – bringing in water from the sacred lake and chanting spells over it to ensure its ritual purity; killing an ox and cooking it, together with other meats – in other words, making breakfast. Everything would be prepared before dawn, for the use of the chief officiant in the morning ritual, in theory, the king, in practice, the high priest of the temple.

At dawn, the priest entered the temple and made his way to a room called 'The House of the Morning'. There, he ritually purified himself with water, incense and natron, and dressed himself in the vestments to be worn for the ceremony. Then he made his way to the entrance to the Sanctuary, in which there was a locked and sealed shrine containing a statue of the god, Horus. The priest burned incense before the Sanctuary and chanted spells to ensure absolute purity. He then entered the Sanctuary and broke the clay seal on the shrine, which had been attached the previous evening at the end of the Evening Service.

The officiant then opened the door of the shrine and 'revealed the face of the god'. He fell upon his face before the god and kissed the ground. Next, he offered incense to the god to purify him. He then 'laid his hands upon the god' – that is to say, he lifted the statue of the god out of its shrine. He then removed the cloths in which the statue had been draped the previous evening, in effect, removed the god's nightgown; and censed the statue, in other words, gave the god his morning bath. Then the priest dressed the god for the day: he put a white cloth upon the statue and offered it four balls of the natron the Egyptians

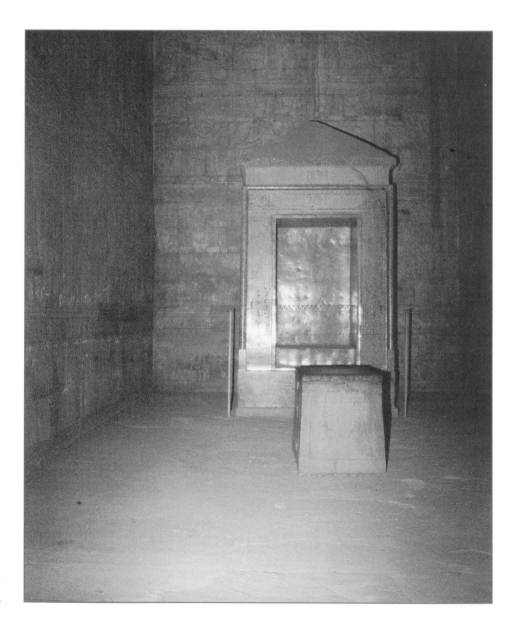

Naos (shrine) in the god's sanctuary, Temple of Horus, Edfu.

called *bd*. Then he put on a green cloth and offered four balls of Upper Egyptian natron from El-Kab. Next came a red cloth and four balls of natron from Wadi Natrun. Lastly, the priest fixed a jewelled collar round the statue's neck, and purified it with water and incense.

The statue was then put back in its shrine, and invested with its regalia – crook, flail, crown and sceptre, and jewels such as bracelets and anklets. The priest then left the sanctuary, walking out backwards and, as he went, smoothing the sand with which the floor of the Sanctuary was covered with a special plant called the *hdn* so that his footsteps were obliterated. He then walked round the Sanctuary censing it to restore it to a state of perfect purity.

The god was then ready for his breakfast. But first, all the other gods who were in the temple, either permanently or as visitors, had to be ritually purified. The ceremony for these gods, or rather, their statues, was an abbreviated version of that performed for Horus himself; and it was probably undertaken by lesser priests who began the ritual while the chief priest was attending to Horus. The gods were thus made ready for breakfast together.

Breakfast consisted of a selection of the offerings brought daily into the temple. They were placed in front of the statue of Horus (and some in front of the statues of the other gods), who was supposed to partake of them. The offerings then reverted to the priests. This Reversion of the Divine Offerings was very important to the priesthood of a temple because it was the means by which they received their 'daily bread'. The offerings were divided among the priest according to rank, the high priest, of course, receiving the largest share.

The Midday Service was much shorter than the Morning Service, and probably consisted of offering libations, and displaying jewels 'for the god's delight'. The Evening Service took place just before sunset and was basically a repetition of the Morning Service, except that the god was prepared for the night by having his coloured cloths and regalia removed. He was then 'put to bed' for the night: his shrine was locked and sealed and the god was left to sleep until dawn next morning.

Most of the important ceremonies particular to Edfu were based on the myths concerning Horus, his birth and his struggles against Seth. Several major deities had their own legends in which the deity was credited with the creation of the world, and Horus was no exception. At Edfu, the story is told of how, in the beginning, Chaos reigned, all was in darkness and the waters of the Nun – silent, inert, deep – covered the earth. And then, two amorphous deities, the Great One and the Distant One, appeared above a small island that had emerged out of the Primeval Waters. From the flotsam that clung to the edges of this island, one of the deities picked up a stick, split it into two pieces and stuck one of them into the ground, near the water's edge. No sooner had he done so than a falcon emerged from the surrounding darkness and alighted on the stick. Immediately, light broke over Chaos, and the falcon sitting on his perch transformed the island into a holy place. The antiquity of this tradition is attested by the fact that, in the Archaic Period, the hieroglyphic sign for 'god' consisted of a falcon sitting on a perch. Eventually, the waters of Chaos receded; the island became bigger and bigger until it became the earth, which, to the Egyptians, was Egypt. Men appeared, and built a shelter round the falcon to protect him, thereby creating the first temple. Thus did Horus the Falcon become the creator of the world, and incidentally the owner of the first temple.

We have seen already that Horus-son-of-Isis was at one time King of Egypt until he handed on the throne to mortal kings. It was natural, therefore, that one of the great ceremonies held in his temple of Edfu should be the annual celebration of the Coronation of the Sacred Falcon. This took place during the first five days of the first month of winter (the fifth month of the Egyptian year – November). The statue of the falcon Horus was taken in procession out of the main body of the temple into a small building outside – the Temple of the Sacred Falcon. The statue was carried by four priests – the two in front wearing falcon masks and the two behind, jackal masks, representing the ancient kings of *Nekhen* and *Pe* respectively. The whole procession continued in silence, 'no man speaking to his fellow'.

In the Temple of the Sacred Falcon, the new 'king' was chosen – not from among men, but from among several falcons that had been brought in from the special grove near the temple where they had been bred for the purpose. Once the Sacred Falcon had been chosen, it was taken to the bridge that linked the two wings (pylons) of the main gate of the temple. There, the statue of Horus presented his newly chosen heir, the living falcon, to the people, after which the procession made its way back to the interior of the temple where the sacred falcon was crowned and invested with the royal regalia. At the end of the day, the living falcon, having played its role in the great ceremony of the day, was returned to the grove of the sacred falcons, there to live out its life until, when it died, it was mummified and buried in the necropolis that had been set aside to receive the sacred birds.

The Coronation of the Sacred Falcon was much more than the yearly selection of a new sacred falcon: it commemorated the coronation of the King of Egypt. Thus the date of the festival was significant – the first day of the fifth month; in other words, the day after the month in which the resurrection of Osiris took place (see page 70), the day on which his son Horus ascended the throne.

Another major annual festival at Edfu was the Festival of Victory, celebrated for five days, starting on the twenty-first day of the second month of winter (December). It is, in effect, a sacred drama, concerned with the victory of Horus over his enemy, Seth. The 'script' of this drama is found on the inner surface of the great wall that runs round the main body of the temple, on its western side, and it is said to be the first play ever written. In AD 1971, it was revived by students of Padgate College, Lancashire, in a performance entitled *The Triumph of Horus*.[11]

It is probable that, in ancient Egypt, although not at Padgate, *The Triumph of Horus* was concluded with a recitation of *The Legend of the Winged Disk*, which is carved on the same wall as *The Triumph of Horus*. This legend, 'dated' to the 363rd year of the reign of Re-Horakhty, tells of how Re and his soldiers were in Nubia when the inhabitants of that land began to talk seditiously against him,

Scene from *The Triumph of Horus*: inner side of the western enclosure wall, Temple of Horus, Edfu.

for which reason Nubia was thereafter called *Wawat* (a pun on the Egyptian verb 'to conspire'). Re commanded Horus the Behdetite to deal with the rebellious Nubians. And Horus flew up into the sky in the form of a great winged sun-disk and shone so ferociously upon the rebels that they were blinded and in panic killed one another.

Re was pleased and decreed that Horus should thenceforward be his champion and gave him a new name, 'He-of-the-Dappled-Plumage'. In the form of the winged disk, Horus pursued the enemies of Re. Whether these enemies took the form of crocodiles or hippopotami, whether they fled from him on land or on sea, Horus defeated them with his axe and his spear. And at each place where he did this, his achievement was commemorated by Re who gave the place a new name; and often, Horus a new epithet.

Eventually, Re's enemy was seen in his true guise: Seth, who raged and cursed and earned the name 'Stinking Face'. Horus of *Behdet* waged war against Seth for a long time until, finally, he overthrew his ancient enemy and brought him in chains before Re. Then Horus-son-of-Isis cut off the head of the enemy (Seth) and dragged him by his feet through the land, with his spears stuck into his back. An image of the winged disk was set up in every temple in every town; Seth was despatched to thunder in the sky, and Horus became Lord of Egypt.

Horus of *Behdet* had the form of a man with the head of a hawk, crowned with the Double Crown of Egypt and wearing two plumes and two cobras on his

Gilded statuette of
Tutankhamun showing him
balanced on a skiff with
harpoon in hand, ready to
stab Seth in the manner of
Horus. (Cairo Museum)

head. In his hands he held a metal axe, a harpoon and a chain. Horus-son-of-Isis
transformed himself and assumed the shape of Horus of *Behdet*; together they
killed the enemies of Re. Their followers were called *mesentiu*, 'The
Harpooners', and Horus was named Lord of *Mesen* (The Place of the Harpoon –
another name for Edfu), Prince of the Two Halves of Egypt.

The cult statues of Horus at Edfu show him in purely falcon form, and in reliefs he
is usually depicted as a falcon-headed man. Horus-son-of-Isis was never a falcon god;
however, it is clear that long before the Ptolemaic Temple of Edfu was built, the
images of the two gods had become inextricably mixed in the minds of the Egyptians.
Thus Horus is often a confusing god for modern man to sort out, and it is perhaps
wise to adopt the attitude of the ancient Egyptians and accept that this confusion
between the attributes and myths of the two deities is nothing to worry about.

Although the worship of Horus, whether distinguished as Horus the Falcon or Horus-son-of-Isis, was pervasive throughout Egyptian history, it is interesting to remember that in predynastic times falcon gods were worshipped under names other than Horus at places such as *Djew-Qa* in Upper Egypt and *Khem* and *Per-Soped* in Lower Egypt; and that only gradually, as the fame of Horus spread, were the cults of these other falcon deities superseded by his.

Djew-Qa (later *Tjebu*; modern name, Qaw el-Kebir, some 180 km north of Luxor) was the capital of the 10th Upper Egyptian Nome, and had worshipped an indigenous falcon god named Anty (He-with-the-Talons) since predynastic times until, sometime in the dynastic period, Anty, like so many other falcon gods, was assimilated with Horus. For some reason, probably because the names had a similar sound, Anty was identified by the Greeks with their mythical giant Antaeus. Antaeus was the son of the Sea God, Poseidon, and Mother Earth, and was King of Libya. He used to challenge strangers to wrestle him, and when they became exhausted he killed them. His final bout was with Herakles, and he lost the contest. However, he is commemorated in the Greek name of the city of *Djew-Qa*, which is not named after either of its falcon gods but after Antaeus, being called Antaeopolis.

At *Khem* (Greek Letopolis; modern name, Ausim), the capital of the 2nd Nome of Lower Egypt, which lies some 13 km north-west of Cairo, a falcon was worshipped originally under the name of *Khenty-khem* (Foremost-One-of-Khem); and then as *Khenty-irty* (which means, perhaps, 'The-Sharp-eyed-One'). At least as far back as Dynasty IV, Horus replaced the ancient falcon god of *Khem* and, incidentally, took on a warlike aspect: his enemies were beheaded there. In the Pyramid Texts, these enemies were called *sabet*-snakes (multi-coloured snakes, possibly cobras) and there was evidently an ancient ritual at *Khem* in which their heads were cut off.

A falcon god of yet another Lower Egyptian Nome, the 20th, also became identified with Horus. This god, Soped, gave his name to the nome capital, *Per-Soped* or 'The House of Soped' (today called Saft el-Hina), a city which lay at the entrance to the Wadi Tumulat, an important route to the Sinai peninsula. Hence, Soped was the guardian of Egypt's eastern border and considered to be lord of foreign lands. Coalesced with Soped, Horus became Lord of the East.

As the cult of Horus grew, he was welcomed at places that did not have falcon gods of their own but worshipped other forms of animal, which, once Horus had arrived on the scene, were absorbed by him. One such case was *Kem-wer*, which lies on the east bank of the Damietta branch of the Nile, and was the capital of the 10th Lower Egyptian Nome. Its modern name, Tell Atrib, is derived from the Greek, Athribis, and owes nothing to the original name of the town, *Kem-wer*, which means 'The Great Black Bull'. The oldest name of the town refers to the bull that once was worshipped there until, in dynastic times, it was replaced by a crocodile god named Khentykhai. Perhaps as early as Dynasty IV, Horus had become the most important deity at *Kem-wer*, not only syncretizing with the indigenous crocodile god but also taking over the name of Khentykhai.

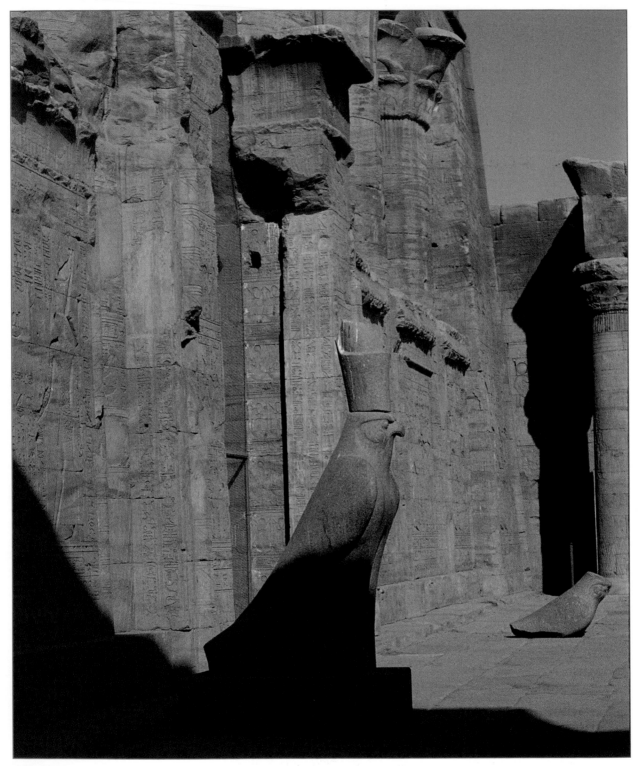

Statue of Horus, Edfu
temple.

At *Kem-wer*, Horus-Khentykhai was also worshipped in the form of a falcon-headed man holding two eyes (*Wadjet*) representing the sun and the moon in his hands. He is called *Hor-merty*. The second syllable of this name, *merty*, is written in hieroglyphs using the sign that usually means 'to love'; hence it is possible that the translation of the name *Hor-merty* should be 'Horus-with-the-two-Precious-Eyes'. *Hor-merty* is only one of several names of Horus which connect him with eyes. To the Egyptians, as to many peoples, the eye was extremely important. We still say that the 'eye is the mirror of the soul'; and many people today, in Egypt and elsewhere, fear the Evil Eye. Hence, the Divine Eye was, to the Egyptians, a symbol of great significance.

It could take many forms. It could be a deity – the goddesses Wadjet, Tefnut and Hathor, for instance, were each known as the Eye of Re; or it could be the *Wadjet*-eye of Horus (see page 86) with its religious and protective connotations. The *Wadjet* symbol became one of the most potent and popular of Egyptian signs, used as an emblem, or as an amulet, worn as a protective piece of jewellery, or in the wrappings of mummies. Painted on the prow of a boat, the Eye of Horus was thought to be able to 'see' the way ahead; and, above all, to protect the boat and its crew from the Evil Eye. Even today, boats all over the Mediterranean can be seen with eyes painted on their prows, their owners little realizing that the origins of the custom lie in the mists of ancient Egyptian mythology.

Whenever the Egyptians depicted the Divine Eye, it was not a human eye that formed the inspiration for their model, but the eye of a peregrine falcon, stylized to show a bright pupil set in the socket of a human eye drawn full-face, under which is the characteristic mark that is found under a peregrine's eyes, the so-called 'moustachial streak', which on the actual bird is black and stands out conspicuously against its white chin and cheeks.

The cult of Horus was also found at *Hebenu* (modern name Zawyet el-Amwat, sometimes known as Zawyet el-Maiyitin). *Hebenu* was the capital of the 16th Upper Egyptian Nome, the Oryx Nome. It lies on the east bank of the Nile, a few kilometres south of Minia. The sacred animal of this nome was the desert oryx, the graceful antelope that had become associated with Seth. When the cult of Horus was introduced into *Hebenu*, Horus was regarded as the vanquisher of the oryx, symbolically representing his great enemy, Seth; and in the Late Period this aspect was reflected in the drawing of the nome sign, which depicted Horus as a falcon, standing with his talons sunk into the back of an oryx.

Another place where Horus displaced an original god who was not a falcon was *Tjel* (or Sile), the modern Tell Abu Sefah, a town which lay within the 14th Nome of Lower Egypt, some 3 km east of Qantara on what is now the Suez Canal. The name of the nome capital, *Khent-iabet*, which means 'Front of the East', illustrates the strategic importance of the area: *Tjel* itself was the site of a great fortress, possibly called *Mesen*, that the Egyptians built to guard their north-eastern frontier. The indigenous god of *Tjel* was a lion whose special function was to protect Egypt against foreigners and invaders from the east. Horus took over from the Lion of *Tjel* as guardian of Egypt's north-eastern border and by so doing became the Lord of *Mesen*.

Horus was worshipped at another *Mesen*. It is not certain where this *Mesen* was, but it is known to have been in the Western Delta, and was, perhaps, near the city of *Pe*. According to legend, Isis bore her son, Horus, on the island of Khemmis, near *Pe*, where he was protected by Wadjet, the goddess of the neighbouring city of *Dep*. *Pe* was a city whose god was originally a heron, or perhaps some kind of hawk, which was ousted by Horus. In Chapter 112 of the Book of the Dead, the inhabitants of *Pe* are asked whether they know how it came about that *Pe* was given to Horus and are told, 'Re gave it to him in compensation for the injury to his eye'.

Apparently, Horus woke up one day with a sore eye and took himself off to Re to ask him to inspect it to see if he could find the cause of the soreness. Re examined the eye, and said, 'Look, can you see that black pig?' Horus looked, and was immediately smitten with a blow on his eye, rendering it even more painful than it had been before. Horus was very angry at this; it seemed obvious to him that it was the second time that Seth (who was, of course, the black pig) had inflicted a blow upon his eye. Re healed the injured orb and decreed that henceforward all pigs should be an abomination to Horus. And *Pe* was given to him as compensation for his injury.

Although Horus was usually depicted as a falcon, or as a falcon-headed man, there is one famous instance of him appearing in another guise: the Sphinx of Giza, that most illustrious symbol of ancient Egypt. In Dynasty IV, when Khafre's pyramid was being built at Giza, it may have been decided that a knoll of limestone some 400 metres to the east of the pyramid resembled the body of a crouched lion; and that, as a compliment to the king, the front end of the knoll should be carved, not into the head of a lion but into a likeness of Khafre, who thus became identified with the Heliopolitan tradition of the horizon being guarded by lions (see page 31), not, however, by Shu and Tefnut this time, but by Horakhty (Horus-of-the-Two-Horizons; see page 23) in the guise of a lion.

Statues of lions with heads representing kings, gods or the animals associated with those gods – the ram of Amun, for instance – became very popular in Egypt, especially when arranged in double rows along the path that led to the entrance of a temple, as guardians of the sanctuary, for they were thought to have the power to protect both kings and gods. The Egyptians called such statues *shesep-ankh* or 'living statues'; today, they are known by the Greek word, sphinx.

The Greeks themselves had a sphinx, but this sphinx was the cruel winged lioness with a woman's head who appeared in the story of Oedipus challenging travellers on the road to Boeotian Thebes with the riddle, 'What goes on four legs, on two and then three, but the more legs it goes on the weaker it be?' Those who could not answer correctly were killed; but Oedipus destroyed the sphinx with the answer to her riddle: man. As a baby, he crawls on all fours; in the prime of life he walks on two legs; but in old age he has to use a third 'leg' – a stick.[12]

The Great Sphinx of Giza, which is about 70 metres long, is the largest and most renowned of Egyptian sphinxes. Some thousand years after it was constructed, a young prince of Dynasty XVIII was hunting in the desert near the

Giza plateau. He decided to rest near the Sphinx, whom he called Horakhty-Re-Atum-Khepri, and fell asleep in its shadow. The Sphinx sent him a dream in which it promised him the throne of Egypt if he would clear the sand that the wind had blown over its body. The prince had the encroaching sand cleared away, and when in due course he became king, he, Thutmose IV, left a record of his actions between the paws of the Sphinx – the Dream Stele,[13] still to be seen there today; and from thenceforward, the Great Sphinx of Giza was identified, not with the long-dead Khafre, but with Horus alone, under the name of *Hor-em-akhet* – Horus-on-the-Horizon – whom the Greeks called Harmakhis.

A visitor to Giza today, looking at the impressive Sphinx Harmakhis might consider that the old Arabic saying, 'The world fears time, but time fears the pyramids', could equally well be applied to the Sphinx. But perhaps the most impressive image of Horus is to be seen in the courtyard of his temple at Edfu, where a giant statue of the falcon god, magnificently carved to show all his strength and ferocity, gazes imperiously from his piercing eyes at those who enter his domain.

SETH

· ·

Seth was one of the oldest Egyptian deities. In predynastic times, he was worshipped as an idol that seems to have been assembled from the features of several animals into an elegant imaginary beast, the so-called 'Seth-animal' – a creature that has the body of a greyhound; a long, fork-ended tail standing upright from its body; an elongated, curved muzzle or snout; long, pricked-up ears with flattened tips; and almond-shaped eyes. It has been suggested that the Seth-animal was a species of dog, now extinct but resembling a saluki; or a pig, a jerboa, a giraffe, an ant-eater, a wart-hog or an okapi! However, there is no known zoological equivalent for the fabulous Seth-animal.

The earliest centre of the cult of Seth was at *Nbt*, which lay on the west bank of the Nile some 30 km north of Luxor near the modern town of Tukh. *Nbt* was close to the entrance of the Wadi Hammamat through which the Eastern Desert with its gold deposits could be reached. It was probably due to gold that the town achieved its importance, a fact that is reflected in the name of the place – *Nbt* means 'Gold Town'. Seth himself was called *Nbty*, 'He-of-Gold-Town'. The importance of *Nbt* dates back to the predynastic era; some of the oldest settlements of Upper Egypt have been found in the area, notably at the nearby site of Naqada, which the English Egyptologist Flinders Petrie (1853–1942) excavated in AD 1895, afterwards using the name to describe the last two predynastic cultures of the whole of Upper Egypt, Naqada I and II.

Other predynastic centres of the cult of Seth were found in northern Upper Egypt, two major sites being in the 11th and 19th Nomes. The original nome standard of the 11th Nome consisted of a Seth-animal on a pole. In dynastic times, this animal was depicted with a dagger sticking into its head, a sign that by this time Seth was regarded as a force for evil, and his animal as potentially harmful. This aspect is reflected in the ancient Egyptian name for the capital of the 11th Nome, *Sha-shtp*, which means 'The Pig [i.e. Seth]-is-Pacified'. The Greek name for the town was Hypselis; today it is called Shutb. It lies some 8 km south of Assiut.

The capital of the 19th Nome of Upper Egypt, *Pr-mdjd*, which today is called el-Bahnasa, lies some 160 km north of Assiut. In ancient times, Seth was worshipped there, as was a fish, *Mormyrus kannume* – an appropriate pairing since the penis of Seth's great enemy, Osiris (see page 62), was supposed to have

Seth, worshipped by
Aapahte, deputy foreman
of the gang (of workers),
Dcir el-Medina, Dynasty
XIX. (Stele, Turin Museum)

been swallowed by the fish. Little is known of the town from Pharaonic times
but it became prominent in the Graeco-Roman period when it was called
Oxyrhynchus. Today, it is famous chiefly because of what Grenfell and Hunt
found during their excavations between AD 1896 and 1907: thousands of papyri
lying in its rubbish heaps or used as stuffing for the mummified bodies of sacred
crocodiles.

From earliest times, Seth was regarded as the Upper Egyptian god *par
excellence*. Legend had it that Geb, the Earth God, divided Egypt into two
halves, giving the northern part to Horus and the southern to Seth. The famous
limestone mace-head found at Hierakonpolis, known as the Scorpion Mace-head
because it is carved with reliefs showing episodes from the life of a predynastic
king of Upper Egypt named Scorpion, shows two standards bearing Seth-

animals. This would seem to indicate that the followers of Seth were allies of Scorpion, himself an adherent of Horus, when he initiated the conquest of Lower Egypt by the South.

After the Unification, the kings of Egypt adopted Horus names (see page 83); but they allotted to Seth a role as representative of Upper Egypt. The queens of the period were given the titles 'She-who-unites-the-Two-Lords' [i.e. Horus and Seth] and 'She-who-sees-Horus-and-Seth'. In the reign of the fourth king of Dynasty II, Sekhemib, a religious revolution of some sort seems to have taken place. Horus was displaced as royal god, and Seth received the allegiance of Sekhemib, who changed his name to Peribsen, and, whereas the *serekh* (see page 83) bearing the former name was surmounted by the Hawk God, that bearing the latter name was instead graced by the figure of the Seth-animal. Although Sekhemib/Peribsen's successor, Sendji, reinstated Horus, the last king of the Dynasty did not entirely forsake Seth in favour of Horus, since the *serekh* carved with his name, Khasekhemwy, bears both hawk god and Seth-animal, a sign, perhaps, that a reconciliation had been achieved.

For a long time, Seth was regarded as a beneficent god by a large part of the population of Egypt. However, he was also at all times identified with the desert that lay to the east of the centre of his cult, *Nbt*; an association which extended eventually to all deserts. To the Egyptians, the desert which lay to the east, the west and the south of their land was inhospitable, arid and dangerous, a place where gods, wild animals and the dead held sway. The fertile land of Egypt on which they grew their crops was called the Black Land; the desert was the Red Land. As god of the deserts, Seth was called the Red God, and associated with every frightening element that the Egyptians thought emanated from them: wind and rain, storm and thunder.

The roads that led out of Egypt passed through deserts, and, indeed, one of the words commonly used by the Egyptians for 'desert' (*ḫ3st*) was the same as that for 'foreign land'; inevitably, Seth became known as Lord of Foreign Lands. Around 1650 BC, Semitic invaders from the foreign lands which lay to the east of Egypt began to infiltrate the eastern part of the Delta, gradually establishing a hold over the Delta and Lower Egypt. These invaders are known as the Hyksos, and they flourished for over a hundred years until they were driven out of Egypt by Ahmose, the founder of Dynasty XVIII. The major group of Hyksos – Manetho's Dynasty XV – established its capital at Memphis; but its offshoot, Dynasty XVI, founded a capital in the North-eastern Delta at the site of the modern village of Tell ed-Dab'a. This capital was called *Ḥwt-w'rt*, 'The-Mansion-of-the-Leg', the leg in question being that of the dismembered Osiris; thus, the city was identified with Osiris rather than with Seth. Today, the city is better known by the Greek form of its name, Avaris.

Seth had long been worshipped in the Eastern Delta, and the Hyksos, identifying him with the Semitic god of war, Baal, worshipped him under the name Sutekh. Although Seth had a wife – his sister, Nephthys – at Avaris he was given two other consorts: the western Semitic goddesses Anath and Astoreth. Anath was a war goddess who was represented in human form equipped with shield and battle-axe and wearing on her head what appears to be the Upper Egyptian crown surrounded by plumes. She was regarded as the daughter of Re. Astoreth was a goddess of war who was identified with Sekhmet, and, more particularly, a goddess of love and therefore equated with Hathor. She could be depicted with the head of a lioness, but she appeared more often as a naked woman standing in a chariot and driving a team of horses. Even after the departure of the Hyksos, these two consorts of Seth were worshipped by the Egyptians themselves, with Anath achieving the height of her popularity during the Ramesside period, while Astoreth was venerated from Dynasty XVIII to the Ptolemaic era.

After the expulsion of the Hyksos shortly before 1550 BC, the city of Avaris sank into obscurity. Then, in 1295 BC, Horemheb, last king of Dynasty XVIII, died childless and was succeeded by Pramesse, one of his generals, who ascended the throne as Ramesses, first king of Dynasty XIX. Ramesses I came from a Delta family which seems to have been particularly devoted to Seth of Avaris. His son and heir, Sety I, was named after the god; and on a stele found at Tanis (see below), Sety's son, Ramesses II, records that when his father was still Crown Prince and a commander in the Egyptian army, he went to Avaris to celebrate the 400th anniversary of the foundation of the city and its dedication to Seth. However, Avaris was destined to be used as a quarry during the building of *Pi-Ramessu* (House of Ramesses), the city built for Ramesses II a short distance away; and *Pi-Ramessu* was itself used as a quarry by the kings of the Twenty-first and Twenty-second Dynasties for the building of their capital city, Tanis. The site of Tanis lies some 130 km north-east of Cairo, and is today called San el-Hagar. In ancient Egyptian times, the place was called *Dja'net*, the meaning of which is lost but thought to refer to a topographical feature connected with water. The Greeks pronounced it Tanis, the Copts Tjanni, which was eventually given the Arabized pronunciation, San. To this was added *el-hagar*, meaning 'the stones', an appropriate appellation since the Pharaonic structures there were for centuries robbed of their stone for use in local buildings.

Although the state god of Egypt at that time was Amun of Thebes, in the Delta Seth was of greater importance. Ramesses II emphasized his allegiance to him by naming his favourite daughter Bint-Anath, that is, Daughter of Anath, Seth's consort, and by building a temple for Anath at *Pi-Ramessu*. In addition, as we learn from a description of Ramesses' famous battle against the Hittites at Kadesh, one of the divisions of the Egyptian army was named after Seth's warlike form, Sutekh (see page 110). In the Ramesside period, Seth was not regarded as merely the deity of the harmful elements in the desert but as the patron of the life-sustaining oases.

Seth had always had two aspects to his character: one good, the other malevolent. Throughout their history, the Egyptians held an ambivalent attitude towards him: they feared his capacity for harm yet they had a sneaking admiration for his power and ferocity. From time to time, political expediency or the personal preference of the ruler dictated that he should be a favoured god; but his role at other times was that of the personification of all things harmful: the Greeks called him Typhon.

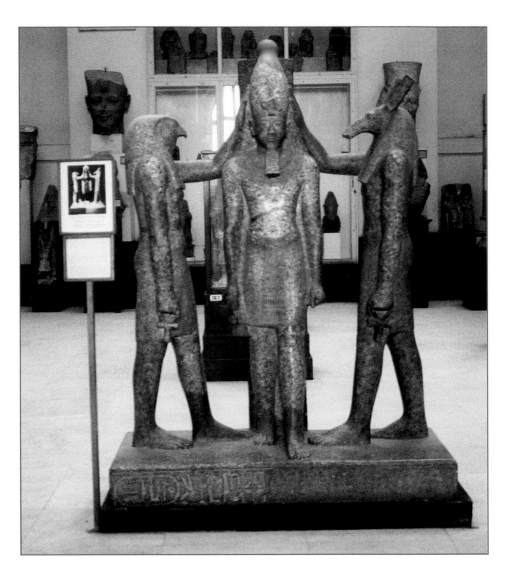

Ramesses II flanked by
Horus (left) and Seth
(right): statue from Medinet
Habu, Luxor. (Cairo
Museum)

In Greek mythology, Typhon, the child of Mother Earth and Tartarus (the place of torture in Hades), was the largest monster ever born. He had an ass's head and immensely long arms which ended in countless serpents' heads instead of hands. In place of legs, the lower part of his body was yet more serpents. He had vast wings which blotted out the sun; from his eyes he flashed fire; from his mouth, he belched forth flaming rocks. Some authorities believe that the myth of Typhon was based on an actual event – the flight of priests and priestesses from the volcanic eruption on the Aegean island of Thera (Santorini) which destroyed Minoan sites on Crete. After his birth, Typhon rushed towards Olympus, from which the gods fled in terror at his coming, only pausing in their flight when they reached Egypt. There they disguised themselves as animals so that they would not be noticed among the Egyptian gods! Only Athene stood against Typhon, until eventually Zeus overcame him with his thunderbolts. The severely wounded monster fled to Sicily where Zeus threw a mountain on top of him. Typhon's breath and the fire from his eyes turned the mountain into a volcano – Etna – and to this day, Typhon sometimes hurls molten rocks and fire from its cone.

Typhon, like Seth, was a god of violence and turmoil. The colour red became associated with them both: with Typhon because he became a volcano and with Seth because of his links with the desert. Hence, red-haired animals, and even red-haired people, were held in abhorrence by Greeks and Egyptians. Seth's turbulent nature was apparent from his very begetting. Plutarch says that Seth entered the world by bursting through his mother's side. All kinds of dangerous and unpleasant animals were associated with him: the scorpion, the serpent, the hippopotamus, the crocodile, the wild ass, the wild boar, and the pig.

In ancient Egypt, as in Syria-Palestine, the pig was held in abomination. Although the Egyptians kept pigs and are said to have used them during the sowing season to trample seed into ground left soft and muddy by the receding water of the Inundation, pigs were, according to Herodotus, considered unclean; and swineherds lived apart from the rest of the community.[14] Herodotus also claimed that pigs were only ever sacrificed during the festivals of Dionysus and the Moon, after which the flesh was eaten – but only on the day of the full moon; and that people of slender means ate models of pigs made from dough. However, judging from the number of pig bones found at the Twelfth-Dynasty pyramid-workers' town at Kahun, and in the Eighteenth-Dynasty workmen's village at Amarna, pork was a not insignificant part of the diet of many Egyptians.

Any reluctance to eat pork was probably for practical reasons: pig meat rapidly becomes unfit to eat in a hot climate. However, just as Jews and Muslims were later to be forbidden to eat pig by religious law, so the Egyptians invented a mythological reason for not doing so. The pig was a representation of Seth, probably because in predynastic times it had been an object of worship in one district or another of Egypt associated with him. Had not Seth, in the guise of a black pig (see page 98), wounded the eye of Horus? Had not a wild boar, a near relative of the pig, killed Attis and Adonis? In all probability, there was once an Egyptian myth that told of Osiris being slain by the same animal, thus rendering the pig as Seth's representative inimical to followers of Osiris. Herodotus stated that there was a legend current among the Egyptians that explained the reason for their abhorrence of sacrificing swine at any festivals except those of the Moon and Dionysus; but he declined to elucidate, saying, 'though I am well aware of what it is, I think it would be unseemly to mention it'![15]

Seth's oldest role was as the foe of Horus the Elder. Whereas Horus as Sun God was regarded as the face of the sky by day and therefore as a god of light and sunshine, Seth was his opposite, the face of the sky at night and therefore a deity of darkness and terror. According to the Pyramid Texts, Seth, aided by the seven stars that make up the Great Bear, attacked Horus, the Sun God. This story was probably a relic of the time when the gods were regarded as stars and constellations; the attack by Seth on the sun probably represented for the Egyptians the 'attack' on the sun by showers of meteorites and shooting stars; or even an eclipse.

By the New Kingdom, Seth's relationship to the sun had changed. His ferocity, his reputation as a 'most valiant god', had earned him a place in the Barque of Re, where he defended the Sun God from attack by his enemies. As a god of storm, Seth was himself regarded at times as a threat to the Barque of Re, but its greatest enemy was the serpent, Apophis (see page 44). Although by the Late Period, Seth had become identified with the monstrous serpent, in the New Kingdom he was thought to stand in the prow of the Barque warding off its attacks.

Chapter 39 of the Book of the Dead gives a graphic account of Seth's efforts to perform his task, enraged by Apophis' taunts. In a reference to an episode in Seth's long-drawn-out fight against Horus, in which Horus tears out Seth's testicles, Apophis jeers at him, saying, 'What was done to you was so terrible that you will suffer from it forever. You will never go a-wooing, you will never make love!' Seth overcomes Apophis, only to be driven away from the Barque by its divine crew, ostensibly for boasting but in reality for fear lest he himself harm it. Obviously, even when being valiantly helpful, Seth was not trusted.

Seth's most famous role was as the implacable enemy of Horus, son of Osiris. One legend relates that Geb decided to divide Egypt between Horus and Seth in equal halves. Horus ruled wisely and well, but Seth proved to be an unjust king. Geb was so displeased that he deposed Seth and handed over his throne to Horus. Thus began the great quarrel between the two gods. Later versions of the feud, influenced by the popularity of the cult of Osiris, give as its cause the murder of Osiris by Seth, exacerbated by Seth's attempts to prevent Osiris' son, Horus, inheriting the throne of his father.

The most entertaining version of the great quarrel is found in *The Contendings of Horus and Seth* (see page 86) although Seth is not shown to great advantage in this account, being wont to appear slightly stupid and blundering, easily tricked by both Isis and Horus. In a letter to the Tribunal of the Gods, the goddess Neit recommends that Horus should be confirmed in the office of kingship, while Seth is fobbed off with an increase in his possessions and the gift of the two erotic goddesses Anath and Astarte – a move obviously calculated to appeal to Seth's lecherous nature.

Seth's lust for women enabled Isis to trick him by disguising herself as a beautiful young girl (see page 78) but he was equally capable of an act of homosexual rape. *The Contendings of Horus and Seth* tells of one such episode, relating it in a frank manner that, until quite recently, would have been translated into Latin rather than the native languages of scholars who considered it to be an offensive part of the text, preferring, like Gibbon,[16] that their versions should be 'chaste, and all licentious passages . . . left in the decent obscurity of a learned language'[17] – presumably to ensure that their servants and womenfolk, having no Latin, should not read and be corrupted by such indecency. However, the ancient Egyptians would not have understood such a convention, being an earthy people not at all inhibited or prudish about sexual matters.

Having been commanded by Re-Horakhty to stop quarrelling day after day and to let him have some peace, Seth invited Horus to his house, and, in all innocence, Horus accepted the invitation. When night came, a bed was made up for the two gods and they lay down together – an unwise move on Horus' part because, in the night, Seth made his penis become stiff, and he put it between the thighs of Horus. Thereupon, Horus put both his hands between his thighs and caught Seth's semen in one of them.

Alarmed, Horus ran to his mother, crying, 'Help me, Isis, my mother! Come and see what Seth has done to me!' When he opened his hand and showed Seth's semen to Isis, she was horrified, and, seizing her knife, she cut off his hand and threw it into a nearby canal. Isis then made Horus a new hand to replace the one that had been defiled by Seth's semen. Next, she took a little sweet ointment and rubbed Horus' penis with it until the penis became stiff. She then inserted the penis into a jar and Horus made some of his semen drip into the vessel.

Early next morning, Isis went to Seth's garden carrying the jar containing Horus' semen and asked the gardener what Seth's favourite vegetable was. She was told that he only ever ate lettuce, a vegetable that the Egyptians thought had aphrodisiacal qualities (see page 195). Isis put Horus' semen on the lettuces so that when Seth arrived and consumed his daily portion of the vegetable he 'became pregnant with the seed of Horus'. Shortly after this, Seth challenged Horus to come before the Tribunal of the Gods again, confident that this time he would win his case, for he knew that to subject an enemy to an act of homosexuality, such as the one he had perpetrated against Horus, was considered by the Egyptians to be the worst indignity a conqueror could inflict upon his foe. He was sure that once his attack upon Horus became known, Horus would become an object of scorn to all.

Sure enough, when Seth stood up in the Tribunal and pointed to his victim, saying, 'As for Horus, this creature who is standing here, I have performed a sexual act against him!', the Ennead uttered a loud cry and spat and belched in Horus' face. Undismayed, Horus laughed at them and swore that Seth was lying. He demanded that the semen of Seth be summoned so that everyone could hear whence it answered. Then Thoth laid his hand upon Horus' shoulder and cried: 'Come forth, Oh semen of Seth!" And it answered him, not, as expected, from inside Horus' body, but from the water into which Isis had thrown it.

Then Thoth laid his hand upon Seth's shoulder and cried, 'Come forth, Oh semen of Horus!' To which it replied, from inside Seth's body, 'Whence shall I come forth?' And Thoth said to it, 'Come forth from his ear!' But the semen said to Thoth, 'Is it from his ear that I should come forth seeing that I am a divine essence?' And so Thoth said to it, 'Come forth from his forehead!' And it came forth as a golden disk upon Seth's brow. Seth was exceedingly angry and stretched out his hand to seize the golden disk, but before he could do so, Thoth took it and set it upon his own head. Then the Ennead gave their judgement: 'Horus is right, Seth is wrong.'

Seth, furious at being tricked, issued yet another challenge, this time to a race using boats made of stone. Horus accepted the challenge, but, instead of making a boat out of stone, he fashioned one of cedarwood and coated it with gypsum, and launched it at night when there was not a soul around to see the boat close-to. When Seth looked at Horus' boat, he was taken in by the gypsum coating, which made the boat look as though it were made of stone as had been agreed. Accordingly, he sliced off a mountain peak and used it to make for himself a boat '138 cubits [over 63 metres] long'. And then the two contestants boarded their boats in the presence of the entire Ennead. Horus' boat, being made of wood, floated beautifully; Seth's sank like the stone it was. Immediately, Seth transformed himself into a hippopotamus and overturned his rival's craft. But this was his final fling. Before long, the Tribunal had exchanged letters with Osiris (see page 86) and found that Horus' case was proved.

Atum commanded that Isis should fetch Seth into the Tribunal tightly bound in a wooden collar. Isis took great delight in obeying the command and the hapless Seth was brought in as a prisoner. When Atum charged him with being unwilling to accept the judgement of the gods that the office of kingship should be given to Horus, Seth made no further attempt at bravado but cravenly denied the charge, saying, 'Not so, my good lord. Let Horus, son of Isis, be summoned and let the office of his father, Osiris, be given to him.' In the midst of the general rejoicing and relief that at long last the case was over, the god Ptah asked what was to be done with Seth, and Re-Horakhty decreed that he should live with him as his son. Horus was set upon the throne of Egypt, and Seth was set to thunder in the sky and put fear into the hearts of men.

In the Late Period, the unpopularity of Seth grew; from about 700 BC, hymns were composed celebrating his defeat by Horus. During the Ptolemaic Period, Seth came to symbolize the Macedonian Greeks who ruled Egypt, and in the Temple of Horus at Edfu in particular (see page 87) he was reviled both as the enemy of Horus, who was the symbol of Egyptian nationalism, and as the representative of the despised conquerors of Egypt. Late in Egyptian history, Seth's name and image were often cut out of ancient monuments; and his statues were remodelled by having the characteristic long ears of the Seth-animal cut off and replaced by ram's horns so that the statues were transformed into representations of Amun (see page 136).

In spite of this, compromise could still be reached. The most famous example of the accommodation that could be achieved between the two great enemies is the Graeco-Roman temple that was built some 170 km south of the earliest centre of the cult of Seth, *Nbt*, which the Copts called Embo and the Greeks Ombos. The new site was also called Ombos after the god of the ancient city – who was, of course, Seth, He-of-Ombos or the Ombite. Kom Ombo (Mound of Embo), as this temple is now called, was begun in the reign of Ptolemy V Epiphanes and decorated in the reigns of several Roman emperors, Tiberius, Domitian and Caracalla among them. The decorations are some of the best examples of Graeco-Roman art.

Kom Ombo is unique among Egyptian temples because it is dedicated jointly to two deities: Haroeris, or Horus the Elder, and Suchos, or Sobek, the crocodile god, who was worshipped at many places in Egypt but especially at Gebelein and in the Fayum. At Kom Ombo, the temple stands on a stretch of river that was infested with crocodiles until the latter half of the nineteenth century AD.

Opposite: Sobek: relief from Kom Ombo Temple.

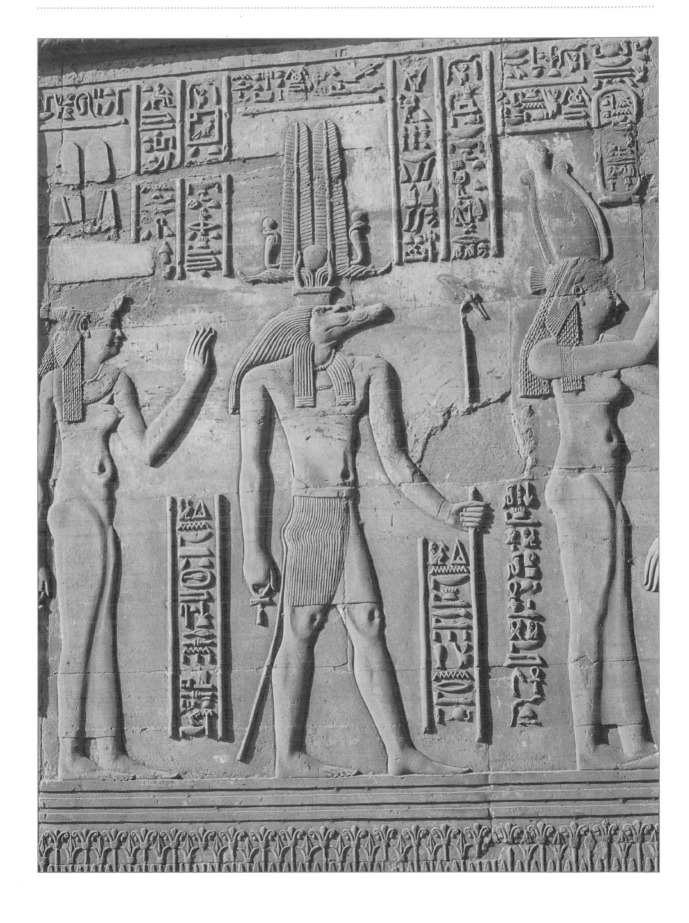

Evidently the people of the district felt that Sobek was a god to be placated. However, Sobek was a form of Sutekh, the Semitic name for Seth, while Haroeris was a form of Horus. In spite of the fact that only a short distance away at Edfu, Horus was worshipped as the vanquisher of Seth, and was even depicted in some reliefs on the walls of the temple in the act of slaying crocodiles, at Kom Ombo the two adversaries share a temple, the left-hand side of which is dedicated to Haroeris together with his wife, Hathor-ta-sent-nefert (Hathor-the-good-sister) and their son, Panebtawy (Lord-of-the-Two-Lands); and the right-hand side to Sobek, who is not accompanied at Kom Ombo by his usual consort, the cobra goddess Renenutet, but by Hathor, who is normally the wife of Horus, with Khonsu, son of Amun and Mut, being allotted the role of their son.

Although Kom Ombo Temple was not dedicated to Seth under his own name, the fact that a form of Seth could still be worshipped there proves that he was not entirely out of favour. It seems probable that there were two separate priesthoods in the temple who tended their respective gods in perfect amity. However, in many places in Egypt, the worship of this turbulent deity had for a long time been proscribed, and by the Christian era Seth had been demoted from ancient and powerful god to a mere evil demon.

Manifestations of Seth can be both surprising and pervasive. The god, reviled in many places in the Nile valley for the murder of Osiris, was worshipped in el-Khargah oasis in the Western Desert as the deity who would ensure the fertility of the oasis. In the temple of Hibis, begun in the fifth century BC during the reign of the Persian king Darius, and completed over one hundred and fifty years later in the reign of Nectanebo II, a relief in the hypostyle hall shows a winged figure of Seth in the act of slaying the serpent Apophis, a depiction which some scholars claim was the inspiration for the Christian story of St George and the Dragon.

Opposite: Nephthys and Isis on the right and left corners respectively of Horemheb's sarcophagus, in his tomb in the Valley of the Kings, Luxor.

NEPHTHYS

• •

Nephthys was normally depicted as a woman with no special attributes except for the hieroglyphs which form her name worn as a headdress. Her name, ☥, in Egyptian *Nbt-ḥwt*, means 'Lady of the House'; which house or to whom it belongs is not known. Neither is anything known about Nephthys before she became a part of the Heliopolitan myths. She seems never to have been the object of a cult, and no temple or shrine has yet been discovered that is dedicated to her alone.

Nephthys figures only in the Heliopolitan myths: she was one of the five children born to Nut on the extra days that she won from Thoth (see page 129). Although Nephthys was the wife of Seth, at all times she was loyal to her siblings, Osiris and Isis. She helped Isis collect together the pieces of Osiris' dismembered body and then to wrap them in bandages; with Isis, she was chief mourner for Osiris as the two sisters wailed for the dead god.

Her participation in the protection and resurrection of Osiris, and her mourning for her dead brother, was later extended so that she became the protector of the dead in general: she is one of the four guardian-goddesses of Canopic jars (see page 85), and was carved on the corners of sarcophagi and shrines for the protection of their contents, in which position she was often equipped with the wings of a kite like her sister, Isis (see pages 63 and 79).

There is a legend that tells of how Nephthys was enamoured of Osiris and went to him at night. In the darkness, Osiris mistook her for Isis and made love to her, the result of their adulterous union being Anubis.

Nephthys: faience amulet. (Photograph: Roger Dickenson, courtesy of the School of Archaeology and Oriental Studies, Liverpool University)

HATHOR

· ·

In an agricultural society such as that of ancient Egypt, it was natural that the cow should become a sacred animal; worship of a cow goddess, therefore, was found throughout Egypt from a very early date. In predynastic times, the cow represented fertility; she was the great mother. Statuettes of naked women with arms upraised in imitation of a cow's horns have been found in graves of the period, placed there presumably because they had been used as votive offerings to the mother goddess, perhaps in supplication for a child. A fetish of the fertility goddess was found in a tomb at Naqada dating to the fourth millennium BC. It is in the shape of a vase, the exterior of which is decorated with a relief of a human head flanked by cow's horns, and a pair of arms holding breasts.

Other predynastic vases are painted with arms holding breasts, or figures of women dancing with their arms held up and curved towards their heads. Such 'cow-dances' are performed to this day by the women of the Dinka and Shilluk tribes of the southern Sudan. On many of the vases, the fertility goddess is accompanied by a representation of a young man with twigs or feathers in his hair, performing a ritual dance. He is the son or lover of the goddess who, in later times, was called the *Ka-mut-ef* or 'The-Bull-of-his-Mother', and impersonated in temple ceremonies by a priest. On one vase, the goddess and her lover are shown in a boat standing together under an awning: the first representation of the sacred marriage of the fertility goddess.

The most famous cow goddess was Hathor. Her name, *Ḥwt-Ḥor*, means 'The-Mansion-of-Horus', a reference to the fact that she was the sky in which the sacred falcon flew. The hieroglyphs that represent her name, 🏠, show a house or temple with a hawk inside it. She was not only a symbol of fertility but also a sky goddess, regarded as the Eye of the Sun God, Re; and as the personification of the sky itself. The Egyptians thought of her as a gigantic cow which straddled the earth, her legs marking the four cardinal points. Between her horns she carried the sun's disk; her belly was the sky, her hide and udders were the stars and planets. The iconography of Hathor as cow and sky goddess is not dissimilar to that of Nut (see page 37) but Hathor was by far the more pervasive and popular of the two goddesses.

In dynastic times, Hathor could be depicted as an actual cow; as a woman with a cow's head; or as a woman wearing upon her head a sun-disk set between

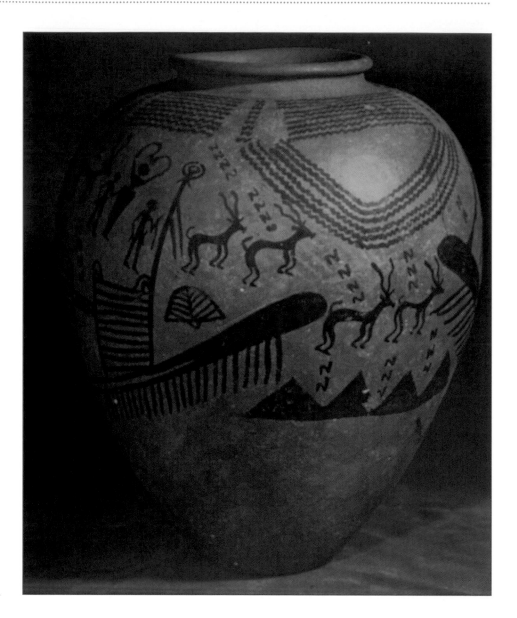

Woman performing 'cow
dance' (see page 113):
predynastic vase, Naqada II
period. (Cairo Museum)

a pair of cow's horns. The earliest certain representation of Hathor is on the
great ceremonial palette that was found at Hierakonpolis, the ancient capital of
Upper Egypt: the Narmer Palette, now in Cairo Museum. Palettes, often made of
slate, were used by predynastic Egyptians as surfaces upon which to grind
cosmetics, especially the malachite that, mixed with fat, was employed as a
protective eyeliner. Towards the end of the predynastic period, palettes were
often used, not for mundane, utilitarian purposes but as decorative votive
objects.

The Narmer Palette, which is made of slate, was designed to commemorate the
union of Upper and Lower Egypt, and was probably made as a votive offering
for the local shrine of Hathor. Carved at the top of each of the two sides of the
Palette are heads of Hathor, showing her with a cow's horns and ears but with a

human face. This depiction of the head of the goddess was perhaps based on her fetish, the form in which she was worshipped in predynastic shrines and which was probably composed of a wooden post or pillar topped by the skull of a cow. In the dynastic period, this was stylized into the *Bat*-symbol (𓅱) of Hathor (see page 118).

Hathor's head as depicted on the Narmer Palette was later developed so that whenever the Egyptians used her head alone in decoration, she could be shown as what at first glance seems to be a woman with a round, somewhat flattened, face, wearing a wig which falls into thick ringlets on either side of her head. Only on closer inspection can it be seen that the ears of the goddess, protruding from beneath the wig, are not human ears but those of a cow. The ringlets of the wig are often plaited, with tapering ends that curl outwards, and are reminiscent of cow's horns.

The full-face depiction of Hathor broke the normal conventions of Egyptian art which decreed that the human head should be shown in profile; indeed, Hathor is the only goddess ever to be shown full-face in reliefs, and in her shrines and temples use was made of this special form of head in the decoration of the capitals of columns. These capitals are four-sided, with each side bearing the face of Hathor.

Hathor was a goddess of many attributes and functions. The story of how Re sent his Eye in the form of Hathor the cow to destroy mankind has already been

The Narmer Palette (recto): the top edge is carved with the head of Hathor in the form of a cow with a woman's face. (Height of palette 64 cm)

Hathor-headed column-capitals, Pronaos, Temple of Hathor, Denderah.

Ihy (left) and Hathor
(middle) receiving offerings
from king: exterior wall,
mammisi, Temple of
Hathor, Denderah.

told (see page 43) and illustrates that Hathor had a fierce aspect as an agent of destruction. However, the most popular concept of Hathor was not as an angry, vengeful goddess, only pacified because she became drunk, but as a beautiful young woman who brought joy and happiness not only to mankind but also to gods, even to the Lord of the Universe himself, as an indelicate episode from *The Contendings of Horus and Seth* relates. The story goes that Re, having been insulted by one of the lesser gods, retired to his booth to sulk. And Hathor came and stood before him and uncovered her vagina in front of his face; an act that cheered up the Lord of the Universe so much that he laughed and rejoined his Company of Gods.

Hathor was often described as the Beautiful One, the Golden One, the Lady of Drunkenness, of Song and of Myrrh, Mistress of Maidens who gives husbands to her favourites. The Greeks chose to equate her not with the age-old Mother Goddess, who for them was Artemis, but with their goddess of love and beauty, Aphrodite. The ceremonies performed in Hathor's temples laid great emphasis on the presentation of wine, and of the beer that had become especially sacred to her because of the part it had played in saving mankind from destruction; and on music and movement: the king himself sang and danced before the goddess.

Music played an important part in all Egyptian temple rituals: one instrument much used in them was the sistrum, a kind of rattle that was sacred to Hathor. Sistra were made of metal or faience and formed in the shape of a Hathor-head or *Bat*-symbol (see page 87) with horns bent round to form a loop. Three thin metal rods were threaded through holes and passed across the loop from one side to the other. The rods were either threaded with metal disks or left loose in their sockets so that when the sistrum was shaken they rattled. The sistrum-player *par excellence* was Ihy, the son of Hathor. He is always depicted as a young boy whose head is shaved except for one long lock of hair – the so-called side-lock of youth which human boys, and sometimes girls, wore until puberty, at which time it was shaved off and offered to a favourite god. In his hands he holds a sistrum which he shakes in honour of his mother.

Hathor was especially revered by women. As the goddess of love and beauty, she looked after the interests of unmarried girls. In an association of ideas, she is often found on the handles of the mirrors, which could themselves be objects of beauty, that women used to inspect their faces. The mirrors were made from disks of polished copper, bronze or silver (there were no silvered glass mirrors in ancient Egypt), a reminder of the disk that Hathor sometimes supported on her head. As a fertility goddess, Hathor was clearly associated with childbirth: she protected pregnant women and helped them during their labour, aided by her son, Ihy, who soothed them with his music; and by Bes.

Bes was a very ancient god, possibly of Sudanese origin. He is usually depicted as a squat male figure – a dwarf, or perhaps a pygmy – with a large head, a lion's mane, protruding ears, flat nose, bow-legs, a tail and a long penis. He sometimes wears a panther skin wrapped round his body and a crown of feathers on his head. His ugliness, and the fact that he was shown pulling tongues at his beholders, made people laugh and supposedly frightened away demons. He was

Bes: statue at Temple of Hathor, Denderah.

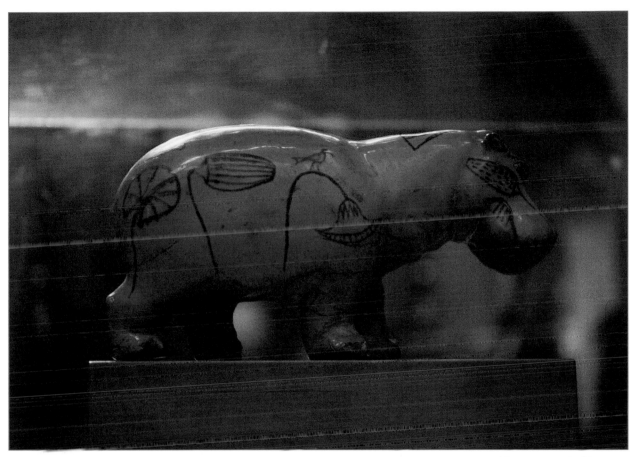

Hippopotamus in faience,
Dynasty XVIII. (Cairo
Museum)

believed to kill snakes and harmful animals. Women in labour looked upon Bes
as their protector, and children thought of him as their particular friend. Even
queens might turn to the ugly little god for comfort during childbirth, as a relief
in the memorial temple of the Eighteenth-Dynasty Queen Hatshepsut at Deir el-
Bahri illustrates. In the relief, Bes is shown attending Queen Ahmose as she gives
birth to her daughter, Hatshepsut. Even goddesses did not scorn the comforting
presence of Bes during their travails, and carvings of him are found in the Birth
Houses of several temples.

Bes was allotted a consort in the shape of a pregnant female hippopotamus:
Ta-weret (Greek: Thoueris). Hippopotami in general are not popular with an
agricultural people such as the Egyptians. Although these ungainly animals are
not vicious by nature, they do have the habit of invading carefully tended fields
and trampling on anything that they do not actually eat. In ancient Egypt, male
hippopotami were identified with Seth and regarded as symbols of evil. However,
females, with their broad flanks, were considered to be symbols of fecundity and
were worshipped under names and epithets such as 'The White One' or 'The
Great One'. Ta-weret ('The Great One') helped every woman, whether divine,
royal or ordinary mortal, in childbirth. She was identical in form with the
hippopotamus goddess of Luxor, Ipet (see page 142). Ipet's name means 'She-of-

the-Inner-apartments', an appropriate appellation since the inner rooms of a large house were those occupied by the women of the household.

The concern of Hathor with childbirth did not, in the case of royal babies, end with the birth of the child, for the goddess was the royal nurse, also. In her cow form she suckled the adult king. Special attention to this aspect of Hathor was paid at Deir el-Bahri, the locality traditionally associated with the cult of the cow goddess as practised in Western Thebes. Here, in Hatshepsut's memorial temple, a shrine was dedicated to Hathor, and in reliefs on its walls Hatshepsut and her stepson, King Thutmose III, are shown crouched under figures of the cow goddess, drinking from her udder. This theme is taken up in the magnificent statue of the Hathor-cow suckling Thutmose III that was discovered at Deir el-Bahri during the Egypt Exploration Society of London's excavations in AD 1905. When found, the statue was still standing in its chapel of painted sandstone; and both statue and chapel are now in Cairo Museum.

The Seven Hathors were a group of goddesses, all of whom were forms of Hathor, who had the power to foretell the fate of a new-born child and to bestow gifts upon it. The Seven Hathors were thus analogous to the Greek *moirai* (Fates); or even to the Good Fairy who attended the christening of the Sleeping Beauty. Thus, they are found in stories such as *The Tale of the Two Brothers*,[18] in which they prophesy that the beautiful maiden who has been created to be the wife of the younger brother, Bata, will meet a violent death – as she does. In another story, *The Doomed Prince*,[19] sometimes called The Prince who Knew his Fate, they decree that the princely hero shall die either by means of a crocodile, or by a snake, or by a dog. Unfortunately the papyrus is damaged, so we do not have the end of the tale and perhaps we shall never know whether the prince evaded his Fate.

Hathor, the cow goddess, suckling the female king: relief from the memorial temple of Hatshepsut, Deir el-Bahri.

Hathor offered help to the deceased as well as to the living. It was thought that in the Afterlife she had her abode in a sacred sycamore tree. The deceased found refuge under its branches while Hathor leaned out to offer him food and drink. One of her epithets was Lady of the Sycamore, and at Memphis in particular she was worshipped as a tree goddess. From Dynasty XVIII onwards, she served as the patron deity of the Theban necropolis in the guise of Mehet-weret. Mehet-weret, whose name means 'The Great Flood', a reference both to the primeval ocean and also to the celestial ocean across which Re was thought to sail in his Barque every day, had been the local cow goddess, second only to Hathor in importance; but at an early date, the two were merged so that she became another form of the great Hathor. Mehet-weret was depicted as a cow standing partially concealed in a papyrus thicket at the foot of the Western Mountain of Thebes, with only her head visible through the reeds. The gilded head of a cow with elegant lyriform horns found in Tutankhamun's tomb, and now in Luxor Museum, was probably meant to represent this aspect of Hathor.

The equipment with which Tutankhamun was furnished for his journey to the Afterlife shows that Hathor played an important part in the king's protection, either under her own name, or in the guise of Mehet-weret. Apart from the gilded head described above, he was provided with three giant funerary couches, one of which has sides shaped like two long, slender cows, each of which carries a sun's disk between her horns. An inscription on the couch places Tutankhamun under the protection of Isis-Mehet (Mehet probably being an abbreviation of Mehet-weret). Just as Re journeyed to heaven on the back of the goddess Nut, who had assumed the form of a cow for the purpose (see page 43), so Tutankhamun must have believed that he, too, would journey to heaven reclining on his Mehet-weret couch. Even before his death, Tutankhamun was protected by Hathor. The seat of one of the thrones found in his tomb – the so-called Ecclesiastical Throne – is inlaid with ivory and ebony in imitation of a cow's hide. Cowhide was sometimes used for chair seats, but the seat of the Ecclesiastical Throne is not merely an artificial reflection of this: the inference was that by sitting on it Tutankhamun associated himself with the cow goddess.

Temples dedicated to Hathor were built at many places in Egypt. One of the oldest centres of her cult was the town that the Greeks called Diospolis Parva, the capital of the 7th Upper Egyptian Nome. In predynastic times, its nome standard consisted of the skull of a cow suspended from the top of a pole. Later, probably during the Middle Kingdom, the emblem of a cow's skull was replaced by the head of Hathor as a woman, surmounted by a sistrum – the *Bat*-symbol – which was evidently felt to be a less crude motif than the original skull. The local temple of Hathor, which was called the *Ḥwt Sekhem* (Mansion of the Sistrum) gave its name to the whole town. By the Coptic period, *Ḥwt Sekhem* had been abbreviated to *Hoo*, which today has become Hiw. At Gebelein, a temple of Hathor first built in Dynasty III was still functioning in the Graeco-Roman period. The name of this temple, Per Hathor (House of Hathor), which the Greeks pronounced Pathyris, caused them to call the locality Aphroditopolis (City of Aphrodite). Other major temples of Hathor

New Abu Simbel:
foreground – memorial
temple of Nefertiri;
background – memorial
temple of Ramesses II. Note
the colossi of the king,
which became the focus of
a royal statue cult (see page
210).

were built at Atfih (also called Aphroditopolis) and Cusae; and at Deir el-
Medina, Western Thebes.

At Deir el-Medina, a village was built to house the workers who constructed
the tombs of the Theban necropolis during the New Kingdom. Just outside the
village, a sanctuary was built for use by the workmen and their families; it was
dedicated to Hathor, who was a particularly popular deity at Deir el-Medina
because of her status as goddess of the Western Mountain of Thebes. Many years
later, during the reign of Ptolemy IV Philopator, a new temple was built on the
site of the old; this was dedicated to Hathor, to Imhotep (see page 168) and to
Amenhotep, son of Hapu, the Chief Minister and Master Builder of Amenhotep
III (see page 209), a very unusual dedication since temples normally belonged to
gods and kings.

The Egyptians made Hathor goddess of foreign lands such as Punt (northern
Eritrea) and Byblos in the Lebanon; and she was worshipped in places as far
apart as the Sinai Peninsula and Nubia. From Dynasty III until the end of the
New Kingdom, the Egyptians mined in Sinai for turquoise, copper and
malachite, and, at Serâbit el-Khâdim, they built a temple for Hathor in which she
was worshipped as 'the Lady of Turquoise'.

Nubia was the land from which the Egyptians obtained gold, the metal sacred
to Hathor who was often referred to as the 'Gold of the Gods'. In Dynasty XIX,
Ramesses II built a temple there for his favourite wife, Nefertiri, next to his own
temple at Abu Simbel; and dedicated his wife's shrine to Nefertiri herself and, in

Hathor-headed columns,
interior of Nefertiri temple,
Abu Simbel.

a graceful compliment to the queen, to Hathor, goddess of love and beauty. Nefertiri's temple was cut into the face of a cliff and its façade is fronted by six colossal statues, each about 10 metres high, two of the queen and four of Ramesses II. The main hall of the temple contains six square pillars, each decorated with the typical Hathor head surmounted by a sistrum. In the sanctuary, a recess holds a figure of the Hathor-cow protecting the king.

The most famous of Hathor's temples is that at Denderah, dedicated to the triad of Hathor, Horus of Edfu and their son, Harsomtus. At Denderah, Hathor was worshipped in her most important role, that of wife to the falcon god Horus. Denderah, which lies some 60 km north of Luxor, was the ancient capital of the 6th Nome of Upper Egypt. The antiquity of the site is shown by the existence of an ancient necropolis there, and its connection with Hathor by the number of cow-burials in this cemetery.

In predynastic times, the fetish of Hathor worshipped at Denderah was a pillar, giving Hathor the epithet 'She-of-the-Pillar' (in Egyptian, *Iunet*); thus, the earliest name of the place was *Iunet*. The modern name, Denderah, is derived from a reference to Hathor as 'The Goddess', which in Egyptian was *Ta-neteret*. In Greek, this became Tentyris, in Arabic, Denderah. The predynastic shrine of

Hathor was rebuilt in Dynasty IV by Khufu and dedicated to Hathor, Lady of the Pillar, and to her son, the musician god Ihy; it was enlarged, refurbished and embellished at various times over the next thousand years or so, notably during the reigns of Mentuhotep III of Dynasty XI and Thutmose III of Dynasty XVIII.

The Temple of Hathor at Denderah as it stands today dates from the Ptolemaic and Roman periods, most of it being constructed between 116 BC and AD 34. It is the most imposing and elaborately decorated structure of its period, rivalled only by the Temple of Horus at Edfu. The roof of the great hall of the temple is supported by twenty-four cylindrical columns, some 15 metres high, with a diameter of close-on 2 metres. Their capitals are four-sided and each side is decorated with a head of Hathor. The outstanding features of the temple are the thirty-two long, narrow chambers built into the thickness of the walls and under the floors, with entrances covered by slabs of stone. Such 'crypts' are to be found in other temples, but only at Denderah are they decorated. Although some of them may have been used for the secret rituals of the goddess, most, prosaically enough, were used as storage places for temple equipment.

The roof of the temple is flat, and on it are several shrines or kiosks. One of these is formed from twelve Hathor-headed columns joined together at the top by stone architraves. The usual practice would have been to fill in the spaces between the architraves with slabs of stone to form a roof, but in this instance the shrine has been left open to the sky. It was in this specially designed shrine that the most important rites in the New Year Ceremony were performed, the culminating point of which occurred when the statue of Hathor, which had been carried up from its sanctuary within the temple, was placed in the roofless kiosk

New Year Chapel on the roof of the Temple of Hathor, Denderah.

The Denderah Zodiac.
(Plaster copy; original in the
Louvre Museum, Paris)

so that the dawn sun could shine on the face of the goddess in the ritual entitled
'Uniting with the Sun's Disk'.

Denderah was one of the many places which laid claim to being the site of
Osiris' burial (see page 62); and it was for the celebration of his resurrection that
the other roof chapels were intended. The ceiling of one of these chapels was
decorated with a map of the sky, the so called Denderah Zodiac, with its thirty-
six decans, the constellations that enabled the Egyptians to tell the time at night.
Each decan was visible on the horizon for about ten days at a time, its point in
the sky determining the hour according to a set of rules that had been worked
out over years of observation by priests. Only a plaster copy now remains in the
temple: the original 'Zodiac' is in the Louvre in Paris.

Outside the temple proper are subsidiary buildings: to the south, a small
temple, the Iseum, in which was celebrated the birth of Isis. Ironically, the Iseum
was built for Octavian (Caesar Augustus) within a few metres of the rear wall of
the main temple which is decorated with a relief showing his vanquished enemy,
Cleopatra, with her son by Julius Caesar, Caesarion. To the west of the temple lie
dozens of mud-brick cubicles and two Birth Houses. The cubicles, sometimes

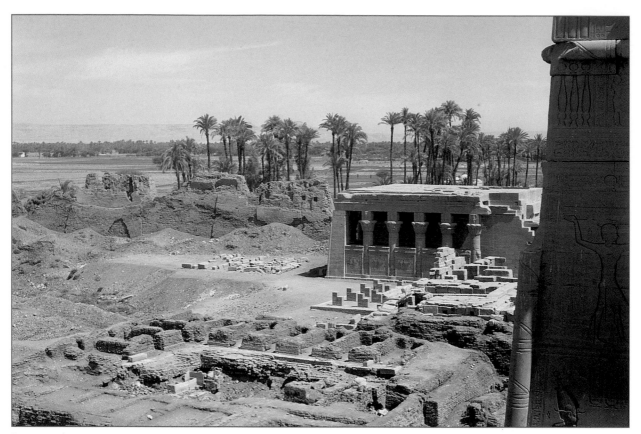

Foreground, sanatorium;
background, *mammisi*:
Temple of Hathor,
Denderah.

called the 'sanatorium', were used by the sick as places in which to sleep in the
hope of having a healing dream sent by Hathor; or as places in which to be
bathed in water that had been blessed by the goddess, or run down over statues
inscribed with magical texts, a process that was thought to impregnate the water
with the magic inherent in the texts so that the patient would be imbued with its
potency.

One of the Birth Houses was built on behalf of Nectanebo I and renewed
under the Ptolemies. Reliefs in it depict the divine birth of Nectanebo, showing
Hathor as his mother and Amun of Thebes as his father, in conformity with the
old tradition of theogamy (see page 16). The other Birth House was built for
Caesar Augustus; in it the birth of a divine child is depicted, in this instance not
the king but the young son of Hathor, Ihy.

The birth of another Divine Child of Denderah, Harsomtus, was a result of
one of the great events in the Festival Calendar of both Denderah and Edfu
temples. This was the Sacred Marriage between Hathor and Horus, an annual
event which took place at Edfu Temple during the third month of summer (May)
on the night of the New Moon. Fourteen days before the New Moon, the statue
of Hathor was carried out of her temple at Denderah in a great procession that
wended its way down to the Nile, where the statue of the goddess was placed in
her state barge, after which the barge, accompanied by a flotilla of lesser boats

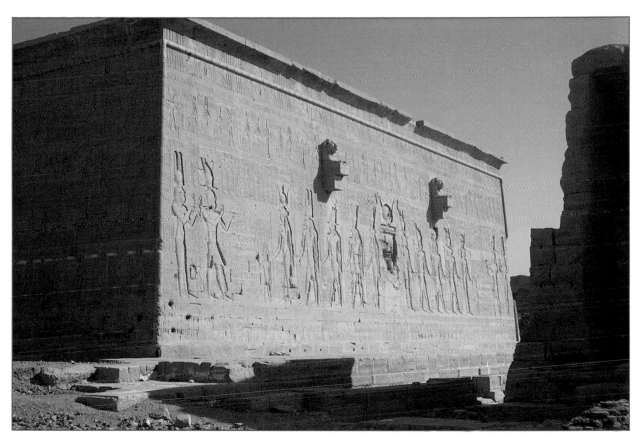

Left: Cleopatra and Caesarion dressed in Egyptian royal costume making offerings to the gods: rear wall, Temple of Hathor, Denderah.

bearing priests and notables of Denderah, was towed up-river towards Edfu, a journey of some 70 km.

The journey was a slow one. Not only was Hathor's progress impeded by numerous pilgrims who joined her glittering cavalcade along its route, but she delayed her arrival at Edfu by stopping at several places along the way to visit local deities. At Thebes, for instance, she was taken ashore to visit the goddess Mut at Karnak; at Hierakonpolis, she greeted the local form of Horus. At each place she visited, more boats were added to her ever-growing procession, all crammed with local dignitaries and enthusiastic devotees of the goddess.

Eventually, on the afternoon of the day of the New Moon, Hathor reached Edfu, where she was met at the quayside by Horus and his retinue. For the rest of the afternoon, the statues of Horus and Hathor were carried to each of the sacred sites outwith Edfu Temple for the performance of certain rituals until the time came for them to enter the temple itself. There, the rites celebrating their marriage were enacted. Finally, they were led to the Birth House and there they spent their wedding night.

For the next fourteen days, the city and district of Edfu, crowded with visitors from all over Egypt, especially from the area between Denderah to the north and Elephantine (Aswan) to the south, rejoiced, and celebrated the sacred marriage with the food and drink supplied free to them by the temple staff. An inscription in the temple describes the scenes of festivity and celebration that were typical on such an occasion, and tells us that countless provisions were available – all kinds of bread in loaves numerous as grains of sand; oxen abounding like locusts; roast fowl, roasts of gazelle, oryx and ibex; free-flowing wine. The whole city was festive:

> Its youths are drunk, its citizens are glad, its young maidens are beautiful to behold; rejoicing is all around it and festivity is in all its quarters. There is no sleep to be had in it until dawn.[20]

On the fourth day of the Festival, the son of Hathor and Horus was conceived. However, before then the nature of the Festival had undergone a subtle change: it was no longer just a sacred marriage but a celebration, called the Festival of *Behdet*, in which a great ancestral ritual was combined with a harvest festival. On the last day of the Festival of *Behdet*, the day of the full moon, the time came for Hathor to return home. She was escorted to the quayside by Horus and his followers to embark on her journey down the Nile to Denderah where, in due course, she gave birth to Horus' son, Harsomtus or *Hor-sma-tawy*, whose name means 'Horus-who-unites-the-Two-Lands' (Egypt).

In every large town in Egypt, there was a shrine in which Hathor was worshipped; in many of them she was regarded as a form of the indigenous goddess. Thus, at Elephantine she was identified with Sothis; at Thebes, with Mut; at Buto, with Wadjet. She was identified with Isis in so many places – Coptos, Panopolis, Aphroditopolis and Kanopus among them – that by the Late Period these two greatest of Egyptian female deities were inextricably mixed together.

Throughout ancient Egyptian history, Hathor was given a place of honour in every Company of Gods: Hathor, their Golden One, the joyous goddess of love, music and intoxication, the bringer of happiness.

WADJET

· ·

Wadjet, the goddess whom the Greeks called Edjo, is known to us by a variety of different names: she is sometimes called Buto; and in older books her name is spelled variously as Wadjet, Wadjit or Uadjit. Since we do not know how ancient Egyptian was pronounced, it is not possible to be dogmatic about the form her name should take. Its meaning is more clear: in hieroglyphic script, it is written using the symbol of Lower Egypt, the papyrus plant ⚬, and means 'She-of-the-Papyrus.'

In predynastic times, Wadjet was worshipped in the form of a cobra at Dep, a town in the North-western Delta. She is one of several cobra goddesses, of whom Renenutet (see page 80) and Meretseger (see page 208) are lesser examples, a popular form of deity throughout Egypt, for cobras are found all over the land. Wadjet rose to pre-eminence thanks to the proximity of her city, Dep, to Pe, where the residence of the Kings of Lower Egypt is believed to have been situated. Pe, which means 'seat' or 'throne', and Dep merged gradually, so that by the New Kingdom they had become one city, named after its chief temple which was dedicated to Wadjet and called *Per Wadjet* (House of Wadjet), rendered by the Greeks as Buto and known today as Tell el-Fara'in (Arabic meaning 'Mound (tell) of the Pharaohs'). 'The Souls of Pe and Dep' was a term often applied to the falcon-headed figures in reliefs and inscriptions which are thought to be representations of early kings of Lower Egypt; and thanks to her association with them, Wadjet became tutelary goddess of the North.

The crown most closely connected with Wadjet was, naturally, the diadem of Lower Egypt, the Red Crown, which she is usually seen wearing. Reliefs in many temples show the coronation of a king, and an important part of the coronation ritual was the crowning of the ruler first with the Red Crown of Lower Egypt, an act undertaken by Wadjet, who is depicted in such reliefs in human female form; then with the White Crown of Upper Egypt by Nekhbet, also in the shape of a woman.

Except for coronation scenes, Wadjet, like Nekhbet, was seldom depicted in human form: she was usually represented as a cobra. From the earliest times, the Egyptians considered the cobra to be a sign of royalty and sovereignty, presumably because the cobra goddess of Dep was so closely connected with kings. Legend says that Wadjet guarded the infant Horus, son of Isis and Osiris,

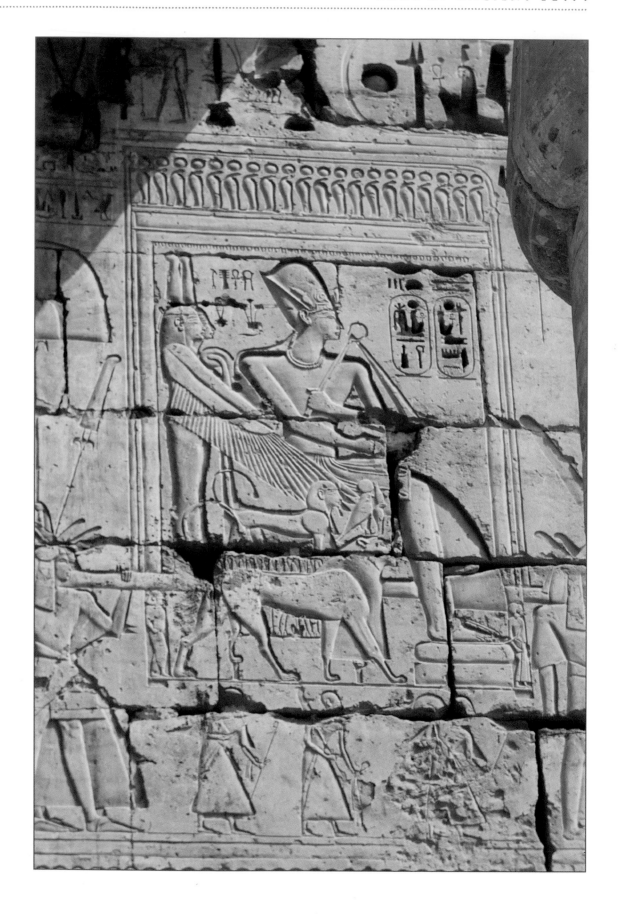

after his birth on the island of Khemmis, near Dep. Later it was her task to guard every King of Egypt, who was regarded as the Living Horus on the throne of Egypt. The sun-disk of Re was usually depicted with a cobra coiled round it as a symbol of his kingship, a convention which led to the cobra being thought of as the Eye of Re which could spit fire against his foes.

The cobra goddess could also spit fire against the enemies of the king. Representations made of gold of Wadjet, the royal cobra, sometimes alone, sometimes accompanied by Nekhbet either in her own vulture-form or in the guise of a cobra, made up the special emblem, the Uraeus, that was borne by kings and gods. The Uraeus (a word which comes from the Greek for cobra, ouraios) was worn on the brow attached to crowns or fillets, and both protected the wearer and indicated that he had dominion over the whole land, with Wadjet symbolizing sovereignty over Lower Egypt and Nekhbet over Upper Egypt. Outstanding examples of uraei were found in the tomb of Tutankhamun, those on the gold funerary mask that covered the head of his mummy and on the fillet that encircled the head, being particularly fine. The most interesting were perhaps the two uraei made of gold and faience beads embroidered onto the linen skull-cap that covered the king's mummified head.

Wadjet was the Royal Cobra. It is fitting that the last Queen of Egypt, Cleopatra, should have chosen to kill herself with the bite of what the Greeks called an 'asp', but which was probably a cobra. Thus Wadjet, by helping 'Egypt' to die with dignity rather than to be paraded in a Roman triumph, extended her protection of the rulers of Egypt to the end.

Opposite: Cobra-frieze at the top of the Opet shrine of Ramesses III: relief in his memorial temple at Medinet Habu.

Left: Coronation of the king by Wadjet (left) and Nekhbet (right): relief in the Temple of Horus, Edfu.

NEKHBET

· ·

Nekhbet, the local goddess of the ancient city of Nekheb, was worshipped by the Egyptians in the form of *Vultur auricularis*, the Sociable Vulture, a species which today is reasonably common in southern Egypt but hardly ever seen in the north. Nekheb, which lies on the east bank of the River Nile some 80 km south of Luxor, was one of the oldest settlements in Upper Egypt, dating back to at least 5000 BC. Because of the city's geographical position, it had great strategic importance in that it had control over the western outlets of the routes that led through the Wadi Abbad and the Wadi Mia to the Red Sea, and to the areas of the Eastern Desert that were exploited for flint, as well as for metals such as lead, tin and gold.

On the west bank of the Nile opposite Nekheb lay the earliest capital city of Upper Egypt, Nekhen (to the Greeks, Hierakonpolis; modern name, Kom el-Ahmar). Because of the proximity of Nekheb to Nekhen, and because of the importance of Nekheb itself, Nekhbet, its goddess, whose name means 'She-of-Nekheb', became the principal goddess of Upper Egypt during the predynastic period. In dynastic times, Nekhbet was elevated to the role of protectress of the King of Upper Egypt. Her northern counterpart as tutelary goddess was Wadjet. When Menes united Upper and Lower Egypt, he symbolized the event by adopting a title which identified him with the two deities: the *nbty*-name, which in hieroglyphic script is written showing a vulture and a cobra sitting on baskets – the Two Ladies (*nbty*) Nekhbet and Wadjet. From thenceforward, the *nbty*-name formed part of the titulary of every King of Egypt.

Nekhbet's role of protectress is reflected in the design of royal jewellery: the broad collars and pectorals which were worn on the chests of kings, for instance, were often made of gold and semi-precious stones shaped to represent vultures. Outstanding examples of these vulture-collars were found at Thebes in the tombs of Smenkare and his brother, Tutankhamun. Whenever Nekhbet was used as a motif in jewellery, she held in her claws the hieroglyphic sign Ω, which reads *shen*, 'to encircle', and denotes that Nekhbet offers a king sovereignty over all that the sun encircles. Even the cobra goddess Wadjet could sometimes be equipped with claws in which to hold a *shen*-sign so that she, too, might offer a king mastery over the world.

Mud-brick city wall, El-Kab.

Nekhbet was particularly concerned with the crown of Upper Egypt. As the embodiment of this, the White Crown, she was often called 'The White One of Nekhen', and she was normally shown wearing the diadem. She could appear on the head of a king, not only as the White Crown, but also in vulture, or even in cobra, form, as part of the Uraeus (see page 131) which he wore on his brow attached to his headdress.

On monuments, Nekhbet is usually shown with wings outstretched, hovering protectively over the figure of a king. She was also depicted attending royal births, an aspect of the goddess which caused the Greeks to identify her with their own Eileithya or 'She-who-comes-to-the-aid-of-women-in-childbed', and to call her city of Nekheb Eileithyiaspolis.

During the New Kingdom, Nekheb was the capital of the 3rd Nome of Upper Egypt. From predynastic times until the Roman era, kings built or renewed shrines and temples there and dedicated them to Nekhbet. Occasionally, Hathor, with whom she was sometimes equated, was honoured alongside her, as in the Eighteenth-Dynasty temple built in the reigns of Thutmose IV and Amenhotep III for Nekhbet and Hathor, Mistress of the Entrance to the (Nile) Valley.

Nekheb suffered considerable damage over the centuries. Today, little remains to be seen of this once great city. El-Kab, as it is now called, is of interest mainly because of the biographical texts in the tombs of men such as Ahmose-

Double Uraeus (cobra and
vulture) on the brow of
Tutankhamun: the second of
the king's mummiform
coffins. (Cairo Museum)

Uraeus on the brow of
Ramesses II: statue of the
king at Memphis.

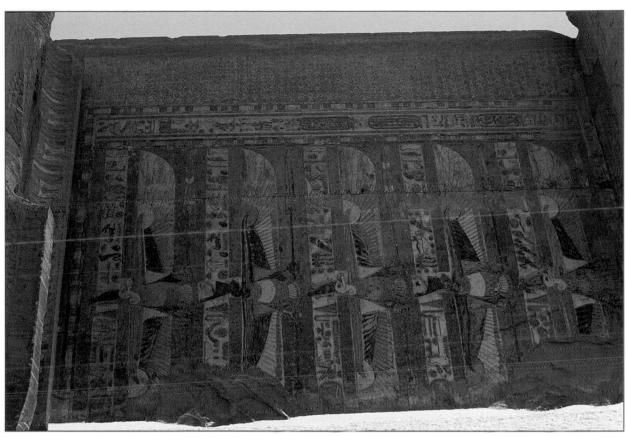

Nekhbet: architrave decorations in the memorial temple of Ramesses III at Medinet Habu.

Pennekhbet (Pennekhbet meaning 'The Man who Belongs to Nekhbet') and Ahmose, son of Abana, who fought against the Hyksos, and in Nubia, Syria and Palestine in the early part of Dynasty XVIII. However, the traveller who passes by the site, whether by road, by train or by boat, cannot but be impressed by what remains of the massive mud-brick ramparts which once surrounded the city of Nekhbet.

AMUN

The name Amun means 'Hidden-' or 'Invisible-one', and he was a deity of the air. The oldest god known by the name Amun was a member of the Ogdoad of Hermopolis (see page 182); but at the end of the First Intermediate Period, a god named Amun appeared in the 4th Nome of Upper Egypt, the *Waset* or Sceptre Nome. Whether this Amun is to be identified with the Hermopolitan Amun is not certain. What is certain is that within a matter of a hundred and fifty years or so, Amun had displaced the indigenous god of the Sceptre Nome, Montu, and had begun the rise to power that was to make him King of the Gods.

A particular kind of sheep, found nowhere else in Egypt, was native to the area of the Sceptre Nome. This sheep belongs to the fat-tailed species *Ovis platyura aegyptiaca*, the ram of which has a characteristic peculiar to it in that its horns are particularly large, curved and down-turned. It is possible that the original deity of the Sceptre Nome, older even than Montu, was a ram of this type. Amun not only displaced Montu, but he adopted the ram with down-turned horns as his own symbol.

Although the ram, famed like Amun himself for its virility and pugnacity, was Amun's sacred animal, Amun was never depicted in the form of a ram, or as a man with a ram's head. He was always portrayed in human shape wearing a cap surmounted by two tall plumes and a sun's disk. The mysterious, hidden part of his nature, implicit in his name, was expressed by the custom of covering the shrine that held his statue with a shroud. The soul of Amun was supposed to be enshrined in a serpent-shaped sceptre known as *Kem-at-ef* (He-who-has-finished-his-moment) which was perhaps his original fetish. The virility and fecundity of Amun was manifest not only in the ram but also in the bird associated with him: the goose.

At least as early as the Middle Kingdom, a temple was built for Amun in the Sceptre Nome, at *Waset*, the town named after the nome although not then its capital, which was further to the south at Armant (see page 196). Very little is known of the early history of *Waset*, the town, except that it had strategic importance due to its geographical position: it lay on both banks of the Nile, close to the deserts, with their natural resources; and not too far away from Nubia which supplied the Egyptians with manpower and gold. After the arrival of Amun, *Waset* grew ever more important and Amun flourished.

Ram-headed sphinxes,
Temple of Amun, Karnak.

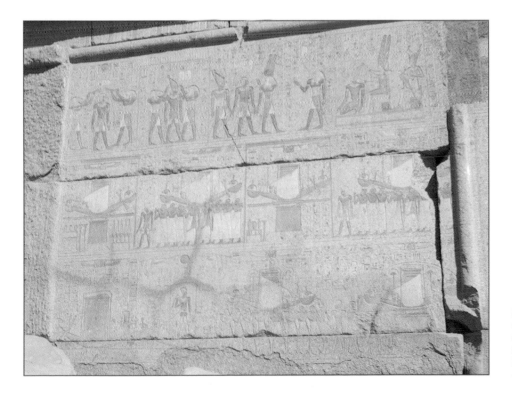

Portable shrines of Amun,
covered with white veils:
exterior of the innermost
sanctuary in his temple at
Karnak.

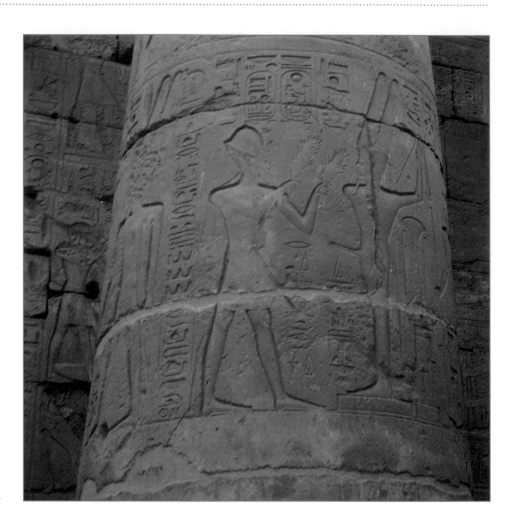

Ithyphallic Amun: relief in the hypostyle hall at Karnak.

Eventually, *Waset* became known as 'The City of Amun' or just as 'The City' – named in the Bible as No Amon (Nahum 3: 8) and No (Ezekiel 30: 16). The Greeks equated Amun with Zeus and therefore called *Waset* Diospolis (City of God). Earlier, Homer had described it as:

> Proud Thebes . . .
> The world's great empress on the Egyptian plain
> That spreads her conquests o'er a thousand states,
> And pours her heroes through a hundred gates,
> Two hundred horsemen and two hundred cars
> From each wide portal issuing to the wars.[21]

Why Homer called *Waset* Thebes we do not know, unless as a compliment to the Boeotian city of the same name. However, it is often convenient for Egyptologists to call the City of Amun, Thebes, although today it is usually known by the names of the two famous temples on its eastern bank, Karnak and Luxor (see page 142).

A century or so after Amun arrived in Thebes, the kings of Dynasty XI, who were natives of the Sceptre Nome and adherents of its chief god, Montu, made

Thebes the capital of Egypt, a position that it held for some fifty years. Then, in 1963 BC, the last king of Dynasty XI, Mentuhotep IV, was overthrown by his chief minister, himself a follower of Amun. The new King of Egypt, the founder of Dynasty XII, called himself Amenemhat, 'Amun is Supreme', a practice followed by three of his successors; and not only honoured Amun by including him in his name, but began to have built for him a temple at Thebes which he called *Ipt-swt*, a name which means 'The Most Select of Places'. Today, the site of this temple is known as Karnak. Karnak was enlarged and embellished over the succeeding centuries, up to and including the Roman period. From the fourth century AD, the temple, abandoned by its priests, was used as a dwelling place by local villagers and their animals. Gradually, it was buried under their debris until eventually only the tops of the windows in the main hall were visible, earning for it the Arabic name, Karnak – 'The Town of the Windows'.

Amenemhat decided that Egypt could not easily be governed from Thebes and so he built a new capital on the boundary between Upper and Lower Egypt, some 30 km south of Memphis, which he called *Itje-tawy*, 'The Seizer of the Two Lands' (Egypt), better known today as Lisht. However, Thebes remained the administrative centre for the South. In Dynasty XIII, the capital was shifted to Memphis. However, in 1648 BC Memphis was captured by the invading Hyksos (see page 102). Thebes fell into obscurity for a hundred years or so until the descendants of the Theban rulers of Dynasty XIII, having made the city into a rallying point for Egyptian resistance to the Hyksos, formed themselves into what Manetho later designated Dynasty XVII.

The Hyksos were finally driven from Egypt in about 1550 BC by the Theban king Ahmose, the founder of Dynasty XVIII. Ahmose chose Thebes to be the capital of the newly unified Egypt; and, as the glory of Thebes grew, so did the glory of her chief god, Amun, who became state god of Egypt. Under Thutmose III, Thebes became the capital of the mighty empire that he won for Egypt in the Near East, and Amun was given sovereignty over the deities of the countries that were subjugated. Amun thus became the supreme god of the then known world and was given the title 'King of the Gods'; he himself was thought of above all as a god of war who brought victory to the kings of Egypt.

Amun, and his city of Thebes, achieved great importance during the New Kingdom, especially during the reigns of the warrior kings Thutmose III and Ramesses II, each of whom made great conquests in the Near East and Nubia and donated much of the wealth gained therefrom to Amun of Thebes. Thutmose III was a particular devotee of Amun, and with good reason. He was the son of Thutmose II and a concubine named Ese. Several years after he came to the throne, he recorded in an inscription at Karnak that when he was a mere child serving as an acolyte in the Temple of Amun at Thebes, his father the King came to make offerings to the God. Prince Thutmose was standing in the hall outside the Sanctuary as his father's procession passed by, and the God (presumably the statue of Amun, carried by priests in a portable shrine with carrying poles) began to search for him:

On recognizing me, lo, he halted . . . I threw myself on the pavement, I prostrated myself in his presence. He set me before him and I was placed at the Station of the King [i.e. the place usually occupied by the Ruler].[22]

And so, by means of a divine oracle, the young boy was chosen to be Crown Prince. The oracle, of course, must have been worked by the priests of Amun, who had marked out the young Thutmose and were prepared to back his claim to the throne.

When Thutmose II died, his wife, Thutmose III's stepmother, Hatshepsut, ruled Egypt, first as regent for the young Thutmose III, then as Female King (note, not queen) in her own right, for twenty-two years. She, too, favoured and was favoured by Amun, claiming him as her heavenly father in reliefs in her memorial temple at Deir el-Bahri showing her divine birth; and erecting obelisks for him within his temple at Karnak. On Hatshepsut's death, Thutmose III came to the throne as undisputed ruler, ready to show his gratitude to the god. The Thutmoside kings who followed him attributed their successes at home and abroad to the favour of Amun, and even claimed their rights to the throne of Egypt by virtue of the fact that each of them was the son of the god he spoke of as 'his father, Amun'. For over a hundred and fifty years, Amun reigned unchallenged.

Throughout Egypt, new shrines and temples were built to Amun, often replacing those of other deities. Small chapels dedicated to these deities were erected within the precincts of Amun's own vast temple at Karnak, thus emphasizing their subordination to Amun. The titles of High Priest of Re and High Priest of Ptah were included among the titles of the High Priest of Amun, who claimed jurisdiction over all other priesthoods. The dead as well as the living came under the jurisdiction of Amun's priesthood, for it governed not only the east bank at Thebes where the temples were situated but also the west bank where the great necropolis of the city lay. They had charge not only of the royal tombs belonging to the kings and queens of the New Kingdom, but also of those of the nobles; and they ran the memorial temples that stretched along the western bank of the Nile for over 7 km. The size and number of the temples and tombs of the Theban necropolis as seen today never fails to impress a visitor with the immensity of the task.

From about 1390 BC, the character of Amun began to change. It was no longer claimed that he was just a god of war; instead, he usurped some of the functions of Ta-tenen of Memphis and Re of Heliopolis. His priests proclaimed that he was a cosmic creator god, self-engendered, who 'had no mother or father but shaped his own egg, mingled his seed with his body to make his egg come into being and took the form of Tanen to give birth to the gods'. It was claimed that Thebes was the birthplace of the whole universe, where the never-sleeping Amun ruled as 'Lord of Time who makes the years, rules the months, ordains nights and days'. Eventually, the priests added Re's name to that of Amun, so that he was thenceforward known as Amen-Re, King of the Gods (*Amen-Re-Nesu-neteru*), which the Greeks rendered as Amonrasonther. The power of

Opposite: Amun (right) and Re-Horakhty (left) greeting Thutmose III: relief on exterior of the sanctuary, Karnak.

Amun was such that it proved oppressive: so much so that before the end of Dynasty XVIII there was a religious revolution (see page 156).

The eclipse of Amun that followed was short-lived. Within a few years, he was reinstated by the last kings of Dynasty XVIII, and by Dynasty XIX had regained his supremacy. In the papyrus now known as the Great Harris and preserved in the British Museum, the Twentieth-Dynasty king, Ramesses IV, recorded that in the reign of his father, Ramesses III, the practice of flooding the coffers of Amun continued until the estate of the God owned:

> 86,486 serfs, 421,362 head of cattle, 433 gardens and orchards, 691,334 acres of land, 83 ships, 46 workshops, 65 cities and towns, plus gold, silver, incense and other valuables in unmeasured amounts.[23]

By the end of the reign of Ramesses III, all the temples of Egypt, not just those of Amun, owned vast amounts of property. It has been calculated that one fifth of the inhabitants of the country and about one third of the cultivable land belonged to the temples, and that some three quarters of all this wealth was owned by Amen-Re of Thebes. It is not surprising that the possession of such wealth gave the High Priest of Amun an enormous amount of power and influence not only in Thebes itself but throughout Egypt.

During the New Kingdom, with the exception of the Amarna Period (see page 152), Thebes flourished as the centre of the cult of Amun. Numerous shrines were built for him: on the west bank he was worshipped in the memorial temples of the kings; on the east bank, his cult temples at Karnak and Luxor were enlarged year by year. The site of Karnak does not contain one temple only: it is, instead, a vast complex of religious buildings in which at least twenty major shrines have been identified. The sacred enclosure covers some 1¼ sq. km and the main temple, dedicated to Amun, was in its final phase at least 1½ km long. The approach to the Temple of Amun was along an avenue of sphinxes that led from the Nile, which lies to the west of the temple; and an avenue of sphinxes linked the Temple of Amun with another temple lying within the precinct of Karnak, that of the goddess Mut. The sphinxes are not human-headed but ram-headed in recognition of the sacred rams of Amun. Karnak, which Champollion called a 'gigantic wonder', was for over two thousand years built, rebuilt, enlarged and embellished by numerous rulers of Egypt. The last-known embellishment of the temple on behalf of a native Egyptian king was undertaken during the reign of Nectanebo I, when Karnak was linked with Luxor Temple by an avenue of human-headed sphinxes.

Luxor Temple, where Amun was worshipped in ithyphallic form in the guise of the fertility god Min, lies just over 2 km to the south of the Temple of Amun. Once a year, during the second month of the Inundation season, the cult statue of Amun was carried in procession from its home at Karnak to spend a holiday with his *alter ego* at Luxor; and to celebrate his union with his divine consort, Mut, during the Beautiful Festival of Opet. As seen today, the temple is largely the result of work carried out during the reigns of two kings: Amenhotep III, for

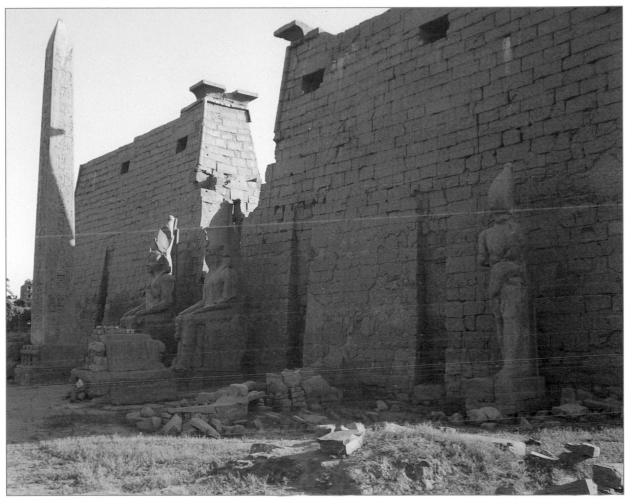

Façade of Luxor Temple
showing obelisk and
colossal statues of
Ramesses II.

whom the sanctuary and its forecourt, and a processional colonnade, were built;
and Ramesses II, who commissioned a peristyle court and a pylon in front of
which were colossal statues of the king, and obelisks, one of which was removed
to the Place de la Concorde, Paris, in AD 1833 (see page 50).

The ancient Egyptians called the temple *Ipt-rsyt*, or the Inner Apartments of
the South. In the Graeco-Roman period, the settlement that had grown over the
accumulated debris of centuries in the area, even encroaching upon the site of the
great temple, was given the name Ophieum, derived from the ancient name Ipet
or Opet. Late in the third century AD, the Romans stationed a legion within the
sacred precinct, and turned one of the inner rooms of the temple into a chapel in
which the insignia of the legion were venerated. From the Latin word for fort,
castrum, was derived the Arabic *al-qasr*, meaning castle; and it is the plural of
this word, *l-uqsor*, 'The Castles', that has given us the name Luxor.

A Christian basilica was erected in the north-east corner of the forecourt built
for Ramesses II; and in the thirteenth century AD, a small mosque dedicated to
Abu'l Haggag, a noted pilgrim to Mecca, was erected on top of the debris that by
then filled the court. Today, the forecourt has been cleared of the debris, but the

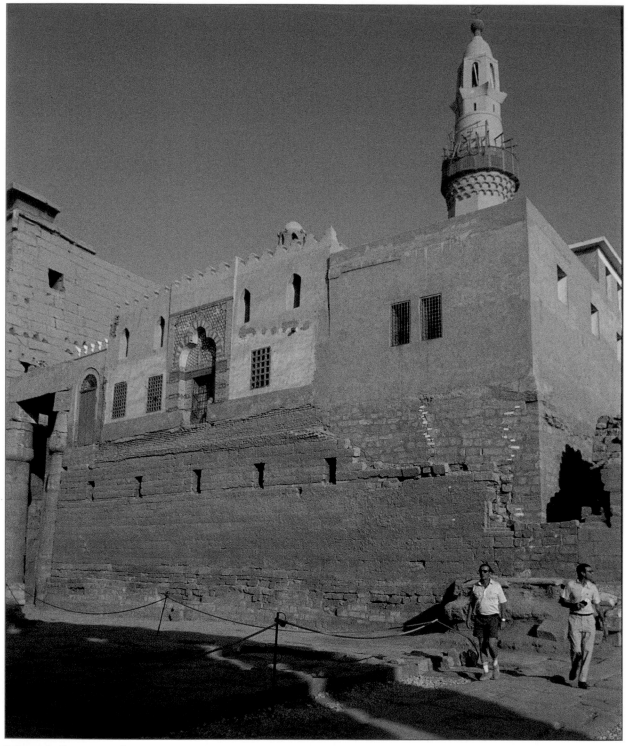

Entrance to the mosque of
Abu'l Haggag at the top of
the eastern wall of the
courtyard, Luxor Temple.

ancient door of the mosque is still in position near the top of the court's eastern wall. The mosque, which is still in use, has a new door on its eastern side; and to this day, a boat which is stored on the roof of the mosque is carried annually in procession round the town in unconscious imitation of the ancient days when Amun was carried out in his sacred Barque to visit *Ipt-rsyt*.

The last kings of Dynasty XX were weak; little by little, the High Priests of Amun usurped their power in Upper Egypt until finally, during the reign of Ramesses XI, a military man named Herihor became High Priest of Amun. Herihor had himself portrayed as a king and founded a dynasty of priest-kings at Thebes which ruled the Theban district if not most of Upper Egypt during the period when the Twenty-first Dynasty of Egyptian Kings proper ruled from Tanis in the North-eastern Delta. Relations between Tanis and Thebes during Dynasty XXI were friendly. The Theban Triad of Amun, Mut and Khonsu were worshipped in Tanis where they displaced the old deities Sutekh and Anath. Princesses were sent from Tanis to Thebes to become wives of the High Priests of Amun.

Maatkare, daughter of Psusennes II, the last king of Dynasty XXI, married Sheshonq, commander of the Egyptian army and formerly commander of the Meshwesh, a special force recruited from among Libyan tribes. When Psusennes II died, the Libyan, Sheshonq became the first king of a new Dynasty, the Twenty-second. The line of Tanite kings ended simultaneously with the line of High Priests of Amun as an independent dynasty, for Sheshonq I proved to be a strong king. He reigned from Bubastis in the north, and Thebes was never again to be a capital city, although it took another three hundred years before it became a fully integrated part of Egypt

During Dynasty XXI, a custom arose that a daughter of the reigning king should be consecrated to Amun to be his wife. The Divine Wife of Amun, who was also called 'The Hand of the God', a reference to an ancient belief that the creation was achieved through an act of masturbation (see page 25), was required to be a virgin: hence the device of adoption was resorted to. Each Divine Wife adopted a daughter to succeed her; and successive kings in their capital cities of Tanis, Bubastis and Sais, and even the kings of Dynasty XXV who were of Sudanese origin, ensured that it was one of their own daughters who travelled to Thebes to become the heiress of the Divine Wife of Amun. Thus, Shepenupet, daughter of Osorkon III of Dynasty XXII, Amenirdis, daughter of Kashta of Dynasty XXV and Nitocris, daughter of Psammeticus I of Dynasty XXVI, and others less well known, reigned, in Thebes at least, not as Queen but as High Priestess of Amun, with a court of her own, surrounded by the 'concubines' or priestesses of Amun, the owner of vast estates with the privilege of making offerings in the temple. Having wielded great power in her lifetime, the Divine Wife of Amun, when she died, was buried in the same manner as a King of Egypt, usually on the west bank of Thebes at Medinet Habu, the great memorial temple of Ramesses III.[24]

Despite the fact that Amun was King of the Gods, and a very close associate of the Kings of Egypt, his priests were at pains to encourage Egyptians to see him as

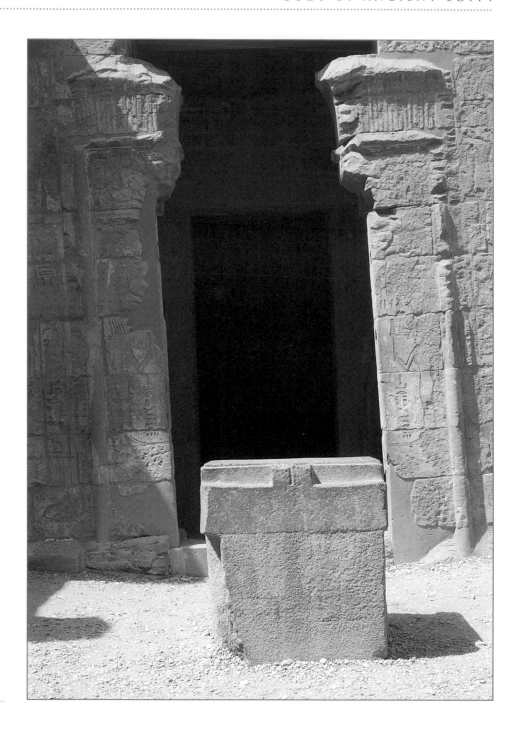

Chapel of the Divine Wife of Amun, Amenirdis, Dynasty XXV, at Medinet Habu.

a compassionate deity, one to whom they could turn when they were in trouble. Therefore, they built at Karnak a small temple called 'The Temple of Amun-who-hears-prayers' where the ordinary Egyptian could petition the god by leaving a small stele at the gate. Thus Amun was to many Egyptians a kind god who protected the weak, succoured orphans, defended the oppressed and healed the sick. As was customary in Egyptian religion, he formed part of a triad or holy family, playing the role of husband and father to Mut and Khonsu respectively.

In 663 BC, Assurbanipal the Assyrian sacked Thebes and carried away to
Nineveh a vast amount of treasure looted from its temples. Thebes never
recovered from the blow, although Amun himself continued to receive attentions
from the rulers of Egypt at Thebes and elsewhere. Proof that his power remained
undiminished is provided by the behaviour towards him of Alexander the Great.
In October 332 BC, Alexander conquered Egypt without having to strike a blow,
welcomed by the Egyptians as their deliverer from the hated Persians, who had
ruled them intermittently since 525 BC. As was his usual practice, Alexander
took care to observe local religious susceptibilities. Some three months after his
arrival in Egypt, he took the trouble to make a three-week journey across a
distance of 500 km of burning Libyan desert in order to visit the Temple of
Amun at the Siwah Oasis, and to consult the oracle of Zeus-Ammon. When
Alexander emerged from the consultation, all he would disclose about what the
oracle had said to him was, 'I have been told what my heart desires'.[25] He was
recognized and accepted by the Egyptians, and more importantly by the Egyptian
priesthood, as the son of Amun and therefore the rightful ruler of Egypt. From
thenceforward, Alexander was depicted, on coins especially, wearing the
distinctive ram's horns of Amun.

The Greeks continued the worship of Amun under the name of Zeus-Ammon,
and later, the Romans honoured him as Jupiter-Ammon. And Amun has left to us
a legacy of words: ammonia is so called because the ammoniac salt found at
Siwah was thought, albeit erroneously, to have been formed from dung dropped
by camels used by visitors to the temple; and the fossils called ammonites owe
their name to a resemblance to the ram's horns of Amun.

MUT

Mut was possibly the original deity of Thebes. Although she is always shown on existing monuments in completely human form, she was probably worshipped in predynastic times in the form of a griffin vulture (*Gyps fulvus*). The word *mut*, which is written using the hieroglyph depicting this vulture, is thought to have been old Egyptian for 'vulture', but was replaced in the Egyptian language of later times by another, *neret*, also meaning vulture. Thus the hieroglyph of the griffin vulture was reserved for writing the name of the goddess Mut.

The word *mut* also means 'mother', and so Mut is considered to be a mother goddess. This concept was reinforced by the universal symbolism of the mother-bird with wings outspread protectively over her fledglings. Since, in Egypt, vultures are the birds with the largest wing-span, vulture goddesses such as Mut and Nekhbet became symbols of maternal love and protection.

It seems very fitting that Mut should adorn the head of the principal wife of the king. In the New Kingdom, queens wore headdresses fashioned in the form of a vulture. Although no actual example of this type of headdress has been found, it seems clear from the many reliefs depicting queens wearing it that the vulture's wings were made of small plates of gold wired together to make a flexible covering for the top of the head. In wearing such a headdress, a queen not only associated herself with Mut, consort of the great state god Amun, but also with another vulture goddess, Nekhbet, protectress of Upper Egypt.

When the cult of Amun arrived in Thebes, around 2040 BC, Mut was incorporated into it as his wife. Her temple stands within the precincts of Karnak, in the quarter known as Asher. The major part of this temple was built under Amenhotep III, but later kings, especially the Ptolemies, also delighted in honouring Mut, the Great Mother.

Opposite: Vulture goddess: hieroglyphs from the memorial temple of Ramesses II at Abydos.

KHONSU

• •

Khonsu was the son of Amun and Mut. He was depicted as a youth wrapped in mummy-bandages, holding in his hands a crook, a flail and a *waas*-sceptre (⌐). Like Ptah, he wears a *menat*-necklace; and on his head he wears the side-lock of youth, and a crescent and full moon, for he was a moon god and as such rivalled only by Thoth. Although Khonsu had many sanctuaries throughout Egypt, his cult-centre and principal place of worship was at Thebes, where he had a temple within the precincts of the Temple of Amun at Karnak.

It was once thought that Khonsu's name derived from the words for placenta (*kh*, pronunciation unknown) and king (*nsw*) and that he was the personification of the royal placenta, which was preserved after the birth of the king, wrapped in a cloth, and fixed to the top of a pole, to become one of the four standards that were carried at the head of royal processions. This idea is now generally rejected in favour of the interpretation that Khonsu's name is derived from the verb 'to cross over', thus giving it the meaning 'He-who-traverses [the sky]', which seems an appropriate appellation for a moon god.

As a moon god, Khonsu helped Thoth to reckon time, and under his influence, 'women conceived and cattle multiplied their young'. He was also a god of healing. Khonsu's fame as a god of healing is recorded on a stele[26] that was found in his temple at Thebes, and which is now in the Louvre Museum in Paris. The stele purports to have been erected in the reign of Ramesses II, but was probably set up during either the Persian or the Ptolemaic period in an attempt to recall Egypt's past glories, when its kings ruled over a vast empire. On it is recounted the story of how Ramesses II marched into Naharin (a land lying between the Tigris and the Euphrates which Ramesses II never actually visited) on his annual tour of inspection of the Egyptian Empire. The prince of Bakhtan (perhaps Bactria) brought his daughter and presented her to the king who was 'so pleased with the maiden' that he made her his wife and gave her the Egyptian name of Neferure.

The story goes on to tell of how, in the fifteenth year of his reign, Ramesses went to Thebes to celebrate the Festival of Opet (see page 142). While he was there, a messenger came from Bakhtan to say that the younger sister of Queen Neferure, Bentresh, was ill. And so His Majesty sent one of his most learned men, Dehuty-em-heb, to Bakhtan, to see what was wrong with Bentresh.

Khosu (far left) with, left to
right, Amun, Ramesses II
and Sekhmet: relief in
hypostyle hall of Ramesses
II's Theban mortuary
temple, the Ramesseum.

Dehuty-em-heb discovered that the princess was possessed by an evil spirit and
that he was powerless to help her.

In the twenty-sixth year of Ramesses' reign, a second envoy arrived from
Bakhtan, seeking help for the ailing princess. This time, Ramesses commanded
that the statue of Khonsu, which normally lived in his temple at Karnak, should
be sent to Bentresh. Accordingly, Khonsu was dispatched in a large ship with an
escort of five boats; and equipped with a state chariot and numerous horses, so
that he might make the journey to Bakhtan by sea and by land.

Khonsu arrived in Bakhtan after a journey of one year and five months. He was
taken straight to the princess, and she was healed immediately. On seeing this, the
prince of Bakhtan resolved to keep the healing statue of Khonsu with him in
Bakhtan, and Khonsu was detained there for three years and nine months! However,
the prince was frightened one night by a dream in which Khonsu appeared as a
golden hawk and flew away to Egypt. And so he allowed the statue of Khonsu to
return to Thebes, where it was welcomed home amidst great rejoicing.

Khonsu's fame as a healer was long-lasting. When Ptolemy Philopator, the
fourth of the line of Macedonian Greeks who ruled Egypt as the Ptolemaic
Dynasty, was afflicted with a serious illness, he appealed not to Greek gods but
to Khonsu of Thebes, who intervened (although in what way we do not know)
and cured the king, who ever after called himself 'Beloved of Khonsu who
protects His Majesty and drives away evil spirits'.

ATEN

• •

Aten, or 'The Sun's Disk', is inextricably bound up with King Akhenaten who ruled Egypt for seventeen years or so in the fourteenth century BC, during what has become known as the 'Amarna Period', now a byword for both religious revolution and a distinctive style in art.

No other ruler of ancient Egypt, and few rulers in the entire ancient world, have elicited as much attention as Akhenaten. On the surface, he is a figure sympathetic to modern man; indeed, James Henry Breasted (1865–1935), the founder of American Egyptology, hailed him as the 'first individual in history', a man whose appeal stretches over the millennia. The reason for this is not difficult to find. The kings of Egypt, in their own time, were presented to the world as giants among men, great conquerors who trampled on their enemies, the chosen of the gods with whom they communed. If they had any physical imperfections or human failings, these were never mentioned. For only a brief period, during Dynasty XII, were sculptors allowed to portray the ruler suffering the burden of office, the stresses of which can be seen in the lined, weary expression on the royal face. At all other times, the king was portrayed as the god he was believed to be, confident, untouched by human cares or even feelings; superhuman.

However, Akhenaten broke with the traditions of over a thousand years. He allowed himself to be portrayed kissing his wife in public or chucking her under the chin; sitting her on his lap; dandling his children (and those children daughters rather than the usually preferred sons) on his knee. He is seen in numerous scenes of family intimacy playing the part of a loving husband and doting father, a dutiful son. Not least of the aspects of Akhenaten that have caught the imagination in modern times is the fact that the wife with whom he apparently shared a life of conjugal bliss, whose very name means 'The-Beautiful-Woman-is-Come', was Nefertiti, whose timeless beauty has transcended the ages through the celebrated portrait-bust of her now in Berlin Museum.

Akhenaten is credited with having written poems in praise of Aten, the most famous being the Great Hymn to Aten (see page 159) which has been compared to Psalm 104. He is said to have inspired a new style in art which ignored old conventions in favour of 'truth' and a new honesty in revealing the deformities of its originator. Above all, Akhenaten is admired by those who do not feel

Akhenaten, Nefertiti and daughters, with Aten shining on them. (Stele from Amarna, now in Cairo Museum)

comfortable with Egypt's polytheism for having replaced the myriad deities of his land with one god, monotheism being more acceptable to many people of modern times, and even more so to the many influential Egyptologists of the last century who were committed Christians. Some scholars have viewed Akhenaten as the first monotheist in history, and Sigmund Freud maintained that he was the inspiration for the monotheism of Moses. James Henry Breasted claimed that he was 'such a spirit as the world had never seen before, a brave soul . . . stepping out from the long line of conventional and colorless Pharaohs that he might disseminate ideas far beyond and above the capacity of his age to understand'.

Arthur Weigall, the English Egyptologist whose publications in the early years of the present century helped to popularize Akhenaten, claimed that with Akhenaten we might, for once, look right into the mind of a King of Egypt and may see something of its working. He went on to claim that 'all that is there observed is worthy of admiration'. Others have not been so enthusiastic. To some, Akhenaten was far from being a man in advance of his time, a forerunner of Christ. The doyen of Egyptologists, Sir Alan Gardiner (1879–1963), thought him a fanatic; the archaeologist, John Pendlebury (1904–41), who excavated at Amarna, considered him to be a religious maniac; and, in the opinion of another Egyptologist, S.R.K. Glanville (1900–56), Akhenaten as a king was deserving of nothing but censure.

Even allowing for the modern fashion of debunking heroes, there is evidence enough to show that Akhenaten was not such a revolutionary or inspired figure as previous generations have believed, although such evidence as there is has not been easily come by. The ancient records of Akhenaten's reign are scanty and even more ambiguous than is the case with some other periods of Egyptian history, and are subject to much and varied interpretation.

Whether or not Akhenaten 'invented' the Amarna style of art, or whether this genuinely distinctive style was largely a natural development of traditional Egyptian art, perhaps showing some Cretan influence, it is nevertheless an extremely attractive, sometimes exquisite, genre. At first glance, it seems to be original in its realism and naturalness. However, all the old Egyptian principles and conventions of art are still there, especially in the canon of proportion employed in the drawing of the human figure, and in the convention that the most important person in any group should be depicted larger in scale than the others. The figure of the king himself is shown with all its apparent deformities –the prognathous jaw, the protruding belly, the bulbous hips; and they are often reproduced in depictions of his family or his courtiers, presumably in obsequious deference to the king. This may be 'realism', at least in the case of Akhenaten himself, or 'naturalism'; equally, it may be said to be just a different convention. Akhenaten may not have invented the Amarna style, but at the least he permitted it.

As far as Akhenaten's family life is concerned, that, too, may not have been as idyllic as it first appears. For many people today, the fact that he married his own daughter, Meritaten, had a child by her, passed her on to Smenkare (who was probably his brother and therefore her uncle), married his daughter, Ankhesenpaaten, and had a daughter by her, tarnishes Akhenaten's image as the devoted husband of the beautiful Nefertiti, although the marriage between father and daughter, when that father was the king, was quite acceptable to the ancient Egyptians.

Above all, it is Akhenaten's reputation as the inventor of the one god Aten that suffers most when the evidence is examined. The word *aten* had been in use since at least the Middle Kingdom, with the earliest reference so far discovered being in one of the Coffin Texts. Examples of it are found in the great narrative text of the Middle Kingdom known as *The Story of Sinuhe*,[27] in which a king is described as dying and 'being united with the sun'; and which gives the text of a letter that Sinuhe sends to his king in which he says, 'the sun rises at your pleasure'. In both cases, the word used for 'sun' is *aten* rather than the more usual *re*. The chief source for *The Story of Sinuhe*, Papyrus Berlin 10499, uses the word *aten* in the first example with the sign for god, ⸠, appended to it; a secondary source, an ostracon in the Ashmolean Museum in Oxford, uses the god sign for the second example also.

It seems certain, therefore, that the Egyptians had a sun god called 'Aten' in the Middle Kingdom if not before. In Dynasty XVIII, more is heard of Aten. He probably became a member of the Egyptian pantheon some time during the reign of Thutmose III or perhaps of his son, Amenhotep II. Thutmose III's grandson, Thutmose IV, issued a commemorative scarab on which Aten appears as a war god who goes in front of the king to give him victory. In the reign of Amenhotep III, Aten was further honoured. One of the epithets of the king himself was *Tekhen-Aten*, 'Radiance of Aten', a term found also as the name of a company of the Royal Bodyguard, a town, a lake, and the king's State Barge.

Amenhotep III seems to have favoured the worship of Aten. However, it was left to his son, Amenhotep IV (Akhenaten; see page 156), to develop the worship of the god. The so-called revolution of Akhenaten is now generally thought to have been a political rather than a religious movement, a reaction to events outside Egypt. Thutmose III and Amenhotep II, in particular, were great warriors who were able to take advantage of conditions in the Near East during their reigns, when many countries and petty states in the region were weak and ripe for conquest. Only Mitanni, which lay between the Tigris and the Euphrates, posed a problem for Egypt. Thutmose III and his successors poured much of the booty brought back from their Near Eastern campaigns into the coffers of Amun (see page 141); and the resulting growth in the power and wealth of his priesthood eventually weakened the monarchy. At the same time, foreign influences were brought into Egypt from her new 'Empire', and also from further afield, from places such as Crete; more especially, newcomers from the countries invaded by Egypt were given positions at Court.

When Amenhotep III came to the throne, the situation in the Near East had changed. Mitanni was no longer a threat to Egypt but rather its ally, and was being threatened by the rise of the Assyrians. Egypt's chief enemies were the Hittites. Although their land lay far to the north of Egypt (in what is now Turkey), the Hittites fomented rebellion among the princes of Egypt's Empire in the Near East. The existence of that Empire was threatened unless Egypt were prepared to fight to retain it. Unfortunately, Amenhotep III and his son were not much given to the pursuit of war, and were prepared to let the Empire fend for itself.

From the very beginning of his reign, Amenhotep III had flouted tradition. Before his time, it had been the custom for a son of the reigning king to marry the king's eldest daughter, who was the royal heiress and through whom the royal line was carried. This royal heiress was called the God's Wife of Amun (not to be confused with the later Divine Wife; see page 145) and by marriage with her a prince legitimized his claim to the throne. Amenhotep III did not marry the royal heiress; instead, he married Tiy, a noblewoman, and from that time on, the position of God's Wife of Amun fell into disuse, for Amenhotep III's son, Amenhotep IV, did not marry the royal heiress either.

Although the King of Egypt was thought to be a god, he was not usually worshipped as one until after his death. Amenhotep III was actively deified in his own lifetime, not in Egypt proper but in Nubia, where at Soleb he built a temple dedicated to himself as 'Lord of Nubia', and in which he can be seen in reliefs making offerings to his deified self. Amenhotep III's son went even further than his father in his challenge to the established gods of Egypt. He chose to deal with the threat posed to his throne by the power of the priesthood of Amun especially, by favouring a rival god. And, in a reversal of the age-old device employed by a ruler with problems at home, that is, the distraction of his people by means of a war against a foreign enemy, Amenhotep IV (Akhenaten) distracted attention from trouble in the Empire by initiating action at home against the gods of Egypt.

His choice of weapon for this action was the sun. The cult of the sun was a very ancient one in Egypt: its symbolism could be understood by everybody even if the remoteness of the sun did not endear its cult to all. There had always been an incipient monotheism in Egypt, for the Egyptians were accustomed to having local gods who syncretized with others from time to time. Because every local god in Egypt was identified in the minds of his followers with the state god, in essence this meant that each Egyptian could choose to worship one god made up of his own local god and whichever deity was the state god at the time. In practice, this did not happen, for the Egyptians tended to allot different functions to different gods. However, in Dynasty XVIII, the theoretically possible 'one god' was Re, the Sun God, for by that time it had become the custom for lesser deities to syncretize with Re: even the powerful Amun was known as Amen-Re (see page 141).

However, the sun god chosen by Amenhotep IV was not Re but Aten. Aten represented the physical power of the sun's disk, the life-giving properties of the sun, which were omnipresent. It had been the custom to depict Aten as a man with the head of a falcon surmounted by a sun's disk – not dissimilar from Re-Horakhty. However, early in Amenhotep IV's reign the iconography of Aten underwent a change. The inspiration for this change perhaps dates back to the reign of Amenhotep II. On the stele he erected in front of the Sphinx at Giza (see page 98), the sun is depicted with two arms descending from its disk to embrace the royal cartouche. The Aten of Amenhotep IV is depicted as a solar disk with many rays depending from it, each ray terminating in a hand, with some of the hands holding *ankh*-signs (☥), symbolizing the giving of life.

For the first four years of his reign, Amenhotep IV made no untoward move. Then, in his fifth year, the king changed his name from Amen-hotep (Amun-is-satisfied) to Akh-en-aten, which is often translated as 'Beneficial-to-the-Aten', although a better rendering of the name might be 'Glorious-Spirit-of-Aten'. From the fifth year of Akhenaten's reign, the didactic name of Aten (see page 157), that is, the name which elaborates on the basic appellation Aten in order to reflect what was perceived to be the true character of the god, was divided into two parts, with each part inscribed inside a cartouche, as though Aten were an earthly king. Aten is given regnal years which are identical with those of Akhenaten. And together, the two kings, Akhenaten and Aten, or the two gods, Aten and Akhenaten, celebrate their joint jubilee. From then on, great emphasis was placed on the kingship of Aten. Year five also saw the naturalistic style of Amarna art taken to extremes. The figures of Akhenaten became grotesque almost to caricature. This was perhaps done to emphasize the break with the past.

Part of a limestone relief, now in Cairo Museum, from the Great Temple at Amarna showing Akhenaten and Nefertiti worshipping the Aten. The rays descending from the disk of the Aten terminate in hands, some of which hold the symbol *ankh* (life).

An even more effective break was achieved in the following year, when Akhenaten moved his capital to the new city which he had had built between Memphis and Thebes, on a site that was virgin and therefore not contaminated by any of Aten's rival gods. This site is now known as Tell el-Amarna. It is not actually a tell, which is a mound of rubble or a small hill, but the term was used in the past because of a confusion with the name of the local village, Et Till. El-Amarna is derived from the name of a local tribe, the Beni Amran. Akhenaten named his new city *Akhet-Aten*, 'Horizon-of-Aten'. After the move to *Akhet-Aten*, Aten was supreme: Akhenaten even began to build a temple to Aten in Thebes, in the precincts of the Temple of Amun itself, although he had not yet proscribed Amun or the other gods.

In the ninth year of his reign, Akhenaten made a change in the didactic name of Aten. The earlier form of the name reads: 'Long live Re-Horakhty who rejoices in the horizon'; followed by: 'In his name of Shu who is Aten'. The later form of the name reads: 'Long live Re ruler of the Two Horizons who rejoices in the horizon'; followed by: 'In his name of Re the father who has come as Aten'. The later name reflects a tightening-up of the religion. Shu and Re-Horakhty are dropped from the name and replaced by Re alone, Re being considered to be a more pure form of the sun who was Aten. Amun was a casualty of the tightening-up: his temples were closed down.

Even before the move to *Akhet-Aten*, Aten had become a trinity consisting of Re – the primordial god, the demi-urge – as the father; Aten – visible to man in the form of the sun's disk – as the physical expression of the father; and Akhenaten, the physical manifestation on earth of both Re and Aten. Akhenaten was the son of

Re, the son of Aten; but at the same time, he was the father of both; and further, he was both Re and Aten. This trinity which was at the same time a unity was worshipped in the Temple of the Aten. There, the High Priest was called the High Priest of Akhenaten, indicating that the king himself was worshipped. Atenism was a very exclusive religion. Only the king and the royal family were ever officially depicted worshipping Aten, and it is to them alone that Aten ever holds out the sign of life. The ordinary Egyptian was expected to worship Aten through the medium of the king, and to accept Akhenaten as his personal god.

But Egyptians had always found comfort in their own local gods, and, for a long time, had believed that Osiris offered them the hope of a better life to come. Akhenaten swept away Osiris and the other gods from the official state religion and put nothing in their place. It is not surprising, therefore, that the worship of Aten held no appeal for the ordinary Egyptian; and that it was only at *Akhet-Aten* that Aten held sway with any conviction. Even here, there was some resistance. At the foot of the cliffs beyond the north-east corner of the village in which the men who worked on the official tombs lived, there are over twenty chapels, said by the modern excavators[28] of the site to be tomb-chapels. However, these 'tomb-chapels' have no burial shafts; neither do they display any funerary evidence. It is thought more likely, therefore, that they were used as shrines by the workers and their families, especially since there are benches built along the sides of the front halls. In one of these 'chapels' (number 525), there is a stele dedicated to Isis and Shed (see page 208); and in the village houses amulets of Hathor and Taweret have been found, as well as figures of Bes painted on house walls, proof that these popular deities were worshipped by the workers of Amarna in defiance of the theology of the king.

Even before Akhenaten died, probably in the seventeenth year of his reign, Atenism was dying. His successor, Smenkare, made no attempt to perpetuate the cult: he abandoned *Akhet-Aten* in favour of Thebes, leaving the city of Aten to crumble away, and made his peace with the old religion and with Amun in particular. Scarcely had he done so than he, too, was dead; and his successor, Tutankhamun, having changed his name from Tut-ankh-Aten (Living-image-of-Aten) to Tut-ankh-Amun (Living-image-of-Amun), issued the decree that reinstated Amun in all his glory, thus completing the triumph of Amun over Aten.

Tutankhamun spent the remaining nine years of his short reign restoring the temples of the old gods throughout Egypt, but paying particular attention to Thebes; he was the king who 'spent his life making images of the gods'. However, he did not forget Aten entirely; and on the back of the great golden State Throne that was found in his tomb there is a relief which shows Aten holding out his rays to the young king and his wife, who was none other than Ankhesenpaaten (She-lives-in-the-Aten), the daughter and wife of Akhenaten, who had changed her name to Ankhesenamun (She-lives-in-Amun) on her marriage to Tutankhamun.

Akhenaten's reign was disastrous for Egypt's Empire. Although Aten was supposed to shine in his beneficence on all mankind, Akhenaten ignored the people of his Empire and left them to their fate at the hands of the Hittites and their allies. Akhenaten became known as 'The Heretic', and when Horemheb came to the throne some fifteen years after Akhenaten's death, he dated his reign from the last year of Amenhotep III with the intention of expunging from Egyptian annals all memory of the Heretic King and his successors, whom he considered tainted with the Atenist heresy.

In spite of the work that has been undertaken at Amarna since it was first visited by Sir John Wilkinson in AD 1824, work that is still going on under the aegis of the Egypt Exploration Society, there are still many unresolved problems concerning the Amarna Period, not least the puzzle of the cause of Akhenaten's deformities, or even whether his physical shape was actually as it appears in depictions of the king; the date of his death and that of Nefertiti; their place of burial; his relationship to Tutankhamun. These, and other vexing questions about this perennially fascinating yet tantalizingly ill-documented period, may never be answered.

Even the nature of Aten himself, as envisaged by Akhenaten, is not entirely clear. The fullest statement of Akhenaten's vision of his god is found at Amarna in the tomb constructed for Ay, later to be king and actually buried at Thebes: it is the beautiful poem known as the Great Hymn to Aten, a remarkable work that goes some way towards explaining the appeal of the Amarna Period:

> How beautiful is your appearance on the horizon of heaven,
> Oh Living Aten who creates life.
> When you rise on the eastern horizon
> You fill every land with your beauty.
> You are beautiful and great, gleaming high over every land.
> Your rays, they embrace the earth
> To the furthest limits of what you have created.
> You are Re; you conquer them all,
> Making them subject to your beloved son.
> You are far away yet your rays are upon earth;
> You are on the faces of men yet your paths are unknown.
>
> When you set on the western horizon
> The earth is in darkness in the manner of the dead
> Who sleep in their chambers,
> Their heads covered
> And no eye seeing its fellow.
> All their possessions could be stolen,
> Even though they are under their heads,
> And they would know it not.
> Every lion comes forth from its den
> And all snakes are ready to bite,
> For darkness is the only illumination
> And the earth is silent,
> For he who created it rests in his horizon.

Day dawns when you rise on the horizon,
You shine by day as Aten
Who dispels the darkness.
When you send forth your sunbeams
The Two Lands are festive,
The people awake and jump to their feet
For you have roused them.
Their bodies are washed
And they don their clothing;
Their arms are upraised in adoration at your appearance.

The whole world goes about its work;
All cattle rest in their pastures;
Trees and vegetation are verdant;
Birds fly up from their nests, their wings raised in adoration of your
   Ka.
Goats all jump on their feet and
Everything that flys and flutters lives when you shine upon it.
Boats sail upstream, and downstream likewise,
And all roads are open because you have arisen.
The fish in the river leap before your face,
And your rays are in the midst of the sea.

You are the one who causes women to be fecund,
Who makes seed in men,
Who gives life to a son in his mother's womb,
Who soothes him with whatever dries his tears
By acting as his nurse even in the womb,
Who gives the breath of life to everything that he has made.

When he emerges from the womb
To breathe on the day of his birth,
You open his mouth wide and supply what it needs.
The chick in the egg cheeps whilst still in the shell
For you have given it breath therein so that it might live.
You make for it the strength
With which it breaks it, namely the egg,
And it emerges from the egg at the appointed hour
To cheep and run on its feet as soon as it issues therefrom.

How legion are your works
That are hidden from the face of mankind.
Oh Sole God, who is like none other,
You made the earth according to your will, alone,
Men and women, cattle and all beasts,

Everything on earth that walks upon feet,
Everything above that flies with its wings,
Foreign lands, Syria, Kush
And the land of Egypt.
You set everyone in his place and supply his needs,
Everyone has his provisions
And his allotted life-span.
Their tongues are diverse in speech
And their appearance likewise;
Their skins are different for you have differentiated the peoples.

It is in the Underworld that you make the Nile
And bring it forth at your will
So that mankind might live:
For you have made them for yourself,
Oh Lord of them all, who grows weary on their behalf,
Oh Lord of every land, who shines upon them.
All distant lands, you make whatever they need to live on.
You have set a Nile in the sky
So that it may descend for them
And make waves upon the mountains like the sea,
So that their fields may be watered in their townships.
How marvellous are your schemes, Oh Lord of Eternity.
The heavenly Nile is what you have created for foreign peoples
And for all the game in the desert that walk upon feet;
But the (real) Nile comes forth from the Underworld for Egypt.

Your rays nourish every field and when you rise, they live and flourish
    for you.
It is in order to sustain all that you have created that you have made
    the seasons:
Winter to cool them
And the heat [of Summer] so that they may taste you.
You have made the sky afar off in order to shine therein
And to see all that you have made,
You alone, rising in your form of the living Aten,
Appearing and shining, far off, yet close at hand.
From out of yourself alone you have made myriad forms –
Cities, towns, fields, roads and river.
All eyes see you before them,
For you are Aten the daylight over the earth.
Even when you are done, your eye [still] exists
For you have created their forms.
If you did not see [rest of line damaged].

You are in my heart,
There is none other that knows you
Except your son Nefer-Kheperu-re Wa-en-re,[29] [i.e. Akhenaten],
Whom you have acquainted with your plans and your power.
The earth exists in your hand, just as you have made it.
When you rise, it lives: when you set, it dies.
You yourself are Lifetime
And it is by you that men live.
Eyes gaze upon your beauty until you set,
But when you set in the west, all work is laid aside,
When you rise again, you make [lost] grow for the king.

Movement has been in every leg
Since you founded the earth.
You have raised up [its inhabitants]
For your son who came forth from your flesh –
The King of Upper and Lower Egypt, who lives on Truth,
The Lord of the Two Lands, Nefer-Kheperu-re Wa-en-re,
The Son of Re, who lives on Truth,
Lord of Diadems, Akhenaten, whose life is long;
And for the Great Royal Wife, his beloved,
The Mistress of the Two Lands, Nefer-neferu-Aten,[30]
Nefertiti, may she live and grow young for ever and ever.

PTAH

● ●

Ptah was one of the oldest deities of Egypt. In prehistoric times, he was probably worshipped as a fetish in the district that Menes eventually chose to be the site of the first capital of Egypt, Memphis. The earliest deities to be worshipped at Memphis were Ta-tanen, an earth god, and Sokar, a god of the dead. When Ptah was first established in the city, he coalesced with Ta-tanen and Sokar, thus becoming an earth god with funerary associations.

The standard depiction of Ptah shows him in human form, shrouded like a mummy. His hands, projecting through the mummy-wrappings, are clasped round *waas-* (⬆ meaning dominion) and *djed-* (⬛ meaning stability) signs held in front of his body; and sometimes they hold the traditional symbols of kingship, the crook and the flail, and *ankh*-signs (☥), also. He has a wedge-shaped beard and a close-shaven head upon which he sometimes wears a disk set between two feathers. This feathered disk resembles the crown that Osiris borrowed from Andjety (see page 56). Ptah's shoulders are covered with a broad collar with a counterpoise made of the fertility amulet, *menat* (⬱), hanging from the base of his neck. He often stands upon a plinth shaped like ⬭ which is the hieroglyph for *maat*, Truth; and also a representation of the measuring rod used by workmen.

The original Memphite deity, the earth god Ta-tanen, whose name means 'The Risen Land', was, so his priests claimed, the personification of the Primeval Mound that rose out of the waters of the Nun. This was presumably an attempt to claim a greater antiquity for their god over Atum of On, since the concept of the Primeval Mound was first introduced by his priests. At Memphis, Ptah was considered to be the supreme Creator God who came into existence before both the Nun and the Primeval Mound; hence, he was given the names Ptah-Nun and Ptah-Ta-tanen.

The story of the creation of the world told at Memphis is remarkable in that its concept of the theogony of Ptah is a highly spiritual one, unlike the grosser acts of creation attributed to Ptah's contemporary, Atum. Ptah was said to have created the world by thought and tongue whereas Atum performed his act of creation by masturbation or expectoration. The Memphite Doctrine was probably determined right at the beginning of Egyptian history. When, *c.* 3100 BC, Menes made Memphis the capital of his newly united land, he ensured that his new city became the religious as well as the political centre of Egypt. One of the means to this end was the promotion of Ptah as chief god of Memphis and Egypt, rival of Re-Atum of Heliopolis.

Although the Memphite Doctrine was one of the oldest in Egypt, our version of it is relatively late, dating to the eighth century BC rather than to the end of the fourth millennium, and is to be found inscribed on a large slab of black basalt that was discovered in the nineteenth century AD in the centre of Cairo, being used as a mill-stone. This basalt slab, or stele, was presented to the British Museum in 1805 by Earl Spencer; it is known today as the Shabaka Stone,[31] after the Twenty-fifth Dynasty king who ordered it to be made.

The inscription on the Shabaka Stone is badly worn but enough remains to give a clear idea of Memphite Theology. The opening lines on the stele state that it was copied from an old inscription, written on papyrus (or perhaps wood), which had become worm-eaten. King Shabaka decreed that a fair copy of this ancient text should be cut on a large slab of black stone so that it could be erected as an offering to Ptah in his temple at Memphis. The vocabulary and script of the text on the Shabaka Stone is archaic; however, the grammar is not. There is no evidence that in the Archaic Period, the era to which the original of the text on the stone purports to date, the Egyptians could do more than write short, simple, unconnected sentences. It was only by Dynasty IV that they had developed the ability to write using a more complex grammar. It is doubtful, therefore, whether the text on the Shabaka Stone, which does employ fairly complex sentence constructions and verb-forms, could have been copied from a document composed as early as the Archaic Period; and it is more probable that it was written towards the end of the Old Kingdom as a form of propaganda against Ptah's then rival, Re.

The Shabaka Stone inscription says that in the beginning, Chaos reigned. Then Ptah appeared on the Primeval Mound as a god in whom were embodied several forms: Ptah-Nun; Ptah-Ta-tanen; Ptah-Nefertem and five more, the names of which have been lost. By the effort of his heart and mind, Ptah created Nun and his female counterpart, Nunet. In their turn Nun and Nunet brought forth Atum, who became the Thought of Ptah. Then Thoth came into being as the Tongue of Ptah. Thus did the priests of Ptah give their god an ascendency over his two chief rivals – he had existed before they did, and, indeed, was their creator just as he was the creator and mover of the innermost being of every living thing:

> And it came to pass that Heart and Tongue gained power over every other member, teaching that he, Ptah, was the heart in every breast and the tongue in every mouth of gods as well as of men, of cattle and of all living things.

Memphite theology teaches that Ptah's Company of Gods form part of him as his teeth and lips. The teeth correspond to the seed of Atum and the lips to his hands, but whereas the priests of Heliopolis taught that Atum began the creation of the world through an act of masturbation or, alternatively, by spitting, Memphis insisted on a far more intellectual concept: Ptah's teeth and lips are part of that great mouth which gave all things their names:

Every divine word came into being through that which the Heart of Ptah thought and the Tongue of Ptah commanded. Thus every kind of work and every handicraft, and everything done with the arms, and every motion of the legs and every action of all the limbs takes place through this command, which is conceived by the heart [or mind: the Egyptians thought that the heart was the seat of man's being and of his intelligence] and brought about by the tongue.

Memphite theology was an intellectual concept rather than a warmly-held belief. It may hold a great appeal for modern theologians but it never made a real impact on the ordinary Egyptian, who preferred his religion to have a more concrete expression.

Ptah was more than a creator god. He was credited with the invention of crafts, and his High Priest was called 'Lord of the Master Craftsmen'. The Greeks identified Ptah with their own blacksmith god, the lame Hephaistos; and the Romans thought of him as Vulcan. Ptah was also the patron deity of kings. As such, he was closely connected with the ceremony which, in dynastic times, replaced the prehistoric ritual of the slaughter of the tribal chieftain whose powers had become weakened with age. This ceremony, the *Heb-Sed* or Jubilee, was usually celebrated during the thirtieth year of a king's reign and then repeated at frequent intervals. It was designed to allow a king to renew his vital forces by magical means.

One of the rituals of the *Heb-Sed* was a symbolic race run by the king around the walls of his capital city. During this 'race' the king took possession of the city; and incidentally proved that he was fit to rule. If he felt unable to complete the run himself, he was allowed to employ a runner! During Dynasty III, a tomb was built for King Djoser at Sakkara in the form of a six-stepped pyramid. The pyramid was at the centre of a complex of buildings and courtyards, the whole of which was surrounded by a white limestone enclosure wall, some 10 metres high, with a peripheral length of about 1,600 metres, built in imitation of the white-painted mud-brick walls of Memphis.

The space between the pyramid and the enclosure wall was filled, on the southern and eastern sides, with the ceremonial buildings in which the king celebrated his Jubilee, in this world and the next. The culmination of the ceremony was reached when the king, or his substitute, ran round the enclosure wall; and beneath the southern section of the wall lies a 'tomb' in which Djoser is depicted on blue faience tiles eternally running his *Heb-Sed* race.

Ptah was at the pinnacle of importance during the first three dynasties of Egyptian history, when the kings in Memphis, the site of his cult, flourished. The city of Memphis remained throughout Egyptian history the main home of Ptah. When Menes first built his new capital, he called it *Inb-Hdj* ('The (City of the) White Wall'), by which he probably meant the royal residence rather than the city wall. Ptah was often referred to as 'He-who-is-south-of-his-wall', and, indeed, his temple was built to the south of the city. During the Old Kingdom, kings built their pyramids near The (City of the) White Wall. It is the name of

Heb-sed (Jubilee) Court,
Step Pyramid of King
Djoser, Sakkara.

one of these pyramids, *Mn-Nfr* ('The Established and Beautiful Pyramid'), built in Dynasty VI by Pepi I, that was adopted eventually as the name of the whole city. In Coptic, *Mn-Nfr* was pronounced, and spelled, *Menfe*, which the Greeks turned into Memphis.

The cult of Ptah was popular only as long as the King of Egypt was his patron. Memphite theology held no great attraction for the ordinary Egyptian, who did not find the concept of the world being created by thought and tongue congenial, relying, as it does, on an effort of the imagination. By Dynasty IV, Re of Heliopolis had found favour with the king and had, therefore, become state god of Egypt. Meanwhile, Osiris was making headway in the affections of the Egyptians. By the end of the Old Kingdom, Ptah had been eclipsed. His cult-centre, Memphis, lost its status as capital of Egypt when the Middle Kingdom kings chose as their capital Lisht, which was itself displaced as capital in the New Kingdom when Thebes enjoyed the position. However, Memphis remained throughout ancient Egyptian history one of the foremost cities of the country. It was always an administrative centre, and the seat of an important royal residence.

In the New Kingdom Ptah was again elevated to the position of a state god. The chief centre of his cult was, as always, Memphis; but he was worshipped elsewhere also, particularly at Abydos and Thebes, and in Nubia. In Dynasty XIX, Ramesses II paid special attention to Ptah by building for him temples in Nubia at Gerf Hussein, el-Derr and Abu Simbel. In the 1960s AD, these three temples were all affected by the construction of the High Dam at Aswan, with Gerf Hussein disappearing under the waters of Lake Nasser.

At Gerf Hussein, Ptah was worshipped alongside Ptah-Ta-tanen, Hathor and Ramesses II himself. At el-Derr, which was dismantled and re-erected near Amada in AD 1964, he was worshipped together with Re-Horakhty, Amen-Re and Ramesses II. And at Abu Simbel, perhaps the most famous of the rescued Nubian temples, which was dismantled and re-erected on high ground near the original site, he can still be seen in the restored temple as a statue sitting alongside images of Ramesses II, Amen-Re and Re-Horakhty within the innermost sanctuary.

At Memphis, shrines and temples were erected for many deities; but it was always the Temple of Ptah which was considered to be the most important, worthy of enlargement and embellishment by successive generations of kings. It is the name given to the Temple of Ptah during the New Kingdom – the Mansion of the Soul of Ptah, which in ancient Egyptian was *Hwt-Ka-Pth* – that eventually was taken by the Greeks and applied to the whole land as far south as Aswan, thus giving rise to the name by which we call the country, Egypt. In the Late Period, *Hwt-Ka-Pth* was probably pronounced 'Hi-Ku-Ptah', which the Greeks turned into 'Ai-gy-ptos' – Egypt. Today, the Temple of Ptah, once one of the largest in Egypt, lies under the modern village of Mit-Rahina.

Ptah was worshipped in animal as well as in human form. The ancient Egyptians regarded bulls as symbols of procreation and virility, and, since prehistoric times, a bull had been regarded as sacred in the district around Memphis. When Ptah became god of the city, the local sacred bull was associated with him: it became a manifestation of Ptah, his deputy, his 'blessed soul', and, as such, it was given the name *Hap* (now known by the Greek version of the name, Apis). According to Aelian, the cult of Apis was established at Memphis by Menes and lasted until Graeco-Roman times.

The Apis Bull was black with distinctive markings on its hide; it had white spots on its neck and back, a white blaze in the shape of a triangle on its forehead. Apis was never depicted as a human being but always retained its animal form. Only one bull at a time was regarded as Apis rather than the whole species. The particular bull was kept in a sacred stall immediately south of the great Temple of Ptah at Memphis. It was supplied with a harem of cows and often lived to a great age. People from all over the land came bringing gifts but above all to consult Apis' sacred oracle.

When an Apis Bull died, an event which occurred on average once every fourteen years, the search was mounted for his replacement. Just as the lamas of Tibet travelled round their country seeking the boy destined to become Dalai Lama, so the priests of Apis travelled throughout Egypt searching for a black bull-calf whose hide bore the distinctive Apis markings. When the calf was found, it was taken back to Memphis amidst great rejoicing and installed as the new Apis. The calf's mother was cared for by priests until she died, when she was mummified and buried in a special gallery at Sakkara as 'Mother of the Apis'. The calf's owner was suitably rewarded.

Meanwhile, the dead Apis Bull had been taken to a special embalming house within the temple enclosure. The remains of one of these houses, built in the reign of Sheshonq I, together with the great stone tables on which the dead bulls lay during the mummification process, can be seen today at Mit-Rahina. After mummification, the Apis Bull was taken to his tomb in the Royal Necropolis at Sakkara. The sites of these Apis tombs are known from about the reign of Amenhotep III. In Dynasty XIX, Ramesses II ordered the building of an underground gallery to house the mummified Apis Bulls; the work was probably supervised by one of the king's sons, Khamwese, in his capacity of High Priest of Ptah. The gallery, known as the Lesser Vaults, is about 68 metres long; and large niches, which once contained mummified Apis Bulls, are hewn into its walls.

A second gallery, cut at right angles to the Lesser Vaults, was begun in Dynasty XXVI. It is more than 198 metres in length and is known as the Greater Vaults. The first Apis to be buried there died in the fifty-second year of the reign of Psammetichus I (612 BC). The gallery remained in use until the Graeco-Roman period, when it became especially popular during the reign of Ptolemy I who promoted the cult of Serapis (see page 70). Since Serapis was a composite deity formed from Osiris and Apis, the burial place of Apis naturally became a place of pilgrimage for followers of the new god; and Serapis lent his name to the Apis galleries so that they became known as the Serapeum.

In Dynasty XXX, Nectanebo I and Nectanebo II contributed an avenue of human-headed sphinxes to mark the path that led from Memphis to the Serapeum. It was one of these sphinxes, protruding above the sand, that was said to have led the French Egyptologist Auguste Mariette to rediscover the site in AD 1850. When Mariette excavated the Serapeum, he found twenty-four basalt and granite sarcophagi still intact and in position. Sadly, they had been emptied of their contents – mummified Apis Bulls – but their weight, which was up to seventy tons, had prevented their own removal.

Like many ancient Egyptian gods, Ptah was given a wife and child. His wife was a goddess from the Eastern Delta, Sekhmet (see page 172), a lioness goddess, and his son was Nefertem. Although in deference to his mother, Sekhmet, Nefertem was sometimes depicted as a man with a lion's head, he is more often shown in fully human form as a youth seated upon a lotus blossom. On his head he wears either a crown composed of a lotus flanked by two plumes, with two *menat*-amulets suspended from them; or a lotus alone. The lotus links him with the sun (see page 40) and at Heliopolis he was regarded as the young sun. However, at Memphis he was always the son of Ptah and Sekhmet.

Ptah was said to have another son, not by Sekhmet but by a woman named Khredu-ankh. This son was Imhotep, a real man who lived in Dynasty III and was a high official of King Djoser. Imhotep was a sage and magician; and, although his tomb is as yet undiscovered, he is almost certainly buried at Sakkara, near the Step Pyramid which he is thought to have designed for his master, thus becoming the first named architect of stone buildings. A statue base discovered near the entrance to the Step Pyramid enclosure, inscribed with Imhotep's name and titles, gives us some idea of the man's versatility:

Chancellor of the King of Upper and Lower Egypt, the first after the King of Upper Egypt, administrator of the Great Palace, hereditary noble, High Priest of Heliopolis, Imhotep, the builder, the sculptor.

This statue base, which was also inscribed with one of Djoser's names, is probably contemporaneous with the Step Pyramid.

Imhotep was traditionally supposed to have been the author of several books (long since disappeared) and was regarded as the patron of scribes. Typical statuettes show him as a shaven-headed man seated with a papyrus-roll spread open on his knees. It was the custom with scribes to sprinkle a few drops of water from their pots before they began work, in honour not only of Thoth, the scribe of the gods (see page 183), but also of Imhotep, the sage, the scribe. A temple at Sakkara was dedicated to this most famous of scribes. It stood near the Serapeum and was especially popular as a place of pilgrimage in the Late Period. The Greeks called it the Asklepion, an indication that they identified Imhotep (whom they called Imouthes) with their own great god of healing and medicine, Asklepios. Imhotep's reputation as a god of healing brought sick people, especially cripples, from all over Egypt flocking to his temple at Sakkara, and shrines dedicated to him are found in temples such as Karnak, Deir el-Bahri,[32] Deir el-Medina and Philae.

Although Ptah was not the most popular of ancient Egyptian deities, many people considered it worthwhile to make petitions to him. At his temple in Memphis, a large number of votive tablets have been found, carved with representations of ears, or sometimes of eyes. Similar ear-tablets have been discovered in the temple at Deir el-Medina at Thebes. They are the ears of Ptah-hearer-of-prayers, the stone ears of the god into which a petitioner could make his request for help in the confident expectation that Ptah was not inaccessible, that he would listen, something that the Egyptians did not normally expect a state god to do. It is perhaps appropriate that the concluding chorus of Verdi's *Aida*, which received its première in Cairo on 24 December 1871, should echo evocatively across the centuries:

> Oh mighty Ptah, life-giving spirit of the world, we invoke thee . . .
> Oh mighty Ptah!

SOKAR

· ·

In prehistoric times, Sokar was probably worshipped somewhere in the area around Memphis in the form of a fetish. Later, he was considered to be incarnate in a species of hawk, possibly a peregrine falcon, and therefore took shape as a man with the head of a hawk. In the Old Kingdom, Sokar was normally represented sitting upon a throne holding the *waas*-sceptre and an *ankh*-sign in his hands. In the New Kingdom, he often appeared as a hawk-headed mummy holding a flail, a crook and a *waas*-sceptre.

The essential nature of Sokar is obscured by his early association with Ptah. However, the great annual festival celebrated in his honour took place during the fourth month of the season of *akhet*, that is, on the eve of the winter sowing. Two of the rituals performed during the festival were those of hoeing the earth and driving cattle, which would suggest that originally Sokar was an agricultural deity. One of Sokar's earliest functions was patron deity of artisans; but he lost this position to Ptah, and became more specifically the patron of goldsmiths.

From the earliest times, Sokar was considered to be the guardian of the Memphite necropolis, although he was not just a general necropolis-deity: Sokar was more particularly associated with the darkness and decay of the tomb itself. It is ironic that a hawk god should be connected with graves, since hawks are essentially creatures of light and air. However, the Memphite necropolis was in use for centuries before the city of Memphis was built, and Sokar's connection with it probably pre-dates his manifestation as a hawk to a time when he was worshipped as a fetish. In addition, the Egyptians tended to bury their dead in the desert, and hawks are often seen wheeling above the sand. When Ptah became the principal god of Memphis, Sokar joined him there and fulfilled the role of funerary god to Ptah's creator god.

Sokar had many sanctuaries in Lower Egypt, notably at *Rasetau* on the Giza necropolis and at *Pedjushe* on the Sakkara necropolis. In Dynasty XIX, he joined Ptah in Upper Egypt in the memorial temple of Sety I at Abydos, the domain of the funerary god *par excellence*, Osiris. The site of the chief shrine of Sokar, the *Shetayet*, is so far undiscovered. It was probably near the Temple of Ptah in Memphis; perhaps even within the precincts of that temple; and certainly close enough to it for the High Priest of Ptah to hold office in the Temple of Sokar also.

Early in the Old Kingdom, the proximity of the cult-centres of the two deities led Ptah's priests to claim that Ptah had created Sokar, and to link both gods under the compound name of Ptah-Sokar. By the end of the Old Kingdom, Ptah-Sokar had been eclipsed by another deity with funerary associations, Osiris. The similarity between the nature of Osiris and that of Sokar, both being agricultural deities who were connected with death, facilitated a link between them, and in the Middle Kingdom Ptah-Sokar became Ptah-Sokar-Osiris. Ptah-Sokar-Osiris, whose popularity reached its height during the New Kingdom, was often represented as a squat male figure, rather like a pygmy, wearing a beetle on his head to indicate that he has creative powers similar to those of the god, Khepri.

From the time that the city of Memphis was founded, a ceremony of 'going round the walls' of the city was enacted each year to mark the king's accession. This ritual was eventually incorporated into another ceremony in which Sokar was carried out of his temple to join the king in rites consisting of hoeing the earth and digging canals or ditches. For this ceremony, the cult-statue of Sokar was placed in the portable shrine that was characteristic of Sokar, the *Henu*-Barque. This boat was of a unique design: it had a high prow shaped like a horned, oryx-like animal; and a funerary chest, surmounted by a hawk, stood in the centre of it. The whole thing was set on the runners of a special sledge called the *mefekh* sledge. Originally, the *Henu*-Barque was dragged in procession on this sledge; however, eventually the structure was placed upon carrying poles and transported on the shoulders of up to sixteen priests.

These two ceremonies eventually became the great Festival of Sokar, celebrated annually on the twenty-sixth day of the fourth month of the *akhet* season from at least as far back as the early part of the Old Kingdom. The festival took place not only in Memphis itself but also in the royal funerary temple wherever that happened to be. In Dynasty XX, for instance, the Festival of Sokar was held in Ramesses III's memorial temple of Medinet Habu in Western Thebes, where it was one of the most richly endowed of all the feasts celebrated in that temple.

By the Ptolemaic period, Sokar's festival had become assimilated with the Festival of Osiris; and Sokar himself had turned into little more than a variant of that ubiquitous god.

SEKHMET

· ·

Sekhmet, a lioness goddess whose name means 'The Powerful One', was worshipped wherever a wadi opened out at the desert edge, for in ancient Egypt, those were the places where lions might be found, having come down from the desert to drink at water-holes on the edge of the cultivation; and to prey on cattle and sometimes on people. A late tradition held that the worship of Sekhmet was introduced into Egypt from the Sudan, where lions were more numerous. However, her chief sanctuary was at Memphis, where she was considered to be the wife of Ptah and the mother of Nefertem, and thus a member of the Triad of Memphis.

Sekhmet, who was usually depicted as a woman with the head of a lioness, was believed to be a manifestation of the enraged Eye of Re who devoured the enemies of the Sun God. This fierce goddess was mistress of war and strife; she helped the king to slaughter his enemies against whom he was sometimes said to 'rage like Sekhmet'. Paradoxically, she was also mistress of healing who drove away sickness. The bloodthirsty goddess who could kill could also cure. Just as this Lady of the Messengers of Death could visit them upon Egypt in the form of epidemics, so she could be persuaded to remove them through the performance of the rite of 'appeasing Sekhmet'. The title 'Priest of Sekhmet' came to mean 'doctor', possibly because her priests were entrusted with the task of driving out the evil spirits that the ancient Egyptians thought were the causes of sickness; and who better to fight demons than the goddess of war.

Sekhmet was identified with several other female deities, Hathor, Bastet, Mut and Pakhet (see below) among them. In the original version of how the Eye of Re destroyed his enemies, it was Hathor who played the role of Sekhmet (see page 43). Bastet was a more sympathetic form of Sekhmet in the shape of a cat; and Mut was associated with Sekhmet when the worship of the lioness goddess became popular in Thebes. There, in the Temple of Mut at Karnak, Amenhotep III set up seated statues of Sekhmet, nearly six hundred of which are extant, thirty or so being in the British Museum; these very fine statues, carved in grey diorite, average nearly 2 metres in height.

Pakhet, whose name means 'She-who-scratches', was the local lioness goddess of Beni Hasan, the necropolis of the Middle Kingdom governors of the 16th Nome of Upper Egypt, the Oryx Nome, which lies on the east bank of the Nile

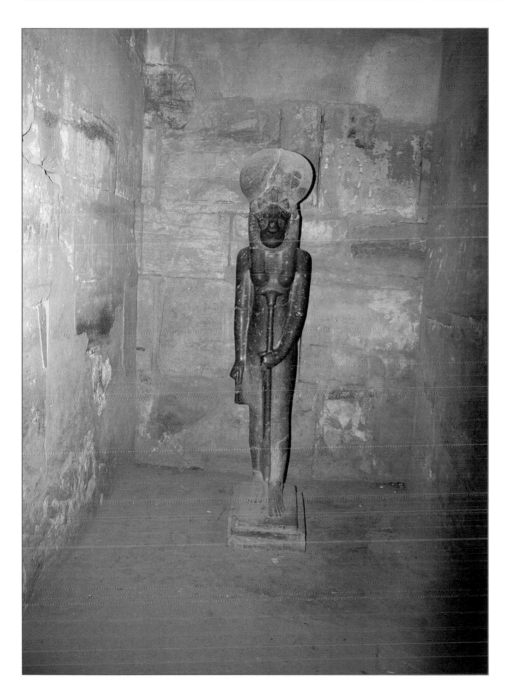

Sekhmet: black granite statue in its shrine in the Temple of Ptah, Karnak. The statue is lit from above through an opening in the roof but is otherwise in darkness. Among local people, the statue has a reputation for evil. One story tells of how, at some unspecified time in the past, seven boys (seven is a magical number to the Egyptians) who were employed on an archaeological excavation as basket boys to remove rubble were buried at the feet of the statue by a fall of sand and stones. Their bodies were never found – the inference being that the goddess had devoured them.

some 23 km south of el-Minya. In Dynasty XVIII, during the reign of Hatshepsut, a temple dedicated to Pakhet was built just south of Beni Hasan. Later on, the Greeks must have thought that Pakhet had more in common with the gentler Bastet than with the fierce Sekhmet, for they called the place Speos Artemidos or 'The Cave of Artemis', the goddess they identified with Bastet. In the Speos Artemidos, Pakhet was worshipped as the 'Goddess-of-the-mouth-of-the-wadi' and 'She-who-opens-the-ways-of-the-stormy-rains', epithets which could equally well be applied to the lioness goddess *par excellence*, Sekhmet.

ANUBIS

· ·

Anubis, a very ancient Upper Egyptian god of the dead, was usually represented as a jackal-headed man. In southern Egypt, jackals are found to this day roaming the high ground at the desert edge, the very place where the ancient Egyptians buried their dead. The jackal has a habit of prowling round cemeteries, scavenging. What more natural, then, than that the ancient Egyptians should associate the animal with death and go on from there to revere jackals out of fear that they might molest the dead in their graves.

Other jackal gods such as Wepwawet (see page 64) were worshipped in Egypt; however, Anubis was the most important of them. Although he was the totem deity of the 17th Upper Egyptian Nome (el-Qeis in Middle Egypt, which the Greeks called Cynopolis or City of the Dogs), from a very early date his worship extended throughout the whole of the land. It was also at an early date that Anubis became identified with an even older deity, *Imy-wt*, 'He-who-is-in-his-wrappings'. The fetish of *Imy-wt*, consisting of a pole from which hangs a headless animal skin containing solutions for washing or embalming a dead body, became the fetish of Anubis.

Before the advent of Osiris, Anubis was the great funerary god and Judge of the Dead. In many Old Kingdom *mastaba*-tombs, the prayers for survival after death that were carved on the walls were addressed to Anubis in his capacity as the god who led the deceased to the Afterlife. When Osiris rose to prominence as chief mortuary god, the priests of Heliopolis gave Anubis a place in their scheme of things as the bastard son of Osiris and Nephthys (see page 112) and the faithful protector of Isis. Anubis it was who embalmed the dead Osiris' body and wrapped him in bandages, thus making the first mummy.

In the beginning, Anubis as mortuary god was chiefly concerned with the king; however, gradually he became the god of death for everyone. His four most important titles reflect his role: he was 'He-who-is-set-upon-his-mountain' (to guard the necropolis); 'Lord of the Necropolis'; 'Chief of the Divine Pavilion' (where mummification procedures were carried out); and 'He-who-belongs-to-the-mummy-wrappings'.

Because Anubis had prepared the mummy of Osiris, he became the patron of embalmers. In the necropolis of Memphis at Sakkara, the embalmers' quarters of at least the Late Period and the Ptolemaic era were specifically under the guardianship of Anubis, so much so that modern Egyptologists who have been excavating the area since the 1960s have named it the Anubieion.

The priests in charge of preparing the body for burial are thought to have worn jackal-headed masks in order to impersonate Anubis. It is probable that the priests who conducted the burial ceremonies at the tomb also impersonated him, for on funerary papyri such as those inscribed for the scribe, Ani, and for the priestess of Amen-Re, Anhai, both of which are now among the finest papyri in the British Museum, Anubis is depicted holding the mummy of the deceased at the door of the tomb. On the arrival of the deceased in the Afterlife, it was Anubis who supervised the weighing of the heart before Osiris at the Judgement of the Dead: he read the scales, and the fate of the deceased depended upon his report, which was accepted without question by Osiris and the Assessor Gods.

Although Anubis is said to be a jackal god, representations of him in wholly animal form sometimes show an animal that is more like a dog, a fox or a wolf. The Greek name for the city of the jackal god, Wepwawet (see page 62), Lycopolis or Wolf City, illustrates the extent of the confusion that was felt. Perhaps the most famous figure of Anubis is that found by Howard Carter in the tomb of Tutankhamun, which he discovered in 1922: at the entrance to the Treasury, a life-sized recumbent Anubis-animal, made of wood overlaid with black resin, lay upon a gilded shrine set upon four carrying poles. The figure of the god was draped with a linen shirt, date-marked to the seventh year of the

Anubis: relief in the tomb of Horemheb, Valley of the Kings, Luxor.

Anubis bending over
mummy: tomb of the
workman, Sennedjem, Deir
el-Medina, Dynasty XIX.

reign of Akhenaten, under which was a gossamer-thin linen shawl, tied at Anubis' throat. A linen scarf was around his neck, like a leash.

Tutankhamun's Anubis, like so many others, bears many features characteristic of a dog: long muzzle, eyes with round pupils, five-toed forefeet and four-toed hindfeet. But the tail, drooping down the side of the shrine, is long and straight; and club-shaped at the tip, more like the brush of a fox than the curved tail of a dog, which is normally carried in an upright position rather than low down like that of a jackal, wolf or fox. Howard Carter recorded having seen two animals resembling this jackal-like dog, one in 1926, the other in 1928, but neither had the characteristic tail, a fact which led him to suppose that the original Anubis-animal may have been a jackal crossed with a sub-genus of the canine family.[33]

Whatever his origin, the ever-vigilant Anubis was deemed to be the lord of the necropolis who presided over burial rites and guarded the dead on their way to the Afterlife.

NEIT

• •

Neit was a very ancient goddess whose cult-centre was at Sais in the Western Delta, on the right bank of the Rosetta branch of the Nile. The ancient Egyptians probably pronounced her name 'Neet'; the Greeks later softened the final 't' to a 'th', and it is this pronunciation, 'Neeth', that is sometimes used today, with many writers spelling her name Neith. The standard depiction of the goddess shows her as a woman wearing the diadem associated with Lower Egypt, the Red Crown. The oldest name of this crown was *Nt*, which leads one to suppose that Neit's name means 'She-of-the-Lower-Egyptian-Crown', making her the personification of the diadem.

There were two emblems sacred to Neit: one consisted of two arrows crossed in front of a shield; the other, ⋈, is often said to be a shuttle, thus connecting Neit with weaving. However, the shape of the emblem is entirely wrong for it to have been a shuttle, which must surely taper at the ends to facilitate movement between the warp threads. Old Kingdom depictions of the object, which show it in detail, reveal that it represents two bows placed back-to-back in a case of some kind. These ancient emblems of Neit, shield, arrows and bows, indicate that in predynastic times she must have been a goddess of hunting and warfare who only later became the personification of the Lower Egyptian Crown. However, Neit had many aspects besides these.

Neit was a primeval bisexual goddess who was said to have created the world and to be the virgin mother of the sun. A late version of how she accomplished this is found in the Temple of Khnum at Esna (see page 189). The Esna Creation Legend tells of how Neit emerged from the Primeval Waters and brought into being the Primeval Mound by uttering its name. She then rested on the mound, which later became the land upon which Esna was built. Next, Neit created light and the primordial gods, and prophesied the birth of a child, the sun. When this child appeared on the horizon, Neit was able to leave Esna and travel through Egypt to take up residence at Sais in the Delta, which became her cult-centre.

At an early date, the worship of Neit was widespread in the Delta and Lower Egypt, where she was regarded as the Great Mother Goddess, the patron of the North, with her crown, the *Nt*-crown, having been adopted as the symbol of sovereignty over Lower Egypt. When Menes united Upper and Lower Egypt, he adopted the title *nsw-bit*, which means, in effect, King of Upper and Lower

Hieroglyphic signs *nsw-bit* from the memorial temple of Ramesses II at Abydos.

Egypt, in other words, *nsw* 'he-who-belongs-to-the-reed' (symbol of Upper Egypt) and *bit* 'he-who-belongs-to-the-bee' (symbol of Lower Egypt). Why a reed and a bee should have been chosen as symbols of their respective halves of the country is not clear; however, in the case of the bee, it is known that the Temple of Neit at Sais was called 'The Mansion of the Bee' (*Ḥwt-bit*), and a connection between Neit and bees would have been ample reason for a bee to become the symbol of Lower Egypt. What this connection was between Neit and bees is as yet unknown – her sacred animal, kept in her temple at Sais, seems to have been a cat.

Menes married a princess of Lower Egypt named Neit-hotep (Neit-is-satisfied), one of three queens in Dynasty I who had Neit as a component in their names, Her-Neit (Pleasing-to-Neit) and Meryet-Neit (Beloved-of-Neit) being the other two. It is possible that the husbands of these demonstrably Lower Egyptian princesses married them in order to legitimize their rule in the North.

Menes' son, Hor-aha, built a shrine for Neit at Sais, the oldest temple for which we have any direct evidence. It was recorded on an ivory label, found in AD 1900 by Petrie at Abydos, on which is engraved a stylized representation of a hut-shrine. The lattice-work hut is surrounded by a fence, also lattice; in front of the hut is a standard bearing the shield and arrows of Neit, and the entrance to the enclosure is marked by two masts with flags.

Neit's cult-centre, Sais (*Sau* in ancient Egyptian; today called Sa el-Hagar), was the capital of the 5th Nome of Lower Egypt, the nome standard of which consisted of her emblem of two arrows crossed over a shield. The city rose to political prominence in the eighth century BC, when, around 725 BC, a local prince, Tefnakhte, challenged the Kushite kings of Dynasty XXV for supremacy in Lower Egypt. In 664 BC, Tefnakhte's successors, whom Manetho grouped into Dynasty XXVI, became the rulers of Egypt. Sais, their native city, became the capital of the country, a great city in which were built the temples and palaces of the kings of the so-called Saite Dynasty, who were buried in the precincts of the Temple of Neit, their patron goddess. The first king of Dynasty XXVI, Psammetichus I, drove out invading Assyrians and Kushites from Egypt, and having restored the country to a unified state, began a period in which every aspect of life in Egypt flourished.

The Saite Period was a mixture of looking back to the past for inspiration for artistic and intellectual achievements; and of opening up – of the country to Greek commerce, and of the written language to a new cursive script, demotic, which made use of an entirely new vocabulary which is obviously derived from the dialect of Egyptian that was spoken in the Delta. The Persian invasion of Egypt in 525 BC put an end to the Saite Period, which had achieved a renaissance in art, architecture and literature. As patron goddess of the Dynasty, Neit prospered. Her shrines were embellished; but so also were those of other deities, including Amun, whose temples at Thebes were left under the direction of the Divine Wives of Amun (see page 145).

Neit was associated with several other deities, chiefly with Khnum, whom she made her deputy as Creator God; with Sobek, the Crocodile God (see page 108) whose mother she was said to be; with Osiris, as one of the four goddesses who protected sarcophagi and Canopic jars (see page 85); and with Amunet, the primordial goddess of Hermopolis (see page 182).

Although Neit herself was a significant figure in the Egyptian pantheon from an early date, she achieved the height of her popularity only very late. This popularity lasted from the Saite Period, through the Persian occupation when Neit continued to receive attention not only from Egyptians but also from Greeks who lived in Egypt, to the time of the Macedonian Greeks who drove out the Persians from the country in 332 BC. The Greeks paid Neit the compliment of identifying her with their goddess of wisdom, Athena.

THOTH

· ·

Thoth was a lunar god worshipped in the form of an ibis (*Ibis religiosa*, the sacred ibis) or a baboon, and usually portrayed in reliefs as a man with the head of an ibis, often holding a reed pen in his hand. His cult dates to Dynasty I, if not before, for his standard appears on slate palettes of the predynastic period. In hieroglyphs, his name was written 𓅝, *Djhuty*, and is thought to mean 'He of *Djhut*', *Djhut* presumably being his place of origin. The whereabouts of *Djhut* is unknown but it was probably in the Delta.

Very little information has survived concerning the progenitor of Thoth. One ancient legend says that he was the son of Horus, and that he emerged from the forehead of Seth whom Horus had succeeded in impregnating with his seed by tricking him into swallowing it hidden in some lettuces. A late version of the legend modified it by making the seed of Horus appear on Seth's forehead as a golden disk which was seized by the already existing Thoth who placed it on his own head as an ornament (see page 107).

From early dynastic times, the main cult-centre of Thoth was a town in Middle Egypt that the ancient Egyptians called *Khemenu*, or 'The Town of the Eight', which is today called el-Eshmunein. When Thoth first arrived there, he found several ancient deities already installed: a hare, a baboon, and the four frogs and four serpents after whom the town was named. Thoth rapidly absorbed or replaced these indigenous deities of *Khemenu*. The hare, a goddess named Wenet, who was sometimes regarded as a demon of the Underworld, survived largely as the name of the nome of which *Khemenu* was the capital, the Hare, or 15th, Nome of Upper Egypt. The baboon became a representation of the spirit of Thoth and was incorporated into his cult. The eight frog- and serpent-deities became his Company of Gods or Ogdoad.

Ogdoad, which means 'group of eight', is the name given to the four pairs of deities who, according to tradition at *Khemenu*, represented the elemental forces that were in play before the creation of the world. The male halves of these pairs were frog-headed, the female halves serpent-headed, and their names were: Nun and Nunet, the male and female personifications of the Primeval Waters; Heh and Hehet, the male and female personifications of infinite space; Kek and Keket – darkness; Amun and Amunet – invisibility. At *Khemenu* they were said to be the oldest gods in the world, the fathers and

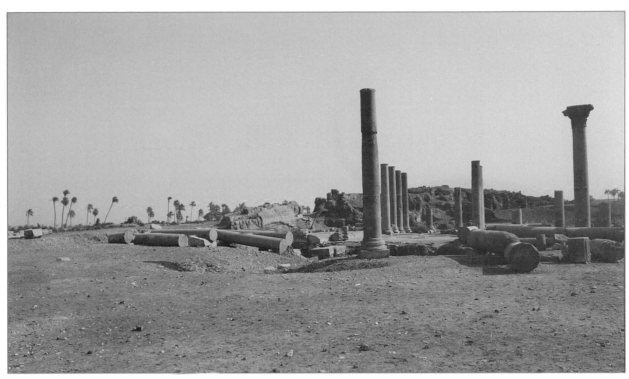

el-Eshmunein: columns of a
Christian basilica built with
the re-used columns of a
Ptolemaic temple

mothers of the Sun God, for whom they created the sacred mound at *Khemenu* so that he could rest upon it.

The Ogdoad of *Khemenu* was greatly respected at Thebes by the priesthood of Amun, for Amun had the same name as one of these primordial deities whose partner, Amunet, was sometimes regarded at Thebes as the Mother Goddess, the consort of Amun alongside the goddess Mut. Amun of *Khemenu* and Amun of Thebes may or may not have been the same god, but certainly during the Graeco-Roman period the Ogdoad was paid particular attention, not least because the Eight Gods were believed to be buried under the temple of Medinet Habu, on the west bank at Thebes, where, every ten years, the last kings of Egypt came to offer libations to these, their primeval ancestors.

Thoth was scribe to the gods, and he was also their messenger. Hence, the Greeks identified him with their own messenger of the gods, Hermes; and during the Graeco-Roman period, Thoth was worshipped by both Greeks and Egyptians as Hermes Trismegistos (Thrice-great Hermes). The Greeks renamed Thoth's town, *Khemenu*, calling it Hermopolis (City of Hermes). Today, the name of the town in which the Ogdoad originated is a reminder of the one that it bore in honour of the Eight Primeval Gods: the Arabic el-Eshmunein is derived from the Coptic 'Shmun', which in turn was derived from *Khemenu*. Thus is the Ogdoad commemorated.

Thoth as a baboon: granite
statue 4.5 metres high
without a base, dated to
the reign of Amenhotep III.
El-Eshmunein.

Thoth was above all the god of wisdom, connected with everything that had to do with intellectual pursuits in both arts and sciences. He was said to be the inventor of hieroglyphic writing, which was called *mdw-nṯr*, 'The words of god';

Ibis-headed Thoth and hawk-headed Horus purifying the king with water in the ceremony known as the Baptism of Pharaoh: relief from Kom Ombo Temple.

and acted as scribe to the gods. Thoth was credited with having written with his own hand forty-two books containing all the wisdom of the world. Some of these books contained the laws of Egypt, of which Thoth was the guardian; others were books of magic, for Thoth was a great magician, rivalled only by Isis; yet others contained the annals of Egypt. Since the moon was regarded as the natural measurer of time, Thoth, a moon god, was the master of chronology and counting; as a moon god he was often depicted wearing a crescent moon on his head. Thoth was also a royal god, who attended the coronation of the king and, together with Horus, purified him before that and other ceremonies in the ritual known as 'The Baptism of Pharaoh', in which Thoth and Horus pour water over the king in order to purify him. Perhaps it was this aspect of the god that was the inspiration for the name of several Eighteenth-Dynasty kings – Thutmose, which means 'Thoth is (re)born'.

The female counterpart to Thoth, who was variously regarded as his wife or daughter, was the goddess of writing and books, the keeper of the Royal Annals, Seshat. Unlike Thoth, Seshat was never a deity of the people: she belonged to the king alone. It was Seshat who wrote the name of the king on the leaves of the *Ished* (Persea) Tree, each sacred leaf representing a year of the king's life as allotted to him by the gods. It was Seshat who helped the king to measure out the foundations of temples; and temple reliefs show her, dressed in a leopard-skin and wearing her fetish, a pair of cow's horns inverted over a flower, upon her

Seshat, flanked by king and Horus of Edfu, performing the ceremony of 'Stretching the Cord': relief in Pronaos, Temple of Horus, Edfu.

head, helping the king to perform this task by 'stretching the cord' to measure and mark them out.

Thoth played an important part in the mythologies of several other deities. At Memphis he was said to be the tongue of Ptah (see page 164); at Heliopolis he was the mind and tongue of Re personified as Sia and Hu respectively; and also the messenger who brought back the Eye of Re and restored it to its rightful place (see page 34). In the Osiris legend it was Thoth who taught Isis the spell for restoring Osiris' ability to procreate (see page 76) and helped her to reassemble the pieces of Osiris' dismembered body (see page 63); and it was Thoth who expelled poison from her son, Horus (see page 78).

In the Osirian version of the Judgement of the Dead, Thoth and his baboon play an important part. Vignettes of the Judgement scene on New Kingdom funerary papyri show Anubis weighing the heart of the deceased in a balance, supervised by the baboon, Thoth's *alter ego*. Thoth is standing by ready to record the verdict.

Some 7 km west of *Khemenu* lies a necropolis that dates from about the fifth

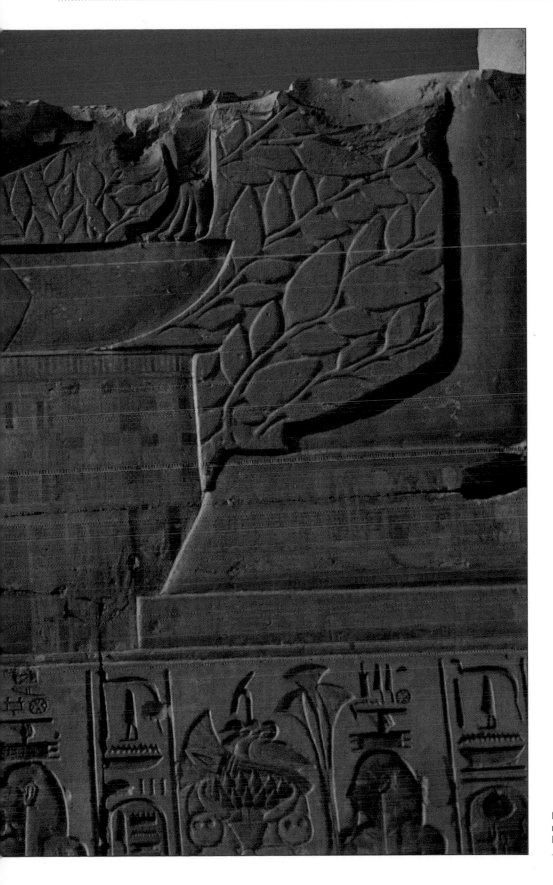

Leaves of a Persea Tree,
memorial temple of
Ramesses II, Abydos.

Thoth, taking Seshat's place, writing the name of Ramesses II on the leaves of the Persea Tree, hypostyle hall, Karnak.

century BC and is now known as Tuna el-Gebel. The necropolis is the site of an extensive underground gallery, the Ibeum, so named because it is the place which houses the mummified bodies of thousands of ibises, and also of baboons, many of them still in the pottery containers in which they were buried – testament to the great popularity of Thoth at that period. Nearby was a large artificial lake which was kept watered by means of a giant waterwheel. Palm trees were planted round the lake, making it into a place fit for the sacred ibises to live in.

Another huge burial place for the baboons and ibises sacred to Thoth is at Sakkara. Since AD 1964 excavations undertaken there by the Egypt Exploration Society of London have uncovered underground galleries for the burials of baboons, out of which lead further galleries crammed from floor to ceiling with mummified ibises in pottery containers. The extent of these catacombs is as yet unknown, for the archaeologists are faced with the daunting task of removing thousands of ibis mummies before exploring further.

Thoth's role as god of writing connected him closely with scribes. It was the custom for scribes to make a small libation to Thoth at the start of each day's work – they simply poured out a drop of water onto the ground from the pot in which they dipped their brushes. In a bureaucratic society such as ancient Egypt scribes enjoyed positions of great power, and the immense popularity of Thoth at all times was due in no small measure to his role as their patron deity. Thoth was the greatest scribe of all.

KHNUM

• •

Khnum was one of the oldest gods of Egypt, revered since predynastic times in the area of the First Cataract on Egypt's southern border. His cult-centre was at *Abu*, capital of the 1st Nome of Upper Egypt, the *Abu* or Elephant Nome, which the Greeks called Elephantine. The town of *Abu* was on an island – Elephant Island – in the middle of the Nile opposite the modern town of Aswan.

Khnum was originally worshipped in the form of a flat-horned ram of the species *Ovis longipes palaeoaegypticus*, which became extinct somewhere around 2000 BC. He can appear as a ram or as a ram-headed man. Because the ram was valued for its procreative powers, Khnum was thought to be a creator of life. He was sometimes depicted as a ram-headed man moulding a human figure, usually a king, and his *ka* or double on a potter's turntable; hence his appellation, 'The Potter God'. The most famous scene of Khnum in this role is found in the Temple of Hatshepsut at Deir el-Bahri, where he is shown modelling the queen and her *ka* on his potter's turntable.

Each person modelled by Khnum was given an allotted life-span. This life-span was personified as Shay or 'That-which-is-ordained', and came to have the broader meaning of 'Fate', which the Greeks rendered as Agathodaimon and the Turks as Kismet. As a deity, Shay was given two partners, the goddesses of fate, Meskhenet (see page 192) and Renenutet (see page 80).

Khnum was closely connected in the minds of the ancient Egyptians with the Inundation, which was thought to start in a sacred pool on Elephant Island; and with the Nile, of whose mythological source at Biga (see page 62) he was the guardian. The cult of Khnum was widespread from an early date, and it is perhaps ironic that his most famous sanctuary should be the Temple of Khnum at Esna, which was built towards the end of Egyptian history. The temple, of which only the great twenty-four-column hypostyle hall, built by the Roman Emperors Claudius and Vespasian in the first century AD, stands today, was dedicated not only to Khnum but also to several other deities, including Neit.

It was the fish sacred to Neit, the Nile perch (*Latus niloticus*), that was the sacred animal of Esna, causing the Greeks to name the town Latopolis (City of the Perch). The Arabic name of the town, Esna, was derived from the ancient Egyptian *(Ta)-sny*. Because of its position, on the left bank of the Nile some 50 km south of Luxor, at a place where the routes across the desert to the Sudan meet, Esna was an important town from at least the Middle Kingdom.

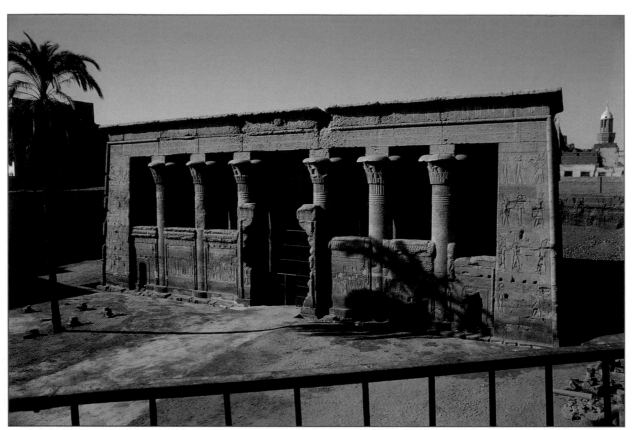

Temple of Khnum, Esna.
Only the Roman hall of
columns remains, standing
in a hollow while all around
has accumulated the rubble
of centuries of later
buildings.

There are numerous ritual and religious texts carved on the walls of the
temple, the last dating to the reign of the Emperor Decius. They tell us, for
instance, that the creation of the world was performed by Neit, who, after her
initial creative work, departed for her own city of Sais leaving Khnum to
continue the task which he did by fashioning living things on his potter's
turntable. After many years of creating and maintaining life, Khnum became
tired of the incessant effort. He therefore thought of a device to relieve him of his
burden: he placed a potter's turntable in the womb of all female creatures, thus
transmitting to them his creative powers. From then on, he was able to
concentrate on his task of maintaining the creation of the life-force.

The Esna theories of the origin of life are exceptionally interesting: once beings
had been created, it was necessary to animate them and fill them with the breath
of life. There were two elements – water and air – which, in certain conditions
and when mixed in given proportions, allowed life to be born and to develop.
This vital breath, which was in the possession of the god, was said to penetrate
the egg to animate the chick before the breaking of the shell; to descend to the
bottom of the waters to vivify the fish; to give colour to the leaves of the trees;
and to cure the sick.

Khnum had three consorts: Heket, Anukis and Satis. Heket was a primordial
creator goddess who took the form of a frog. The oldest centre of her cult was in
the Elephant Nome where she was, for a long time, regarded as the wife of

Part of a limestone relief
from the Dynasty XVIII
Memorial Temple of Queen
Hatshepsut at Deir el-Bahri,
Thebes. The ram-headed
god Khnum is shown
fashioning Hatshepsut and
her *ka* upon his potter's
turntable, with the frog-
headed goddess Heket in
attendance.

Khnum forming a king on
his potter's turntable: relief
in *mammisi*, Temple of Isis,
Philae.

Khnum. Eventually Heket's position in the Elephant Nome was usurped by Satis (see below), and the centre of her cult moved to the Fayum Oasis. Hekat helped Osiris rise from the dead, an activity which was later remembered by Egyptian Christians, for whom the frog was the symbol of resurrection. However, her chief function was as goddess of childbirth: at royal births she acted as midwife.

A story written on papyrus, probably during the Hyksos period (*c.* 1648–1550 BC), and now in Berlin Museum as Papyrus Westcar, illustrates Heket's role as Divine Midwife: the wife of a priest of Re, a woman named Reddjedet, was pregnant with three children sired by Re, each child destined to become King of Egypt. And so Re decided to send a Company of Gods to help Reddjedet in her time of travail. He commanded that Isis, Nephthys, Meskhenet and Heket should go to the aid of Reddjedet, and so the four goddesses set out, disguised as musicians; and Khnum went with them to carry their baggage! The goddesses duly delivered Reddjedet: Isis and Nephthys supported her; and Meskhenet, who was the personification of the birth-stool, stood by ready to act as the good fairy who predicted the future of the newly born child. But it was Heket who brought each of Reddjedet's three children safely into the world.[34]

Anukis, who was a concubine of Khnum, was goddess of the cataract on Egypt's southern border, where her chief shrine was on the island of Seheil. She is normally depicted as a woman wearing a headdress composed of what might be the feathers of a red parrot, perhaps indicating that her origins were in the Sudan, where such birds were found. The Greeks identified her with Hestia, goddess of the hearth.

Satis, whom the Greeks identified with Hera, the wife of Zeus, was the daughter of Khnum and Anukis; she replaced Heket as the consort of her father, probably at a very early date because she herself was an ancient deity who is mentioned in the Pyramid Texts. She was depicted as a woman wearing the White Crown of Upper Egypt flanked by two gazelle horns, suggesting that originally she came from a region where gazelles proliferated – perhaps the Sudan. Her name seems to be derived from the word 'shoot' (arrows) or 'pour' (water), which probably means that she was a local goddess of hunting who became a goddess of the Inundation. Her cult-centre, like that of Anukis, was on the island of Seheil.

Satis became fused with Sothis, presumably because their names have a similar sound. Sothis was the Egyptian name for what we call Sirius, the Dog Star; and was thought to be the goddess responsible for the Inundation. She was depicted as a woman wearing on her head a five-pointed star. In turn, Sothis was fused with Isis; and during the Late Period they were worshipped under the joint name of Isisothis.

Khnum, Anukis and Satis together formed the Great Triad of the Elephant Nome, where above all they played their parts as guardians and donors of the waters of the Nile, who 'dispensed the cool water coming from the Elephant Nome'.

MIN

· ·

Min was one of the most ancient Egyptian gods, a deity of fertility whose origins are lost in the mists of time but whose sacred object (see page 194) is often found on predynastic painted vases. The statues of Min discovered at Koptos by Petrie during his excavations of AD 1893 are probably predynastic in date and, at over 4 metres high, are considered to be the oldest examples of large-scale sculpture in Egypt. They are headless but show Min standing in what was later to become his typical pose. The legs of the statues are not separated but carved in one piece, suggesting the great antiquity of the figures since individual delineation of these limbs in sculpture in the round was not practised until well on in the Old Kingdom.

Min was usually depicted as a man standing upright wearing on his head a cap surmounted by two tall plumes. His legs are never seen, apparently being wrapped in mummy bandages, but more probably copying the style of his predynastic statues. One arm, bent at the elbow, is raised and outstretched, its hand open; above it floats a flail. The other arm is tucked under his robe, from which projects his penis, huge and erect. Any area of skin not covered by a garment is painted black: in dynastic times, it was one of the duties of the High Priest of Min to make up the bituminous substance with which the cult statue of the god was ritually painted, black being the colour of the fertile soil of Egypt and therefore symbolic of regeneration.

The worship of Min was universal throughout Egyptian history; but two cities were particularly associated with him: *Gebtu* and *Khent-Min*. *Gebtu* (called Koptos by the Greeks; now known as Qift) lies on the east bank of the Nile some 40 km north of Luxor, at the terminus of the route which leads from the Red Sea to the Nile. It achieved great importance at an early date because of its geographical position: mining expeditions to the Eastern Desert and trading expeditions to the Red Sea had their starting point at *Gebtu*, which therefore became the obvious choice to become capital of the 5th Nome of Upper Egypt. The original god of *Gebtu* seems to have been a phallic deity named Rahes or Aahes, who appears in the Pyramid Texts as 'Regent of the Land of the South'. Rahes and Min, depicted as falcons, formed the nome standard, although later on, when Horus and Isis became popular in *Gebtu*, the two falcons of the nome standard were identified with Horus and Min.

One of the statues of Min found by Petrie at Koptos, 1893–4. Height: 4.22 metres. (Ashmolean Museum, Oxford)

Min of *Gebtu* (Min of Koptos) was considered to be the tutelary deity of nomads, hunters, miners and travellers, for the Eastern Desert was his special domain. As a deity of the desert, Min was associated with the thunder that was thought to emanate therefrom. Thus, when the Canaanite-Phoenician god of thunder and war, Reshep, was introduced into Egypt during the New Kingdom, it was natural that he should be allied with Min. They were both given the Syrian goddess of love, Kadesh, as partner, with the three deities combining to form a triad of fertility, thunder and love!

Khent-Min (today called Akhmim) lies on the east bank of the Nile some 80 km south of Assiut. Its name means 'The Shrine of Min' and it was once the capital of the 9th Nome of Upper Egypt. Since the Greeks equated Min with Pan, they called the city Panopolis. The emblem on the nome standard was the fetish of Min, which consists of two fossil belemnites flanking a small circle ⊶; this emblem also forms the hieroglyphic symbol for the god's name. The belemnite is an extinct cephalopod related to the cuttle-fish. Although a predynastic green-stone model of a cuttle-fish, now in the British Museum, can be taken as evidence that this mollusc had itself been the object of a cult, the belemnite was probably chosen as Min's fetish for symbolic reasons. It has been suggested that it represents a thunderbolt, which would link it to Min. However, its cigar-like shape could equally well be interpreted as a phallic symbol.

One of the most famous sons of *Khent-Min* was Yuya, the father-in-law of Amenhotep III (see page 52), who served Min as High Priest and Superintendent of Cattle. Yuya's daughter, Tiy, who was married to Amenhotep III, owned extensive estates in the *Khent-Min* region; and even had a lake there, constructed for her by her husband. During the reign of Yuya's son, Ay, who became King of Egypt after

Fossil belemnites.

Tutankhamun, much attention was paid to *Khent-Min* partly because it was Ay's family seat but much more importantly because during Dynasty XVIII, Min became associated with the most powerful god in Egypt, Amun.

At both *Gebtu* and *Khent-Min*, Min was worshipped in the form of a sacred white bull, a symbol of his virility. And wherever he was worshipped, lettuces were offered to him, for these vegetables, whose white sap is reminiscent of semen, were considered to have aphrodisiac qualities. Thus Min was the god of fertility *par excellence*. His cult placed such great emphasis on procreation and fecundity that, in an agricultural country like Egypt, it was bound to be extremely popular. For many Egyptians, the highlight of the year occurred at the beginning of the harvest season, when Min's statues were brought out of their temples for the great 'Festival of the Coming Forth of Min'.

MONTU

· ·

Montu was a falcon god who was usually depicted as a man with the head of a hawk wearing a sun's disk surmounted by two tall plumes. He originated in Upper Egypt, probably in *Iuny*, a town which lay on the west bank of the Nile some 20 km south of modern-day Luxor. Until the Eighteenth Dynasty, *Iuny* was the capital of the 4th Nome of Upper Egypt, the Sceptre Nome. Because of the similarity of pronunciation with *Iunu*, or On, the City of Re (see page 23) *Iuny* was called *Iunu-Montu*, 'On of Montu', to avoid confusion with the Lower Egyptian city. Today, *Iuny* is called Armant, a name which is derived from *Iunu-Montu*, pronounced Ermont by the Copts. The Greeks called it Hermonthis.

The rulers of Dynasty XI probably came from *Iuny* (Armant). Although Montu's name is mentioned in the Pyramid Texts, and he appears in the decorations of Pepi II's funerary temple at Sakkara as one of the representative deities of Upper Egypt, he did not achieve great status until Dynasty XI when, as the patron god of the kings of the Dynasty, he was elevated to the position of one of the major deities of ancient Egypt; and, at about the same time, became particularly associated with war. The kings of Dynasty XI showed their adherence to Montu not only by building temples to him but by including his name in their own; thus there were four rulers in Dynasty XI called Montu-hotep (Montu-is-satisfied).

Montu was often equated with Horus and called Horus-with-the-strong-arm; but by the early Middle Kingdom he seems to have been regarded as the Upper Egyptian counterpart of Re of Heliopolis – a natural development, perhaps, considering that the name – *Iunu-Montu* – given to Montu's cult-centre linked it with the *Iunu* of Re. The two deities were merged as Mont-Re, who was worshipped at several places in the Sceptre Nome either in the form of a falcon-headed man, or in the shape of a bull.

In his falcon form, Montu was the local god of *Djerty* (now called Tod), a town on the east bank of the Nile facing *Iuny* (Armant), which received much attention during the Middle Kingdom. In Dynasty XVIII, Thutmose III had a shrine built there to house the Barque, or carrying chair, of Montu; and later, restoration work was carried out on the shrine during the reigns of several kings, notably Sety I and Ramesses III. A temple was built at *Djerty* (by then called Tuphium) in the reign of Ptolemy VIII; and further work was undertaken there during the Roman period.

At *Iuny* itself, Montu was worshipped in the form of a sacred bull, the Bekh or Bukhis Bull, which was thought to be able to cure diseases, especially those of the eye. It was also renowned for its strength and ferocity. The bull was probably black, although the colour of its hair was said to change every hour of the day; and Aelian,[35] who reported that the animal was called Onuphis, also wrote that its hair grew and lay the contrary way to that of other animals. When a Bukhis Bull died, it was buried on the edge of the desert just north of *Iuny* in a special catacomb known as the Bucheum. The earliest burial so far found dates to the reign of Nectanebo II, and the latest to some six-hundred and fifty years later in the reign of Diocletian. Each mother of a Bukhis Bull was accorded her own burial site near to that of her son.

The Bukhis Bull was worshipped at three other places in the Theban district – in the precinct of Amun at Karnak, where Montu had his own temple, at Tod and at Medamud (see below), although it is probable that there was not a separate live bull in all of them, but rather that the bull regarded as Montu incarnate visited each place at regular intervals and was represented in its absence by a statue.

Nag el-Medamud, the ancient Egyptian *Madu*, lies some 10 km north-east of Karnak, to which it was joined by a canal, allowing worshippers to travel between Montu's temple there and *Madu*. The temple that stands today in Medamud was erected during the Graeco-Roman period on the site of an older

Bukhis Bull: south wall of the Temple of Montu, Medamud.

Temple of Montu,
Medamud, Roman period:
courtyard of Antoninus Pius
(AD 138–161).

edifice begun during the Middle Kingdom and enlarged during the New Kingdom. At *Madu*, the local Bukhis Bull was kept in a special building just behind the main temple. This sacred 'stable' seems to have consisted of two compartments where the bull was allowed to roam at will. From inscriptions in the temple, it seems clear that, during its visits, the Bukhis Bull took part in fights with other bulls, staged in a special arena; and also was consulted by means of an oracle. A relief still to be seen on the exterior of the south wall of the temple, showing the Bukhis receiving the king, marks the place where the oracle was delivered.

Montu enjoyed the supremacy that the rulers of Dynasty XI gave him as chief god of the Sceptre Nome and mighty war god of ancient Egypt only briefly. In Dynasty XII, his position was usurped by Amun, although Montu never lost his appeal to warrior kings such as Thutmose III, who on one occasion called himself 'beloved son of Montu who resides in *Iuny*' and to others who referred to themselves as heroes like Montu, raging on the battlefield 'like Montu in his might'.

BASTET

· ·

Bastet, the cat goddess, was the benevolent counterpart of Sekhmet, the lioness. Bastet herself may originally have been a lioness. However, her worshippers preferred her in the form of the less fierce, more charming, domestic cat. The wild cat (*Felis vercata maniculata*) was native to Egypt, and it was probably this aggressive cat that was the prototype for the Cat of Heliopolis (see page 44); for the cat goddess, Mafdet; and even for the early forms of Bastet herself. In later manifestations Bastet was the domesticated cat, which was introduced into Egypt, according to some authorities, from the west and the south perhaps around 2100 BC. Hence, from at least the Middle Kingdom, Bastet was worshipped as a woman with a cat's head, or in the form of a queen cat, of the type familiar from the numerous statuettes found in museums the world over.

In tomb paintings of the Middle and New Kingdoms, pet cats are sometimes shown sitting under the chairs of their owners at feasts. It was presumably these cats (in ancient Egyptian, *mìw*) that inspired ancient Egyptians to nickname little girls *mìw-sherì*, 'Little Cat' or 'Pussy-cat'. However, cats were more often depicted out hunting in the marshes with their owners. The domesticated cat of ancient Egypt was not just a catcher of mice, the inspiration of the advice given in medical papyri: 'To prevent mice from coming near things – put cat-grease on everything'. It was also a hunter, a killer of the snakes feared by Egyptians. It could also be trained, if reliefs in tombs are to be believed, as a retriever trusted to bring back birds brought down by the throwsticks of its master.

The cult-centre of the goddess Bastet was at *Bast*, which lies some 60 km to the north-east of Cairo; and the name, Bastet, means 'She-of-Bast'. In hieroglyphs, the word *Bast* was written using a picture of a sealed oil-jar 🏺; it is possible, therefore, that the fetish originally worshipped at *Bast* bore a resemblance to such a jar. There were several temples at *Bast*, including one dedicated to Mihos, a lion god who was said to be the son of Bastet. The main temple was called *Per-Bastet* (House of Bastet), and gave its name to the town in the Greek Period when it was called Bubastis, the Greek pronunciation of *Per-Bastet*. Today, it is called Tell Basta. *Bast* controlled the routes from Memphis to Sinai, which in turn led to Western Asia; hence, it was strategically important. During Dynasty XXII it became politically important also, for the kings of that Dynasty originated in *Bast*, which in the Late Period became the capital of the 18th Nome of Lower Egypt.

In the fifth century BC, Herodotus visited *Bast*, which he, of course, being Greek, called Bubastis. In his opinion, there was no temple in Egypt that was a greater pleasure to look at than that of Bastet. In Herodotus' time, the temple stood in the centre of the city and, because the level of the surrounding buildings had been raised over the years since the temple was first built, one could look down and enjoy a fine view of it. The building was surrounded by a low wall, its entrance approached by a stone-paved road about 120 metres wide, lined on both sides with 'immense trees – so tall that they seem to touch the sky'. The main gateway was 18 metres high; and more tall trees stood about the actual shrine, which contained a statue of Bastet. Two canals, each 30 metres or so wide, had been led from the Nile to sweep round the temple, one on each side as far as the entrance, where they stopped short without meeting.

Large cemeteries of sacred cats have been discovered at *Bast*; but it seems that these sacred cats from the Temple of Bastet were not the only ones accorded burial in the cat necropolis of *Bast*/Bubastis. Herodotus maintained that the ancient Egyptians were so fond of all cats that, whenever one of the animals died, they were deeply distressed: they shaved their eyebrows and took the cat to Bubastis, where it was embalmed and buried in a sacred receptacle.

The popularity of Bastet was such that, again according to Herodotus, the most important and best-attended festival was the one held at Bubastis in honour of the goddess, whom the Greeks identified with Artemis. The animal sacred to

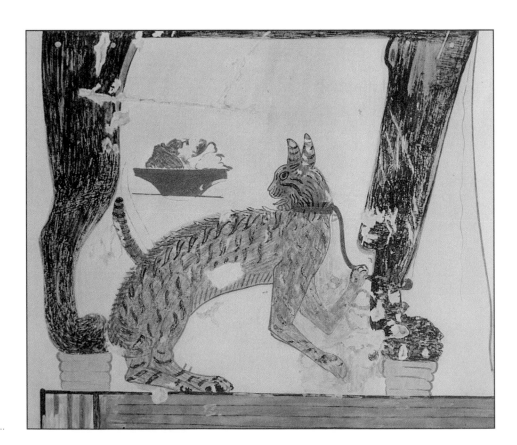

Pet cat: painting in the Theban tomb of May, harbour master in the Southern City, possibly in the reign of Thutmose III.

Hunting cat: painting in the Theban tomb of Menna, Scribe of the Royal Fields, possibly in the reign of Thutmose IV.

Artemis was the she-bear, not the cat; hence the Greeks could not have associated Artemis with Bastet because of any identity between sacred animals. However, they were both virgin goddesses, Bastet being the mother of Mihos notwithstanding, although their worship was orgiastic and in Bastet's case included ritual frenzies.

The evidence of the numerous statuettes, made in the Late Period especially, of beautifully observed cats, lissome, muscular and dignified, testifies to the popularity of Bastet, which never abated from the time when she rose to importance as the local deity of the kings of Dynasty XXII to the Graeco-Roman period. The Romans carried her worship to Italy, to Rome, Ostia, Pompeii; and to Nemi, where she was provided with a silk robe in purple and turquoise-green, a shirt of purple linen with two girdles, one gilt, two mantles, a tunic and a white dress.

PART
III

PERSONAL PIETY
AND
POPULAR RELIGION

PERSONAL PIETY

From literary works such as Instructions on behaviour, which were a popular genre from the Old Kingdom onwards, and for which the New Kingdom sages, Ani[1] and Amenemope,[2] were famous, humility was a prized quality. From biographical inscriptions in tombs, and from funerary stelae, it is clear that good deeds, such as giving bread to the hungry and water to the thirsty, were expected of a man, as were the virtues of truthfulness, modesty and humility. In spite of this, it has to be admitted that many biographical inscriptions seem to be somewhat lacking in modesty and humility.

By the New Kingdom, an awareness of individual responsibility for good behaviour is often demonstrated; and personal goodness, or piety, is much in evidence in votive stelae offered to a deity clearly in the expectation that it will please him. Punishment meted out for wrongdoing was accepted in a penitential manner; thus, a draughtsman from Deir el-Medina, Neferabu, admits that he swore a false oath, for which the god has blinded him:

> I am one who swore falsely by Ptah, Lord of Maat,
> Therefore he made me see darkness by day.[3]

POPULAR RELIGION

The great state temples played a vital role in the economic life of all classes of ancient Egyptian society; and in the social and religious lives of the Egyptian élite, large numbers of whom acted as priests and priestesses, often on a part-time basis. However, the innermost areas of a temple were denied to all but the highest grade of priest, although other parts were open to lesser ranks, and the general public was permitted access to specially designated places. As we have seen (page 169), Shrines of the Hearing Ear, specifically designated for private worship, were a feature of several temples.

Restricted areas of a temple were often indicated by special architectural features and inscriptions such as exhortations on door jambs that only those who are 'twice pure', that is, of priestly rank, may pass through. A private letter written in the Twentieth Dynasty confirms that temple access was according to priestly rank: the writer states that he was in search of the god of the temple to tell him about his problems, but that the god, that is, the divine statue, was shut up in his sanctuary; and he goes on:

> There was nobody having access to it [the sanctuary] to send in to you. But as I was waiting, I met Hori . . . and he said to me, 'I have access'. So I am sending him to you.[4]

Given the nature of ancient Egyptian temples, it is not surprising that ordinary people developed their own forms of religious worship. Popular religion, that is the beliefs and practices of the common people as distinct from the official state religion practised in the temple cults, seems to have been a feature of Egyptian life from an early date. Ordinary people had their own personal gods and expressed their veneration of them in rites performed outside the state temples and without the aid of an official priesthood. Anything might be selected as a personal god – the snake that lived in a hole near the door to a house, or the fox that came down from the desert to scavenge amidst domestic refuse – and since Egyptians were intensely superstitious, they were inclined to be in awe of anything with the potential for harm. Sometimes, the distinction between a personal god and a local god was not clear. For example, the people of Deir el-Medina worshipped a cobra goddess, officially recognized as Meretseger, 'The Lover of Silence'; but the ever-present danger of being bitten by a cobra lurking in the rocks among which the people of Deir el-Medina lived and worked made the veneration of Meretseger a very personal affair!

Occasionally, ordinary Egyptians invented a new deity. An example of this is the New Kingdom god Shed, sometimes called Hor-Shed, who seems to have been a manifestation of *Hor-pa-khred* (see page 85). His name was derived from the noun *shed*, 'saviour', 'rescuer', and he was represented in the garb of a typical Egyptian soldier, treading on crocodiles and subduing snakes and scorpions. His role was to protect his devotees and rescue them when called upon. There is no indication that there was ever an official cult of Shed, and no temple dedicated to him has been found. It is clear, therefore, that he was purely a popular deity worshipped by ordinary people, even at Amarna (see page 158).

In many places, the local popular cult took the form of veneration of a deified man. Deification was not an honour that the ancient Egyptians bestowed lightly, and Herodotus noted that their heroes were not the object of any cult. Nevertheless, there are examples of men who were favoured in this way. One such was Isi, a vizier of the early Sixth Dynasty, who was deified soon after his death and worshipped at Edfu. His *mastaba* was equipped with offering tables for the use of his worshippers, the local people, who also left stelae at the site.[5] A similar cult was established in the Sixth Dynasty at Elephantine for Hekaib, also called Pepynakht, Overseer of Foreign Troops in the reign of Pepy II. The cult of Hekaib was greatly developed in the Middle Kingdom, when the local governor, Sirenput I, built a temple for him on Elephantine Island.[6]

The tradition of worshipping deified men seems to have died out during the New Kingdom, although both Imhotep (see page 168) and Amenhotep-son-of-Hapu were revered. Amenhotep-son-of-Hapu belonged to an obscure family from Athribis in the Delta but, in the reign of Amenhotep III, he rose to become overseer of all the king's works, royal scribe, scribe of recruits and steward of the estates of the princess, Sitamun. Much of the credit for the great buildings erected during the reign must go to the king's namesake, who lived to the age of eighty. He was honoured with a memorial temple on the west bank at Thebes that was comparable to the royal temples nearby, and his statue was erected within the hallowed precincts at Karnak. However, it was not until the Saite era that the cult of Amenhotep-son-of-Hapu flourished: he then became a healer and patron deity of physicians. In the Ptolemaic era, he was worshipped as a god of healing and a giver of oracles, with a sanctuary at Deir el-Bahri, in the upper court of the temple. In the Graeco-Roman era, this became the place to which people went to ask his help in having children. The Greeks called him 'Amenothes Paapis', and linked him with Imhotep.

Occasionally, a king became the recipient of popular worship, in addition to the funerary cult that was observed at his official memorial temple. Popular cults were sometimes centred on royal statues. At Abu Simbel, the colossal statues

Memorial temple of
Hatshepsut, Deir el-Bahri.

Façade of memorial temple
of Ramesses II, Abu Simbel.
The colossi of the king
became the focus of a royal
statue cult.

before the façade of Ramesses II's memorial temple were the objects of a local cult, which was probably practised in a small mud-brick chapel close to the temple; and 60 stelae from *Pi-Ramessu* bear witness to the royal statue-cult there.[7] The most popular deities worshipped at Deir el-Medina were King Amenhotep I and his mother, Queen Ahmose-Nofretari. Amenhotep I was traditionally supposed to have chosen the site at which the men who worked on the royal tombs should live, and he and his mother became the divine guardians of the Theban necropolis. Their original shrine has not been identified, but Sety I had a temple built for them. In this, and in other shrines at Deir el-Medina, it was the village inhabitants themselves who undertook the roles of priests. The cult of Amenhotep I and Ahmose-Nofretari, and its associated oracle, lasted until the Twenty-fifth Dynasty.

Direct communication between deity and mortal was often sought, and could be achieved by several means. Oracles were used not only by kings but by ordinary people, who expected them to give advice on a variety of problems, from enquiries on promotion, to the whereabouts of a piece of lost property, to the treatment of servants. Oracles could be consulted by written message, by casting lots with straws or sticks, and by asking a question – usually demanding the answer 'yes' or 'no' – of the statue of a deity. The statue answered by inclining its head, or by varying its pressure on the shoulders of the priests who carried it to indicate that they should step forward (yes) or backwards (no) – a good deal of interpretation by the priests being essential to this method. In the New Kingdom, if not before, the prophetic voice of the god emanating from his sanctuary was a popular method of consulting the oracle. In the Late Period, in particular, incubation[8] became popular, and Egyptians sought the interpretation of dreams by sleeping overnight within the precincts of a temple, not only at Denderah (see page 126) but elsewhere.

Messages to a deity could be left at his or her shrine. The richer members of society left votive stelae, but the poor could leave their messages on pieces of broken pottery, as at Abydos (see page 67). From the Eighteenth Dynasty to the Saite era, the portico of the tomb of the Twelfth-Dynasty noble, Hapjefa III, at Assiut, was used as a popular shrine to Abydos' ancient deity, Wepwawet. Over six hundred small votive stelae have been found there, the majority dedicated to Wepwawet, others to Amun, Hathor and other deities. One of these stelae (No. 1632 in the British Museum), belonging to a man named Pateweret, is proof that sometimes gods were asked to intervene to save human beings: seemingly, Pateweret was chased by a crocodile, and begged Wepwawet to save him from it. His prayer seems to have been answered, for he erected the stele in thanks for his deliverance.

In the last centuries before Christ, there was an extraordinary revival in animal cults, especially among the poorer sections of Egyptian society. Although the worship of gods made manifest in animals was one of the oldest forms of religion in Egypt, it seems likely that this new-found popularity of animal cults owed much to Egyptian nationalism. Sickened by successive periods of foreign domination, priests may have encouraged Egyptians to turn to what was perhaps the most characteristic feature of Egyptian religion, the worship of sacred animals, mummified after death and buried in tombs. Old animal cults, such as those of the Apis, Mnevis and Bukhis Bulls, enjoyed the patronage of Ptolemaic kings, though the most popular deity was the relative newcomer, Bastet.

At Sakkara (see page 188) and Tuna el-Gebel (see page 188), ibises and baboons, sacred to Thoth, were mummified and buried in subterranean galleries. Eggs found on the site at Sakkara suggest that the birds were actually bred there; one text, written in demotic on a piece of broken pot, refers to the provision of food for sixty thousand ibises.[9] It has been estimated that the average annual rate in the burial of ibises at Sakkara was ten thousand, which would suggest that the birds were ritually slaughtered in large numbers. At Elephantine, rams, as representatives of the god Khnum, were mummified, dressed in their regalia, which included a crown, and buried in large sarcophagi. Crocodiles, representing the god Sobek, were buried at Kom Ombo; and in the Faiyum, large numbers of them, in a variety of sizes, have been found, complete with clutches of eggs.

As Christianity took hold in Egypt, the old gods were seemingly abandoned, parts of some of their temples turned into churches, the rest adapted by the local population as living quarters. With the arrival of Islam, the occasional temple was turned into a mosque. Abhorrence of pagan deities, and fear of the Evil Eye

Osiris on funerary bier:
relief in the memorial
temple of Sety I at Abydos.

that they might turn against trespassers, led to the obliteration of reliefs on temple walls. Yet the ancient deities were not wholly forsaken. Even today, it is not unusual to see a young village bride, Muslim or Christian, accompanied by her mother-in-law and led by her husband, enter the Temple of Hathor at Denderah, where they make their way to one of the crypts to look upon a relief of the goddess with her son on her knee, in the hope that she will help them have their own son. And in a side chapel in the Temple of Sety at Abydos there is a relief of Osiris stretched out on his funerary bier; the erect penis of the god is darkened with the patina formed from the many hopeful fingers of local women who have touched it in the expectation that this most sympathetic of ancient Egyptian deities will come to their aid in their attempts to bear a child.

GLOSSARY

ankh-sign	amulet shaped like the Egyptian hieroglyph ☥ which means 'life'.
Barque (or bark)	a ship (usually mythological, e.g. the Barque of Re) or a portable shrine shaped like a ship.
cartouche	elongated version ⬭ of the hieroglyphic sign ◯ ('*shen*') which means 'to encircle'. Two of the five names which comprised the royal titulary were written inside a cartouche to indicate that the king ruled over everything that the sun encircled.
Coffin Texts	magical spells painted inside coffins belonging to commoners.
Copt, Coptic	originally native Egyptians of Graeco-Roman period onwards, eventually came to mean Christian Egyptians.
crook	hooked staff or sceptre carried as a symbol of authority by the King of Egypt.
cult temple	temple dedicated to the worship of one or more deities.
decans	the (Greek) name given to the period of time (ten days) during which the Egyptians observed the constellations that were visible on the horizon. There were thirty-six decans in the Egyptian year of 360 days. A given constellation appeared at a certain point on the horizon according to the hour; tables were drawn up recording the positions of the constellations enabling the Egyptians to tell the time at night.
demotic	script used on business documents etc. from about 700 BC onwards. By the Graeco-Roman period it had become the ordinary writing of everyday life. Word derived from Greek *demoticos* meaning 'common'.
Dynasty	the divisions into which Egyptian history was divided by the scholar-priest Manetho in third century BC. Dynasties are roughly families of kings.
Ennead	group of nine deities (from Greek meaning 'set of nine') e.g. the Ennead of Heliopolis.
epagomenal days	the five days added on to the Egyptian year of twelve months of thirty days to bring it up to 365 days (from Greek *epagomenal* meaning 'added').

faience	quartz sand heated in crucible with soda until quartz melts then solidifies into glaze. Many colours but most popular was green or turquoise made by adding copper filings before heating. Substitute for lapis lazuli, which the ancient Egyptians obtained from traders, who in turn obtained it from what is today called Afghanistan.
fetish	inanimate object thought to be endowed with magical and mystical powers.
fetishism	worship of such an object.
flail	sometimes called flagellum. Symbol of royal authority.
hieratic	cursive script derived from hieroglyphs. The word comes from Greek *hieratikos* (priestly).
hieroglyphs	picture-writing of ancient Egypt. Word derived from Greek *hieros* (sacred) *glupho* (sculptures).
mastaba	private tomb of the Old Kingdom. In shape rectangular with slightly battened sides, similar to the bench (in Arabic: *mastaba*) sometimes found outside village houses in Egypt; hence the name for the tomb.
menat-collar	bead necklace with counterpoise that hangs down back of wearer.
mortuary temple	*see* memorial temple
memorial temple	temple dedicated to the worship of a dead king.
necropolis	cemetery: from Greek *nekros* (corpse) *polis* (city).
nome	word first used by Greeks to describe the administrative districts of Egypt (forty-two in all).
obelisk	shaft of stone (usually granite) with pointed top (e.g. Cleopatra's Needle); word comes from Greek *obeliskoi* ('little spits').
Ogdoad	group of eight gods (from Greek meaning 'set of eight').
papyrus	plant (*Cyperus papyrus L.*) which once grew prolifically in Egypt, especially in the Delta marshes. Used for making boats, ropes, baskets, sandals, etc. Pith used to make writing material. Papyrus-paper made in 'pages' which could be stuck together to make a roll (standard roll had twenty pages). Pages seldom more than 48 cm deep and 43 cm wide (but note Greenfield Papyrus (No. 10554 in British Museum) which is 49.5 cm wide). Longest known roll is the Great Harris Papyrus (No. 9999 in British Museum) which is 41 metres long. Subject matter on papyrus rolls could be administrative, medical, mathematical, literary, religious (e.g. The Book of the Dead or What is in the Underworld).
predynastic	period of Egyptian history that predates writing and the unification of Egypt into one state. The prehistoric period before 3100 BC.

pyramid	royal tomb in use in Egypt from Dynasty III to Dynasty XVII.
pyramidion	pyramid-shaped tip of obelisk (see above) or capstone of pyramid.
Pyramid Texts	spells and magical inscriptions found inside certain pyramids from end of Dynasty V to Dynasty VI.
sarcophagus	stone coffin: from Greek *sarco* (flesh) *phag* (eat, swallow).
stele (or stela) plural: stelae	slab of stone, usually rectangular in shape with curved top, decorated with relief and inscription.
syncretism	absorption of one god into the cult or persona of another.
theogamy	process by which the supreme god of the time took on the form of the reigning king in order to beget a child upon the queen, the child being destined to become King of Egypt.
Thutmoside	period during which kings named Thutmose ruled Egypt.
The Two Lands	Egypt, i.e. Upper Egypt (South) and Lower Egypt (North).
waas-sceptre	staff with straight shaft split into two at bottom and topped by the head of an animal. Symbol of royal authority.
wadi	Arabic word meaning dry river-bed.

See also general index

NOTES

PART I

Introduction
1.   Juvenal, *Satires*, XV, line 1 foll.

Chapter One
1.   Herodotus, *The Histories*, II, 4.
2.   *Op. cit.*, 97.

Chapter Two
1.   Watterson, 1991, p. 38 foll.

PART II

The Major Gods of Egypt
1.   Herodotus, *op. cit.*, II, 72.
2.   Hoch, 1977.
3.   Griffith, 1890.
4.   Yoyotte, 1959.
5.   The Book of the Dead, Chapter 175.
6.   Some authorities consider that the kings of the First and Second Dynasties were buried at Abydos and that it is the *mastabas* at Sakkara that are the cenotaphs. Since no bodies have been found at either place, the site of the true royal burials remains a matter of conjecture.
7.   Short, 1989, p. 71.
8.   Golenisheff, 1899. For a translation of the Stele, see Budge, 1912, p. 142 foll.
9.   Lichtheim, 1976, p. 214 foll.
10.   Chassinat, vol. I, p. 26 foll.
11.   Fairman, 1974.
12.   Graves, 1981, p. 129 foll.
13.   Breasted, 1906, II, 810–15.
14.   Herodotus, *op. cit.*, II, 121.
15.   *Ibid.*
16.   Edward Gibbon (1737–94), best known as the author of *The Decline and Fall of the Roman Empire*.

17. Gibbon, *Autobiography* (World's Classics edition), p. 212. A similar attitude was taken as recently as 1960 by the prosecuting counsel in the celebrated trial of Penguin Books, prosecuted under the Obscene Publications Act 1959 for publishing a paperback edition of D.H. Lawrence's novel, *Lady Chatterley's Lover*.
18. Lichtheim, 1976, p. 203 foll.
19. *Op. cit.*, p. 200 foll.
20. Chassinat, vol. IV, 3, 5–8.
21. *The Iliad*, Book 9; translated by Alexander Pope, World's Classics edition, Oxford University Press, pp. 176–7.
22. Breasted, 1906, II, 12, 37–8.
23. Breasted, 1906, IV, 156 foll.
24. Watterson, 1991, p. 159 foll.
25. Arrian, *The Campaigns of Alexander*, Book 3, line 4.
26. The Bentresh Stele. For a translation *see* Lichtheim, 1980, p. 90 foll.
27. Lichtheim, 1975, p. 222 foll.
28. Peet *et al.*, 1923, pp. 51–91 (village) and 92–108 (chapels).
29. 'Beautiful-are-the-Forms-of-Re, Sole-One-of-Re'.
30. 'Glorious-are-the-Beauties-of-Aten'.
31. Lichtheim, 1975, p. 51 foll.
32. Laskowska-Kuszal, 1984.
33. Carter, 1972, p. 164.
34. Lichtheim, 1975, p. 219 foll.

PART III

Personal Piety and Popular Religion
1. Aelian, *On the Characteristics of Animals*, XI, 10.
2. Lichtheim, 1976, p. 135 foll.
3. *Op. cit.*, p. 146 foll.
4. Stele now in the British Museum (No. 589).
5. Wente, 1990, 219 No. 355.
6. Alliot, 1937.
7. Habachi, 1956.
8. Habachi, 1969.
9. Sauneron, 1959.
10. Spencer, 1982, p. 210.

BIBLIOGRAPHY AND FURTHER READING

Translations of the classical authors cited in the text are available variously in the Loeb Classical Library, The World's Classics, Penguin Classics and Everyman's Library. Place of publication is given only if outside London.

Aldred, C. *Akhenaten, King of Egypt*, 1986

Allen, T.G. *The Book of the Dead or Going Forth by Day*, Chicago, 1974

Alliot, M. 'Un nouvel exemple de vizir divinisé dans l'Égypte ancienne', in *Bulletin d'Institut Français d'archéologie Orientale*, 37, 1937, p. 93 foll.

Baines, J. and Malek, J. *Atlas of Ancient Egypt*, Oxford, 1980

Boylan, P. *Thoth, the Hermes of Egypt*, Oxford, 1922

Breasted, J.H. *Development of Religion and Thought in Ancient Egypt*, New York, 1959

——. *Ancient Records of Egypt*, Chicago, 1906

Budge, E.A.W. *Egyptian Literature, Legends and the Gods*, 1912

——. *From Fetish to God in Ancient Egypt*, Oxford, 1934

Carter, H. *The Tomb of Tutankhamen*, 1972

Cauville, S. *Edfou*, Cairo, 1984

Černy, J. *Ancient Egyptian Religion*, 1952

Chassinat, E. *Le Temple d'Edfou*, vols i–xiv, Cairo, 1892–1934

Clark, R.T. Rundle. *Myth and Symbol in Ancient Egypt*, 1959, reprinted

Erman, A. *A Handbook of Egyptian Religion*, 1907

——. *The Ancient Egyptians, a Sourcebook of their Writings*, New York, 1966

Fairman, H.W. (ed.) *The Triumph of Horus*, 1974

Faulkner, R.O. *The Ancient Egyptian Coffin Texts*, Warminster, 1973

——. *The Ancient Egyptian Pyramid Texts*, Oxford, 1969

——. *The Ancient Egyptian Book of the Dead*, ed. C. Andrews, 1985

Frankfort, H. *Ancient Egyptian Religion*, New York, 1961

Gaballa, G.A. and Kitchen, K.A. 'The Festival of Sokar', in *Orientalia*, 38 (1), 1969, p. 1 foll.

Gardiner, A.H. *Description of a Hieratic Papyrus*, 1931

——. *Later Egyptian Stories*, Brussels, 1932

Golenisheff, W. *Die Metternichstele*, Leipzig, 1899

Graves, R. *Greek Myths*, 1981

Green, R.L. *Tales of Ancient Egypt*, Harmondsworth, 1967

Griffith, F.L. *The Antiquities of Tell el-Yahûdîyah*, 1890

Griffiths, J.G. *The Conflict of Horus and Seth*, Liverpool, 1960

——. *The Origins of Osiris*, Berlin, 1966

Habachi, L. *Features of the Deification of Ramesses II*, Gluckstadt, 1969

——. 'Hekaib, the Deified Governor of Elephantine', in *Archaeology*, 9, 1956, p. 8 foll.

Hart, G.A. *A Dictionary of Egyptian Gods and Goddesses*, 1986

Hoch, E. 'Reflections on Prehistoric Life at Umm an-Nar (Trucial Oman) based on Faunal Remains from the Third Millennium BC', in *South Asian Archaeology*, 1977, p. 626 foll.

Holmberg, M. Sandman. *The God Ptah*, Lund, 1946

James, T.G.H. *Myths and Legends of Ancient Egypt*, 1969

Jenkins, N. *The Boat Beneath the Pyramids*, 1980

Junker, H. 'Die Onurislegende', in *Denkschrift der Wiener Akademie*, 59 (i), Vienna, 1917

Laskowska-Kuszal, E. *Le Sanctuaire Ptolemaique de Deir el-Bahari*, Warsaw, 1984

Lichtheim, M. *Ancient Egyptian Literature*, vol. I: The Old and Middle Kingdoms, Berkeley, 1975

——. *Ancient Egyptian Literature*, vol. II: The New Kingdom, Berkeley, 1976

——. *Ancient Egyptian Literature*, vol. III: The Late Period, Berkeley, 1980

Lurker, M. *The Gods and Symbols of Ancient Egypt*, 2nd ed. rev. and enlarged by P.A. Clayton, 1981

Morenz, S. *Egyptian Religion*, trans. A. Keep, 1973

Murnane, W.J. *The Penguin Guide to Ancient Egypt*, Harmondsworth, 1983

Otto, E. *Egyptian Art and the Cults of Osiris and Amon*, 1968

Peet, T.E., *et al. The City of Akhenaten*, I, 1923

Posener, G. *A Dictionary of Egyptian Civilization*, 1962

Reeves, N. *The Complete Tutankhamun*, 1990

Sadek, A.I. *Popular Religion in Egypt during the New Kingdom*, Hildesheim, 1988

Sauneron, S. 'Les Songes et leur interprètation', in *Sources Orientales* 2, Paris, 1959, p. 50 foll.

——. *The Priests of Ancient Egypt*, 1960

Short, M. *Inside the Brotherhood*, Glasgow, 1989

Spencer, A.J. *Death in Ancient Egypt*, Harmondsworth, 1982

Watterson, B. *Women in Ancient Egypt*, Stroud, 1991

Weigall, A. *The Life and Times of Akhenaten*, 1922

Wente, E. *Letters from Ancient Egypt*, Atlanta, 1990

Wilkinson, R.H. *Reading Egyptian Art*, 1992

Yoyotte, J. 'Le Bassin de Djarouke', in *Kemi*, 15, 1959, p. 23 foll.

INDEX